The Records of the Medieval Ecclesiastical Courts

I

Comparative Studies in Continental and Anglo-American Legal History

Vergleichende Untersuchungen zur kontinentaleuropäischen und anglo-amerikanischen Rechtsgeschichte

Herausgegeben von

Prof. Dr. Dr. h. c. mult. Helmut Coing

und

Prof. Dr. Knut Wolfgang Nörr

Band 6

The Records of the Medieval Ecclesiastical Courts

Part I:

The Continent

Reports of the Working Group on Church Court Records

Edited by

Prof. Charles Donahue, Jr.

Duncker & Humblot · Berlin

Gedruckt mit Unterstützung der Gerda Henkel Stiftung, Düsseldorf

CIP-Titelaufnahme der Deutschen Bibliothek

The Records of the Medieval Ecclesiastical Courts: Reports of the Working Group on Church Court Records / ed. by Charles Donahue. — Duncker u. Humblot.
NE: Donahue, Charles [Hrsg.]

P. 1. The Continent. — 1989
(Comparative Studies in Continental and Anglo-American Legal History; Bd. 6)
ISBN 3-428-06619-7
NE: GT

Satz: WordTech, Woburn, MA, U.S.A.
Druck: Berliner Buchdruckerei Union GmbH, Berlin 61
Printed in Germany

ISSN 0935-1167
ISBN 3-428-06619-7

Preface

This is the first of two volumes that will contain the reports to date of the Working Group on Church Court Records. The second will deal with England. The Working Group is part of a larger effort: the Research Project on Continental and Anglo-American Legal History. We would like to take this opportunity to thank the Gerda Henkel Stiftung for its generous support for the Project and, in particular, for its support for this Group, which operated quite differently from other Groups associated with the Project.

Many individuals assisted us, too many to name here. We cannot pass over, however, those connected with the Project who did much to get us going in the beginning and who encouraged us along the way, in particular, Professors Helmut Coing, Robert Feenstra, Stephan Kuttner, Domenico Maffei, and Raoul Van Caenegem. Professor Knut Nörr, to whom fell the task of communicating with the Group on behalf of the Project, moved us along with consummate tact. Professor R.H. Helmholz not only wrote the reports on Spain, but he also supported the general editor in his darkest moments. Ms. Kathleen Curley put up with innumerable drafts of the book, making entries and corrections in the computer in strange languages, with a fidelity that is not given to many. Finally, we would like to acknowledge the assistance of the archivists and their staffs in the numerous archives which we visited or with which we corresponded. Theirs is frequently a frustrating task, and their work too often goes unappreciated. Without them these reports could not have been written.

It is in the nature of work like this to be incomplete and to contain mistakes. The *Kanonistische Abteilung* of the *Zeitschrift der Savigny-Stiftung für Rechtsgeschichte* has offered its pages for supplements and corrections to these reports. The Group hopes that these volumes will be but a start on a complete and accurate inventory of the surviving records of the medieval ecclesiastical courts.

Table of Contents

Listings reflect the language of the contents of the reports.

Preface ... 5

Table of Contents ... 7

List of Contributors ... 13

General Abbreviations ... 15

Bibliographical Abbreviations ... 17

General Introduction ... 23

01. The Problem ... 23
02. The Results ... 26
03. How to Use this Book ... 29

I. **Österreich (Kirchenprovinz Salzburg)**
von Othmar Hageneder, Christoph Haidacher, Klaus Lindner und Herwig Weigl

00. Editor's Introduction ... 33
01. Salzburg, Offizialat des Erzbischofs ... 34
02. Salzburg, Bressanone (Brixen), Offizialat des Bischofs ... 38
03. Salzburg, Freising, officiality of the bishop ... 41
04. Salzburg, Gurk, Offizialat des Bischofs ... 43
05. Salzburg, Passau, Offizialat für Österreich unter der Enns mit Sitz Maria am Gestade in Wien ... 43
06. Salzburg, Regensburg, officiality of the bishop ("consistorium ecclesiae Ratisponensis") ... 46
07. Salzburg, Salzburg, Gericht des Archidiakons von Baumburg ... 47
08. Salzburg, Salzburg, court of the archdeacon of Chiemsee ... 47
09. Salzburg, Salzburg, court of the archdeacon of Gars ... 47
10. Salzburg, Salzburg, Gericht des Archidiakons von Gmünd ... 47
11. Salzburg, Salzburg, Gericht des Archidiakons von Unterkärnten ... 48
12. Wien (exemt), Offizialat des Bischofs ... 48

II. **Belgium**
by Monique Vleeschouwers-Van Melkebeek

00. Editor's Introduction ... 51
01. Reims, Tournai, officiality of the bishop ... 53

III. **France**
by Charles Donahue, Jr., and Anne Lefebvre-Teillard

00. Introduction 59
00. Diocese List 61
01. Aix, officiality of the archbishop 63
02. Aix, Apt, officialité de l'évêque 64
03. Aix, Fréjus, officiality of the bishop 65
04. Aix, Sistéron, officialité de l'évêque 65
05. Arles, officialité de l'archevêque 66
06. Arles, Avignon, officialité de l'évêque (jusqu'en 1475) 66
Pour l'officialité d'Avignon depuis 1475 voir III/09.
07. Arles, Marseille, officiality of the bishop 67
08. Arles, Orange, officialité de l'évêque 73
09. Avignon, officialité de l'archevêque (depuis 1475) 74
Voir aussi III/06.
10. Avignon, Carpentras, officialité de l'évêque 74
11. Avignon, Cavaillon, officialité de l'évêque 75
12. Avignon, Vaison, officialité de l'évêque 76
Besançon, officialité de l'archevêque — voir X/01.
13. Bordeaux, officialité de l'archevêque (diocésaine et métropolitaine) 76
14. Bordeaux, Angoulême, officialité de l'évêque 77
15. Bordeaux, Maillezais, officialité de l'évêque 77
16. Bordeaux, Périgueux, officiality of the bishop 77
17. Bordeaux, Poitiers, officialité de l'évêque 78
18. Bourges, officialité de l'archevêque (métropolitaine) 78
19. Bourges, Bourges, officialité du chapitre métropolitain Saint-Étienne 78
20. Bourges, Clermont, officialité de l'évêque 79
21. Bourges, Limoges, officialité de l'évêque 79
22. Bourges, Limoges, officialité du chapitre 80
23. Bourges, Mende, officiality of the bishop 80
24. Bourges, Le Puy, officialité de l'évêque 83
25. Bourges, Rodez, officialité de l'évêque 83
26. Bourges, Saint-Flour, officialité de l'évêque (diocésaine) 84
27. Bourges, Saint-Flour, officialité de l'évêque (officialité foraine d'Arpajon) 84
28. Embrun, Digne, officialité de l'évêque 84
29. Lyon, officialité de l'archevêque (primatiale) 85
30. Lyon, officialité de l'archevêque (métropolitaine et diocésaine) 86
Voir aussi III/33-35.
31. Lyon, Autun, officialité de l'évêque) 87
32. Lyon, Langres, officiality of the bishop 87
33. Lyon, Lyon, officialité de l'archevêque (diocésaine) 88
Voir aussi III/30.

34. Lyon, Lyon, officialité de l'archevêque (Cour des excès) 88
Voir aussi III/30.
35. Lyon, Lyon, officialité de l'archevêque et du chapitre de la cathédrale (Cour commune) 89
Voir aussi III/30.
36. Lyon, Lyon, officialité du chapitre Saint-Jean (justice du glaive spirituel) 89
37. Lyon, Lyon, officialité du chapitre Saint-Just 89
38. Narbonne, Elne, officiality of the bishop at Elne and at Perpignan .. 90
39. Narbonne, Nîmes, officialité de l'évêque 91
40. Reims, officialité de l'abbaye de Corbie 92
41. Reims, Amiens, officialité de l'évêque 92
42. Reims, Beauvais, officiality of the bishop 93
43. Reims, Cambrai, officiality of the bishop 94
Reims, Cambrai, officiality of the bishop at Brussel — see II/00
44. Reims, Châlons-sur-Marne, officiality of the bishop 96
45. Reims, Senlis, officiality of the bishop 98
46. Rouen, officialité de l'archevêque (métropolitaine et diocésaine) 98
47. Rouen, officiality of the abbey of Cerisy 99
48. Rouen, officialité de l'abbaye de Fécamp 100
49. Rouen, officialité de l'abbaye de Montivilliers 101
50. Rouen, officialité de l'archevêque à Pontoise 102
51. Rouen, Bayeux, officialité de l'évêque 103
52. Rouen, Sées, officialité de l'évêque 103
53. Sens, officiality of the archbishop 103
54. Sens, Chartres, officiality of the ?great archdeacon and of the cathedral chapter 104
55. Sens, Orléans, officialité de l'évêque 105
56. Sens, Paris, officiality of the bishop 105
57. Sens, Paris, officiality of the cathedral chapter 106
58. Sens, Paris, officiality of the archdeacon of Brie 106
59. Sens, Paris, officiality of the archdeacon of Paris 107
60. Sens, Paris, officiality of Saint-Germain 109
61. Sens, Sens, officialité du chapitre 109
62. Sens, Sens, officiality of Saint-Julien-du-Sault 109
63. Sens, Troyes, officiality of the bishop 110
64. Toulouse, officialité de l'archevêque (métropolitaine) 112
65. Toulouse, Pamiers, officialité de l'évêque 112
66. Tours, Saint-Brieuc, officialité de l'évêque 113
67. Tours, Le Mans, officialité de l'évêque 113
68. Tours, Nantes, officialité de l'évêque 113
69. Tours, Nantes, officialité du chapitre Saint-Pierre 113
70. Tours, Tréguier, officialité de l'évêque 114

71. Trier, Toul, officialité de l'évêque ... 114
72. Vienne, Die, officialité de l'évêque ... 114
73. Vienne, Grenoble, officiality of the bishop at Grenoble and at Chambéry ... 115

IV. **Germany**
by Klaus Lindner

00. Editor's Introduction ... 117
01. Mainz, Augsburg, officiality of the bishop ... 121

V. **Ungarn (Kirchenprovinzen von Esztergom und Kalocsa)**
von Péter Erdő

00. Editor's Preface ... 123
00. Einleitung ... 124
00. Offizialatsgerichte in Ungarn (1300-1563) ... 125
01. Ungarn, Esztergom, Offizialat des Erzbischofs (Primas) ... 126
02. Rumänien, Esztergom, Offizialat des Dekans von Braşov ... 136
03. Tschechoslowakei, Esztergom, Offizialat des Propstes von Bratislava 137
04. Ungarn, Esztergom, Offizialat des exemten Abtes von Pannonhalma 138
05. Rumänien, Esztergom, Offizialat des Dekans von Sibiu ... 139
06. Tschechoslowakei, Esztergom, Offizialat des Propstes von Spišská Kapitula ... 140
07. Ungarn, Esztergom, Eger, Offizialat des Bischofs ... 141
08. Ungarn, Esztergom, Győr, Offizialat des Bischofs ... 146
09. Tschechoslowakei, Esztergom, Nitra, Offizialat des Bischofs ... 148
10. Ungarn, Esztergom, Pécs, Offizialat des Bischofs ... 148
11. Ungarn, Esztergom, Vác, Offizialat des Bischofs ... 149
12. Ungarn, Esztergom, Veszprém, Offizialat des Bischofs ... 150
13. Ungarn, Kalocsa, Offizialat des Erzbischofs ... 151
14. Rumänien, Kalocsa, Alba Julia (Siebenbürgen), Offizialat des Bischofs ... 152
15. Rumänien, Kalocsa, Alba Julia, Offizialat des Vikars "extra Meszes" 153
16. Ungarn, Kalocsa, Csanád, Offizialat des Bischofs ... 155
17. Rumänien, Kalocsa, Oradea, Offizialat des Bischofs ... 156
18. Jugoslawien, Kalocsa, Zagreb, Offizialat des Bischofs ... 157
19. Jugoslawien, Kalocsa, Zagreb, Offizialat des Propstes von Čazma ... 158

VI. **Italia**
di Giovanni Minnucci

00. Editor's Introduction ... 159
01. Montalcino (cr. 1462), officialità del vescovo ... 159
02. Siena, officialità dell'arcivescovo (vescovo fino al 1458) ... 160
03. Siena (Pisa fino al 1458), Massa e Populónia, officialità del vescovo .. 162

VII. **The Netherlands**
by Carla de Glopper-Zuijderland

00. Editor's Preface . . . 163
01. Köln, Utrecht, officiality of the bishop (archbishop after 1559) . . . 164
02. Köln, Utrecht, officiality of the archdeacon of the chapter of Oudmunster (st Salvator) . . . 173
03. Köln, Utrecht, officiality of the archdeacon of the chapter of st Pieter . . . 175
04. Köln, Utrecht, officiality of the archdeacon of the chapter of st Jan . . . 175
05. Köln, Utrecht, officiality of the archdeaconry of the *chorepiscopus* . . 175

VIII. **Portugal**
par Isaias da Rosa Pereira

00. Editor's Note and Report . . . 177

IX. **Spain**
by R.H. Helmholz

00. Editor's Preface . . . 179
01. Burgos (exempt), officiality of the bishop . . . 179
02. Burgos, officiality of the cathedral chapter . . . 180
03. Tarragona, Barcelona, officiality of the bishop . . . 181
04. Zaragosa (to 1574, Tarragona to 1318), Pamplona, officiality of the bishop . . . 186

X. **Die Schweiz**
von Andreas Meyer

00. Editor's Preface . . . 189
00. Einleitung . . . 189
00. Allgemeine Bibliografie . . . 191
01. Besançon, Offizialat des Erzbischofs . . . 194
02. Besançon, Basel, Offizialat des Bischofs . . . 195
03. Besançon, Basel, Offizialat des Archidiakons . . . 198
04. Besançon, Lausanne, Offizialat des Bischofs . . . 198
05. Besançon, Lausanne, Gericht des Kapitels (Iudex spiritualis capituli) 203
06. Besançon, Lausanne, Gerichte der Archidiakone und Dekane . . . 203
07. Mainz, Chur, Offizialat des Bischofs . . . 204
08. Mainz, Chur, Gericht des Erzpriesters im Dekanat Vintschgau . . . 206
09. Mainz, Chur, Gericht des Dekans im Engadin . . . 206
10. Mainz, Konstanz, Offizialat des Bischofs . . . 206
11. Tarantaise (bis 1510, danach exemt), Sion, Offizialat des Bischofs . . 213
12. Tarantaise (bis 1510, danach exemt), Sion, Gerichte der Dekane von Sitten und Valeria . . . 216
13. Vienne, Genève, Offizialat des Bischofs . . . 217

Index of Persons and Places (Including authors of books and articles cited) . . . 221

Index of Archives . . . 237

List of Contributors

Prof. Charles Donahue, Harvard Law School, Cambridge, MA: General Introduction, Editor's Prefaces and Introductions, France (part), Indexes.

Prof. Dr. Péter Erdő, Pázmány Péter Római Katolikus Hittudományi Akadómia, Budapest: Hungary.

Drs. Carla de Glopper-Zuijderland, Rijksuniversiteit te Utrecht: The Netherlands.

Dr. Christoph Haidacher, Tiroler Landesarchiv, Innsbruck: Austria (Bressanone archives).

Prof. Othmar Hageneder, Institut für österreichische Geschichtsforschung, Wien: Austria (general direction).

Prof. Richard Helmholz, University of Chicago Law School: Spain.

Prof. Anne Lefebvre-Teillard, Université de Paris (II): France (part).

Mr. Klaus Lindner, doctoral candidate, Harvard Divinity School, Cambridge, MA: Austria (Salzburg province: Freising, Regensburg), Germany.

Dr. Andreas Meyer, Historisches Institut der Universität Bern: Switzerland.

Dr. Giovanni Minnucci, Università di Siena: Italy.

Prof. Isaias da Rosa Pereira, Universidade de Lisboa: Portugal.

Dr. Monique Vleeschouwers-Van Melkebeek, Rijksuniversiteit te Gent: Belgium.

Dr. Herwig Weigl, Institut für österreichische Geschichtsforschung, Wien: Austria (Salzburg archives).

General Abbreviations

Archive Abbreviations:

Abbreviations for individual archives are frequently given in the second section of each report. They are repeated in the Index of Archives.

Abkürzungen für Archive werden oft in der zweiten Abteilung des jeweiligen Berichtes sowie im Index der Archive angegeben.

Abréviations des archives individuelles sont données souvent dans la deuxième section de chaque rapport et dans l'Index des Archives.

Cross-references:

I/01/3/1, usw. = Erstes Kapitel (Österreich) (fehlt bei Verweisen innerhalb des Kapitels), Bericht Nr. 01 (Salzburg, Offizialat des Erzbischofs) (00 = Einleitung, Vorwort), Abteilung Nr. 3 (Bestände), erster Abschnitt (KAS—Offizialatsprotokolle), usw.

II/01/3/1, etc = Chapter II (Belgium) (omitted when the cross-reference is internal to the chapter), report no. 01 (Tournai) (00 = introduction, preface), third section (contents of archives), first subsection (Accounts of the bishop's courts), etc.

III/01/3/1, etc = Chapitre numéro trois (France) (manque si la reférence est dans le chapitre), rapport numéro 01, section numéro 3, sous-section, etc., c.-à-d. le rapport sur l'officialité de l'archevêque d'Aix, troisième section, contenu des ADBRA, etc.

Date Abbreviations:

s14/1, s14/2, s14/in, s14/m, s14/ex, etc = first half, second half, beginning, middle, end of the fourteenth century, etc.

s15/1, s15/2, s15/in, s15/m, s15/ex, usw. = erste Hälfte, zweite Hälfte, Anfang, Mitte, Ende des 15. Jhs., usw.

s16/1 s16/2, s16/in, s16/m, s16/ex, etc = première moitié, deuxième moitié, commencement, milieu, fin du seizième siècle, etc.

Other General Abbreviations:

* = An archive that the author of the report has visited or a doc that s/he has examined personally (see further, General Introduction).

[] (in diocese lists) = The see in question is not located within the modern territorial limits of the country covered by the chapter.

abp = archbishop, archevêque

AD = Archives départementales. For shortened forms of the *inventaires* and *répertoires* of the AD see III/00.

AN = Archives nationales (voir III/56/2).

art(s). = Article(s).

BM = Bibliothèque municipale.

BN = Bibliothèque nationale (voir III/18/2; III/40/2).

c (with dates or numbers) = circa (avec dates ou chiffres), um (bei Daten oder Nummern).

cr. (in diocese lists) = creation of the see in question.

dact = manuscrit dactylographié (se trouvant aux archives nommées).

doc(s) = document(s).

Dok. = Dokument(e).

fol(s) = feuillet(s), Folio(s).

MOL = Magyar Országos Levéltár (siehe: V/01/2).

ms = manuscrit (avec un inventaire ou répertoire indique une liste se trouvante aux archives nommées).

nal = nouvelles acquisitions latines de la BN.

no(s) = numéro(s).

Nr. = Nummer.

p(p) = page(s), Seite(n).

sd = undated, sans date.

X (entre dates) = "bracketing dates," i.e., pas avant la première date et pas après la deuxième date.

Bibliographical Abbreviations

Adams/Donahue, *Select Canterbury Cases* = N. Adams and C. Donahue, *Select Cases from the Ecclesiastical Courts of the Province of Canterbury c. 1200 - 1301*, Selden Soc'y 95 (London, 1981).

AKKR = Archiv für katholisches Kirchenrecht.

Aubenas, *Recueil* = Roger Aubenas, *Recueil de lettres des officialités de Marseille et d'Aix*, 2 vols. (Paris 1937-8).

Balázs, *Magyarország levéltárai* = P. Balázs (ed.), *Magyarország levéltárai* (Budapest 1983).

Bándi, *Csehszlovákiai levéltári anyagról* = Zs. Bándi, *Csehszlovákiai levéltári anyagról készült mikrofilmek (1973. január 1-én)* Levéltári leltárak 62 (Budapest: Magyar Országos Levéltár, 1974).

Bautier/Sornay, *Sources* [ou] Bautier/Sornay = Robert-Henri Bautier et Janine Sornay, *Les sources de l'histoire économique et sociale du moyen âge: Provence-Comtat, Venaissin, Dauphiné, États de la maison Savoie*, 3 vols. (Paris 1968-74).

Bónis, 'Entwicklung' = G. Bónis, 'Die Entwicklung der geistlichen Gerichtsbarkeit in Ungarn vor 1526', ZRG KA 49 (1963).

Bónis, *Középkori jogunk elemei* = G. Bónis, *Középkori jogunk elemei. Római jog, kánonjog, szokásjog* (Budapest 1972).

Borsa, *Csehszlovákiai levéltári* = I. Borsa, *Csehszlovákiai levéltári anyagról készült mikrofilmek az Országos Levéltár filmtárában (1963. január 1-én)* Levéltári leltárak 19 (Budapest: Levéltárak Országos Központja, 1963).

Bunyitay, *Egyháztörténelmi* = V. Bunyitay, R. Rapaics, J. Karácsonyi, *Egyháztörténelmi emlékek a magyarországi hitújitás korából*, 5 Bde. (Budapest 1902-1912).

CNRS, *Répertoire des visites* = CNRS, *Répertoire des visites pastorales de la France* 1: *Anciens Diocèses*, 3 vols. to date (Paris 1977-).

Dolezalek, *Imbreviaturbuch* = G. Dolezalek, *Das Imbreviaturbuch des erzbischöflichen Gerichtsnotars Hubaldus aus Pisa, Mai bis August 1230*, Forschungen zur neueren Privatrechtsgeschichte 13 (Köln 1969).

Donahue, 'Canon Law and Social Practice' = C. Donahue, 'The Canon Law on the Formation of Marriage and Social Practice in the Later Middle Ages', *Journal of Family History* (Summer, 1983) 149-53.

Donahue, 'Stubbs vs. Maitland' = C. Donahue, 'Roman Canon Law in the Medieval English Church: Stubbs vs. Maitland Re-Examined After 75 Years in the Light of Some Records from the Church Courts', *Michigan Law Review* 72 (1974) 647-716.

Erdélyi, *Szent Benedek Rend története* = L. Erdélyi (ed.), *A pannonhalmi Szent Benedek Rend története*, 12 Bde. (Budapest 1902-1916).

Fournier, *Origine* = Édouard Fournier, *L'origine du vicaire général et des autres membres de la curie diocésaine* (Paris 1940).

Gottlieb, *Getting Married* = Beatrice Gottlieb, *Getting Married in Pre-Reformation Europe: The Doctrine of Clandestine Marriage and Court Cases in Fifteenth-Century Champagne* Ph.D. Thesis, Columbia University (Ann Arbor: University Microfilms, 1974).

Guide aux fonds judiciaires = [France. Ministère de l'éducation nationale. Direction des archives de France.] *Guide des recherches dans les fonds judiciaires de l'ancien régime* (Paris: Imprimerie nationale, 1958).

Gyetvai, *Egyházi szervezés* = P. Gyetvai, *Egyházi szervezés főleg az egykori déli magyar területeken és a bácskai Tisza mentén* Dissertationes Hungaricae ex historia Ecclesiae 7 (München 1987).

Hageneder, *Geistliche Gerichtsbarkeit* = Othmar Hageneder, *Die geistliche Gerichtsbarkeit in Ober- und Niederösterreich. Von den Anfängen bis zum Beginn des 15. Jahrhunderts* Forschungen zur Geschichte Oberösterreichs 10 (Linz 1967).

Helvetia Sacra 1/1 = *Schweizerische Kardinäle, das apostolische Gesandtschaftswesen in der Schweiz, Erzbistümer und Bistümer* 1, redigiert von Albert Bruckner, Helvetia Sacra 1.1 (Bern 1972).

Helvetia Sacra 1/3 = *Archidiocèses et Diocèses* 3: *Le diocèse de Genève, l'archidiocèse de Vienne en Dauphiné* rédigé par Jean-Pierre Renard, Helvetia Sacra 1.3 (Bern 1980).

Hildesheimer/Giordanengo, *Guide* = Françoise Hildesheimer et Gérard Giordanengo, *Guide sommaire et état des fonds des Archives des Bouches-du-Rhône* (Marseille 1976).

Imbert/Font-Réaux, *Répertoire* = L. Imbert et J. de Font-Réaulx, *Répertoire numérique de la série G* [G I à G LXXI] (Avignon 1956) (voir III/00; III/02/2).

Joosting/Muller, *Bronnen* = J.G.C. Joosting en S. Muller Hz., *Bronnen voor de geschiedenis der kerkelijke rechtspraak in het bisdom Utrecht in de middeleeuwen*, 7 vols. ('s-Gravenhage 1906-1924).

Knauz, *Codices manuscripti* = F.(N.) Knauz, *Codices manuscripti Capituli Posoniensis* (Esztergom 1870).

Knauz, *Monumenta* = F.(N.) Knauz u. C.L. Dedek, *Monumenta Ecclesiae Strigoniensis*, 3 Bde. (Strigonii 1874-1924).

Koller, *Historia Quinqueecclesiarum* = J. Koller, *Historia Episcopatus Quinqueecclesiarum*, 7 Bde. (Posonii/Pesthini 1782-1812).

Kovachich, *Formulae* = M.G. Kovachich, *Formulae solemnes styli in cancellaria, curiaque regum, foris minoribus ac locis credibilibus, authenticisque Regni Hungariae olim usitati* (Pesthini 1799).

Kumorovitz, *Veszprémi regeszták* = B.L. Kumorovitz, *Veszprémi regeszták 1301-1387*, Magyar Országos Levéltár kiadványai 2, Forráskiadványok 2 (Budapest 1953).

Lefebvre-Teillard, *Officialités* = Anne Lefebvre-Teillard, *Les officialités à la veille du concile de Trente* Bibliothèque d'histoire du droit et droit romain 19 (Paris 1973).

Lefebvre-Teillard, 'Une institution inconnue' = Anne Lefebvre-Teillard, 'Une institution inconnue: le conseil archiépiscopal de Lyon', RHD 48 (1970) 226-251.

Magyar Országos Levéltár = *A Magyar Országos Levéltár Fondjainak és Állagainak jegyzéke*, 3 Bde., 2. Ausg. (Budapest: Magyar Országos Levéltár, 1974-1975).

Merlet, 'Registres' = Lucien Merlet, 'Registres des officialités de Chartres', *Bibliothèque de l'école des chartes*, 4e sér. 2 (17) (1856) 574-94.

MHDB = Mémoires de la Société pour l'histoire du droit et des institutions des anciens pays bourguignons, comtois et romands.

MDSR [2.8] = Mémoires et documents publiés par la Société de la Suisse romande [2e série, volume 8].

Muller, *Registers en rekeningen* = S. Muller Fz., *De registers en rekeningen van het bisdom Utrecht, 1325-1336*, 2 vols. (Utrecht/'s-Gravenhage 1889-1891).

Nagy, *Magyarországi katolikus egyház levéltári* = L. Nagy (ed.), *A magyarországi katolikus egyház levéltári anyagának fondjegyzékei*, 1. rész, kézirat gyanánt (Budapest: Uj Magyar Központi Levéltár, 1983).

NRHD = Nouvelle revue historique de droit.

Ollivant, *The Court of the Official* = S. Ollivant, *The Court of the Official in Pre-Reformation Scotland*, Stair Soc'y 34 (Edinburgh 1982).

"O.m., 42" = Oklevélkibocsátói mutató, 42. csoport (vikárius) (siehe: V/00/B.3).

Ortvay, *Geographia* = T. Ortvay, *Geographia ecclesiastica Hungariae ineunte saeculo XIV*, 2 Bde. (Budapest 1891).

Péterffy, *Sacra concilia* = P.C. Péterffy, *Sacra concilia ecclesiae Rom.-Cath. in*

Regno Hungariae celebrata, 1 (Posonii 1741).

Petit, *Registre* = Joseph Petit et Paul Marichal (ed.), *Registre des causes civiles de l'officialité de Paris, 1384-1387*, Collection des docs inédits sur l'histoire de France (Paris 1919).

Pommeray, *Officialité archidiaconale* = L. Pommeray, *L'officialité archidiaconale de Paris aux XVe-XVIe siècles: Sa composition et sa compétence criminelle* Thèse, Paris (Paris: Sirey, 1933).

Poudret, 'Usuriers' = Jean-François Poudret, 'La succession des usuriers selon le concordat de 1430 entre le duc Amadée VIII et le clergé de Savoie', MHDB 36 (1979) 39-51.

RHD = Revue historique de droit, 4e série.

SMÆH = *Scriptoria medii aevi Helvetica. Denkmäler schweizerischer Schreibkunst des Mittelalters.*

Szentirmai, 'Ungarische Diözesankurie' = A. Szentirmai, 'Die ungarische Diözesankurie im Spätmittelalter', ZRG KA 48 (1962) 164-221.

SZG = Schweizerische Zeitschrift für Geschichte.

Tabulae codicum = Academia Caesarea Vindobonensis (ed.), *Tabulae codicum manu scriptorum praeter graecos et orientales in Bibliotheca Palatina Vindobonensi asservatorum*, 10 Bde. (Vindobonae 1864-1899).

Tangl = M. Tangl (ed.), *Die päpstlichen Kanzleiordnungen von 1200 bis 1500* (Innsbruck 1894, repr. Aalen 1959) (*Provinciale* = pp 1-32).

Teutsch, *Geschichte* = G.D. Teutsch, *Geschichte der Siebenbürger Sachsen*, 4. Ausg. (Hermannstadt 1925).

TRG = Tijdschrift voor Rechtsgeschiedenis.

Vleeschouwers/Van Melkebeek, *Liber sentenciarum* = Cyriel Vleeschouwers en Monique Van Melkebeek, *Liber sentenciarum van de officialiteit van Brussel (1448-1459)*, 2 banden, Verzameling van de Oude Rechtspraak in België 7.1-2 (Brussel 1982-3).

Vleeschouwers-Van Melkebeek, 'Archief' = Monique Vleeschouwers-Van Melkebeek, 'Het archief van de bisschoppen van Doornik: een inventaris uit 1477', *Handelingen van de Koninklijke Commissie voor Geschiedenis* 149 (1983) 121-376.

Vleeschouwers-Van Melkebeek, *Officialiteit van Doornik* = Monique Vleeschouwers-Van Melkebeek, *De officialiteit van Doornik. Oorsprong en vroege ontwikkeling (1192-1300)*, Verhandelingen van de Koninklijke Academie voor Wetenschappen, Letteren en Schone Kunsten van België, Klasse der Letteren 47.117 (Brussel 1987).

Wagner, *Analecta* = C. Wagner, *Analecta Scepusii sacri et prophani*, 4 Bde. (Viennae/Posonii/Cassoviae 1773-1778).

Zimmermann, *Urkundenbuch* = F. Zimmermann, K. Werner, G. Müller, G. Gündisch, *Urkundenbuch zur Geschichte der Deutschen in Siebenbürgen*, 5 Bde. (Hermannstadt/Bucuresti 1892-1975).

ZRG KA = Zeitschrift der Savigny-Stiftung für Rechtsgeschichte, Kanonistische Abteilung.

ZSKG = Zeitschrift für schweizerische Kirchengeschichte.

General Introduction

01. The Problem

In the large effort of examining and editing unpublished sources that has characterized the historiography of medieval canon law in the past generation, case material (with the exception of papal decretals), as opposed to legislative and doctrinal material, and archival, as opposed to manuscript material, have tended to be neglected. The reasons for this relative neglect are complicated and probably not very important. So much needs to be done in so many areas that one should hardly criticize scholars for focusing on one thing that ought to be done rather than another thing that ought to be done. What needs asserting is that the history of medieval canon law as a legal system is not going to be written until we have a better idea than we do now of how law and practice fitted together, how the various doctrines of the academic law shaped and were shaped by the societies within which they were applied, what role canon law, as opposed to other bodies of law, played in the lives of different people across the Latin West during the Middle Ages and beyond. Some progress has been made in these areas in the various studies of the interrelationship of canon law and politics, and some attention is now being paid to the *concilia* of later medieval canonists, another important source of the history of the relationship between the academic law and practical reality. There remains, however, one source of that history, the records of the medieval ecclesiastical courts, that until quite recently had hardly been touched.

Recently, a small body of research has been published on the workings of the medieval ecclesiastical courts of the Latin Church both in England and on the Continent. Citing only book-length studies and editions, one might mention:

> Adams/Donahue, *Select Canterbury Cases*; Dolezalek, *Imbreviaturbuch*; Hageneder, *Geistliche Gerichtsbarkeit*; R.H. Helmholz, *Marriage Litigation in Medieval England* (Cambridge (Eng.) 1974); Lefebvre-Teillard, *Officialités*; Ollivant, *The Court of the Official*; Dorothy M. Owen (ed.) *John Lydford's Book* Historical Manuscripts Commission JP 22 (London 1974); Jane E. Sayers, *Papal Judges Delegate in the Province of Canterbury, 1198–1254*, Oxford Historical Monographs (London 1971); Vleeschouwers/Van Melkebeek, *Liber sentenciarum*; Richard Wunderli, *London Church Courts and Society on the Eve of the Reformation*, Speculum Anniversary Monographs 7 (Cambridge (Mass.) 1981).

No complete picture of the medieval officialities has yet emerged, but enough has been done that we can discern striking patterns both of unity and of divergence.

The unity seems to reflect the transnational character both of the academic canon law and of the Church as an institution. We rarely find a sentence of an ecclesiastical court that violates a basic rule of law found in the academic writers; we rarely find a court that does not seem to be applying one or another form of Romano-canonic procedure; and the patterns of geographical jurisdiction almost always reflect the familiar ideal type of the hierarchical church (pope, archbishop (metropolitan), bishop, archdeacon (frequently but not always), with room for occasional courts of rural or urban deans, below the level of the archdeacon, and for 'peculiars', jurisdictions exempt from one or more elements in the hierarchy).

At the same time there are some remarkable divergences. The subject-matter and personal jurisdiction of the church courts varied markedly from time to time and place to place. Sometimes these divergences seem to reflect open or tacit understandings reached between the ecclesiastical and the secular authorities; sometimes they may reflect differences in the underlying societies. An example of the former might be the differing treatment of criminous clerks in England and in France in the later Middle Ages.

Compare, e.g., L. Gabel, *Benefit of Clergy in the Later Middle Ages* Smith College Studies in History 14 (Northampton (Mass.) 1929) and C.R. Cheney, 'The Punishment of Felonious Clerks', *English Historical Review* 51 (1936) 215, with R. Génestal, *Le privilegium fori en France* (Paris, 1929) and O. Martin, *L'assemblée de Vincennes de 1329 et ses conséquences* (Paris 1909).

An example of the latter might be the large number of cases concerning informal, *de presenti* marriages in England and the relative absence of such cases from the French records. (See Donahue, 'Canon Law and Social Practice'.)

The problem is complicated by the fact that jurisdiction in law and jurisdiction in fact frequently differed; knowledge of a court's legal jurisdiction does not always tell the researcher what he will find there. For example, by the s14 the English church courts' jurisdiction over cases concerning lay debts (other than those pertaining to marriage or testaments) was not recognized by the secular courts and was hardly defended as a matter of law even by churchmen; yet the English church courts in fact heard thousands of such cases.

See R. Helmholz, 'Assumpsit and *fidei laesio*', *Law Quarterly Review* 91 (1975) 406-32.

On the other hand, the French church courts' jurisdiction to hear *de presenti* marriage cases seems never to have been disputed, but in fact they heard relatively few such cases.

Not only does jurisdiction in fact differ widely from time to time and place to place, but there are also wide differences in the procedures employed. A great variety of procedures are encompassed under the broad heading 'Romano-canonic procedure'. Some courts seem to have heard practically no civil cases; some courts practically no criminal. There are, for example, no surviving records of civil cases from the diocesan officiality of Châlons-sur-Marne and virtually no records of criminal cases from the consistory court of York (Donahue, 'Canon Law and Social Practice', p 154 n40; Donahue, 'Stubbs vs. Maitland', pp 703-4).

Some courts regularly employed recognizable variants of "long form" procedure; others made use of summary procedures, and there are a bewildering variety of the latter, ranging from the occasional consolidation of terms in a procedure that otherwise follows the long-form *ordo* quite strictly to the one- or two-session hearings typical of criminal cases in the English archdeacons' courts and the northern French diocesan courts. (See Adams/Donahue, *Select Canterbury Cases*, pp *57-9, 68-71*; Lefebvre-Teillard, *Officialités*, pp 71-83.)

Given the state of our knowledge of what was actually happening in the wide variety of English and Continental church courts in the Middle Ages, it would be rash to attempt any definitive explanation of these similarities and differences in jurisdiction and procedure. Before we can even begin to explain the differences, we must get a better comparative sense of what was happening in the church courts in England and on the Continent. To do this we must know where the records are and what is in them. Even when they are available, most archival descriptions are not adequate for our purposes. For example, someone who is examining the question whether there was a shift in the proportion of marriage cases and other kinds of cases in the church courts in the late fifteenth century would not be advised to examine the 1480 register of the provincial court at Sens. The register meticulously records each step in the procedure of the cases but rarely tells us what the case is about. (See III/53/3/2).

This last point leads to another reason why the content of the records must be described: What looks at first glance like differences among the courts may only be differences among the types of records kept or the types of records that have survived. A register may record only criminal cases, but that does not mean that the court heard no civil cases. There may have been a civil register, now lost, or it may have been the practice to keep records of the civil cases in files of documents (libels, depositions, etc.) with the *acta* written on the back, as was done in some periods for the consistory court at York. (See Donahue, 'Stubbs vs. Maitland', p 657 & nn 56, 58.)

The Church Courts Records Working Group, then, undertook a preliminary survey of the surviving records of the courts of the Latin Church in the British Isles and on the Continent prior to 1563. (The date was chosen somewhat arbitrarily to coincide with last session of the Council of Trent. In some cases we stopped short of that. Where we did, the fact is indicated in the editor's preface or introduction that precedes each chapter.) On the basis of this survey we hoped that it might be possible to outline some answers, or possible answers, to the questions just posed. Even if that did not prove possible, the survey would still be valuable, since it would show others where the material that may contain the answers lies.

02. The Results

Our group was joined by one or more correspondents in Austria, Belgium, England, France, Germany, Hungary, Italy, The Netherlands, Portugal and Switzerland. Since we lacked any correspondent in Spain, one of our American members undertook two journeys to that country to make some preliminary soundings of the church court archives there. England proved to be a formidable undertaking. The quantity of surviving medieval church court records in that country is large, and the description of their contents requires substantial space. For this reason, the English reports will be in a separate volume.

Although this volume contains reports on every country listed above except for England, the reports vary in their completeness. Some of our correspondents were not able to complete their work in time for the publisher's deadline. The ZRG KA has offered to publish additional reports of this nature, and we hope that those who were unable to finish in time for this volume will eventually be able to fill the gaps in our reports. Indeed, we hope that others will be inspired to provide similar reports for other archives and to add to and to correct the descriptions of the contents of those archives we have described.

As it now stands, we believe that Austria (which was expanded to include the whole of the medieval province of Salzburg), France, Hungary (which was expanded to include the whole of the medieval provinces of Esztergom and Kalocsa) and Switzerland are complete, or virtually complete. The Belgian report lacks Liège, but is complete or virtually complete for the one see that we believe has left substantial surviving records, Tournai. The report for the Netherlands is complete for the *fonds* of the bishop of Utrecht and three of the five subordinate medieval chapters in that city.

To balance against these substantial achievements, there are disappointments: Our soundings in Germany, Italy and Spain suggest that there are important archival remains of the medieval church courts in those countries, but in all three cases our chapters contain reports on one, or just a few, archives. In the case of both Italy and Germany, the political and ecclesiastical history of the country has separated, in some but not all instances, the archives from their original custodians without placing them under central control, as they have been in France. Thus medieval ecclesiastical court archives may be found in state archives, in city archives, in ecclesiastical archives, or in state, city or university libraries, each with its own system of classification and arrangement, systems which are frequently not published and sometimes not even written down. These systems are so diverse as to defy easy characterization, and in many cases there is no easy way to find records of the officialities without going through the contents of a broad class of general ecclesiastical records.

A striking illustration of the problems created by dispersion of archives is provided by the medieval records of the officiality of Freising (see I/04), broken runs of which exist in both the archiepiscopal archive in München and in the Bayerisches Hauptstaatsarchiv in the same city. When pieced together these records constitute a substantial percentage of the protocol books that probably existed at one time; separated, they are annoyingly broken runs.

In Italy, the problem of partial secularization of the records is compounded by the great notarial tradition of that country. (This problem also exists in the south of France and may exist in Spain.) While the church courts made use of notaries throughout Western Europe, including in England, the notaries in northern Europe do not seem to have kept their records in their own notarial archives. In southern Europe they did so, so that when a notary was appointed to serve a local officiality, he might well keep its records with other records in his notarial archive. Gero Dolezalek was, we believe, the first to point this out in print, and his discovery enabled him to find and publish what remains the earliest published court book of any local ecclesiastical court:

> Dolezalek, *Imbreviaturbuch*; see G. Dolezalek, 'Une nouvelle source pour l'étude de la pratique judiciaire au XIII siècle: les livres d'imbréviatures des notaires de cour', in *Confluence des droits savants et des pratiques juridiques: Actes du Colloque de Montpellier* (Milan 1979), 225-41.

Fortunately, inventories are beginning to be made of the contents of the great southern European notarial *études*, and church court records are appearing in the process. (See, e.g., III/07/2; VI/01/2.)

Not only are our reports incomplete for the central core of Europe, they are simply lacking for its outer orbit. We were unable to obtain a correspondent in any of the Slavic-speaking countries, and the report the provinces of Esztergom and Kalocsa suggests, and in some cases confirms, that there are survivals there. We had no correspondent in any of the Scandinavian countries. Our plans for reports for Scotland and Ireland went awry (although Ollivant, *The Court of the Official* suggests that most of what survives in Scotland has been described in that book).

Granted the incompleteness of our efforts, it is obviously premature to attempt to draw any firm conclusions. We have, however, considerably expanded the list of archival materials known beyond the local areas in which they lie and hence have enlarged the opportunities for comparative research. Further, there do seem to be some patterns emerging from the reports themselves that may be useful in establishing plans for further research:

Leaving aside what has already been found in the Italian notarial archives (much less what remains to found there), the earliest court book found on the Continent of Europe is the court book of Mende from the 1270s (see III/23/3/1), and it is highly experimental in nature. The second volume of reports will show that the earliest court book in England is from the early s14, but that rolls, making continuous recordings of sessions before the court, survive from the

1270s. Prior to the 1270s, we do find in some places individual court documents from litigated cases and, of course, numerous references to cases and to officials. In most places, however, continuous or even broken runs of court documents, much less of court books, do not begin until the late s14 or the s15.

One can, of course, argue that continuous runs of records did exist, at least from the s13, and that they were destroyed. Each archive has its story of why no early church court records exist, a story usually relating their destruction to some calamitous event, either national (the Peasants' Revolt, or the Civil Wars, in England; the Revolution or the Wars of Religion, in France) or local (the Great London fire, the transfer of the Utrecht records to Charles V), etc. There is no doubt that much has been destroyed. The fact, however, that substantial runs of records do survive, at least in some places, from the s15 and s16 suggests that more recent events have not been totally destructive, and the failure of any such runs to survive from earlier periods casts some doubt on the hypothesis that the destruction that has indubitably occurred is completely responsible for the almost total absence of runs of records from the s13 and early s14.

The pattern of surviving records may signify something about the development of local church courts as institutions. Of course, church courts, in the sense of ad hoc or part-time bodies or officers employing canon law to resolve disputes or punish offenses against church discipline, existed in many places from at least the late s12. But the development of a professionalized, separate institution, the officiality as it is classically understood, may be, in many if not all places, a phenomenon of the late Middle Ages.

A second point that emerges from these reports is more mundane but perhaps no less important: There is more variety in modern archival practice and terminology than there is in the underlying records. The typology of church court records that we tentatively suggested in our preliminary report (published in Bd. I of this series) has held up remarkably well: (1) There are individual documents used in litigation (cause papers, *procédures*, *Urkunden* (the last term frequently but not invariably applied)). These are almost always in the forms that a familiarity with the handbooks of Romano-canonical procedure would lead one to expect: libels, exceptions, positions, articles, depositions, sentences, appeals, etc. (2) Proceedings in open court are normally redacted as *acta*. (3) The combination of the individual documents together with the *acta* gives us a *processus*, *(procès* (there does not seem to be a German word for it)). (4) Various combinations of *acta* and/or cause papers can be recorded in books (act books. *registres*, *Protokolle*). The arrangement of these can be more-or-less chronological, or case-by-case, the former having the disadvantage of making the record of any one case difficult to reconstruct, the latter creating considerable problems of composition and running the risk of being incomplete. A few books consisting only of sentences or only of depositions have been found (e.g., III/43/3 (sentences), III/07/3/2 (registers of depositions)).

In areas where the notarial tradition is strong, archivists have attempted to classify these books according to various ideal types of notarial records. These types normally vary according to the stage of redaction of record. Thus, for example, in the south of France we find books of records classified as *plumitifs, brevets, brouillards, manuels, matricules, minutes*. While these classifications may give us some clue as to the immediacy of the record (and also as to its legibility), they generally do not give much help in determining its substantive contents. Each court notary seems to have had slightly different views as to what was useful to record, but the possibilities are quite limited, and there are more similarities than differences in these types of records.

We might add a sixth type of record to the ones that we defined initially. Some courts kept various types of "house-keeping" books. We have found various types of account books, ranging from full annual accounts, listing all the receipts and expenses of the officiality to accounts of receipts of a particular kind, such as fees for gracious acts (documents in non-contentious matters approved by or registered with the court) or fines. There are also books recording fines and excommunications, and books containing lists of proctors or recording proxies. Account books or rolls of various kinds seem to be particularly common in northern France and in the Low Countries, and that fact may give us a clue as to the nature of the officiality as an institution in those areas.

Finally, there are, in addition to the records themselves, a rather large number of formularies drawn from them, and various collections of statutes for the courts, occasionally a style of the court. The pattern of survival with this type of material is almost haphazard, and we have indubitably missed a good deal of it because our focus was on archives rather than on manuscript libraries where this type of material is frequently kept.

03. How to Use This Book

Our correspondents were chosen on a national basis. This makes sense from the point of view of ease of access to archives, but it makes less sense in terms of the geographical divisions of the medieval church, particularly since we committed ourselves to organizing our reports on the basis of officialities rather than of archives. In the end, each report represents a compromise between the two types of organization, and the nature of this compromise is normally given in the Editor's Preface or Introduction at the head of each chapter.

Our search was principally for *court* archives, i.e., records that we had reason to believe had been kept by the officiality itself, as opposed to some person or institution interested in a particular case. This procedure put us, to some extent, at the mercy of archival classifications, some of which were made many years ago, before any of the modern research on officialities. It also meant that court books, as opposed to individual documents, are probably over represented. Our search was also for episcopal officialities, as opposed to subordinate or exempt officialities.

Obviously, where we came across records that had been preserved by parties to litigation as opposed to the officiality itself, we have included them, but our efforts here are certainly incomplete. We have attempted to indicate where a record does not seem to be part of the *fonds* of the officiality itself. Similarly, we have listed individual documents where they are preserved in what seems to be part of the *fonds* of the officiality. But our efforts with individual documents vary considerably in the elaboration of the description. Similarly, where we found records of subordinate or exempt officialities, we have listed them, and in the case of Austria, France, Hungary and Switzerland, we have reason to believe that we have all or most of the organized officialities that have left surviving records.

Each chapter is accompanied by a preface and/or an introduction. These always contain remarks on the completeness of the search and usually contain a list of medieval dioceses in the country or area, derived from Tangl's *Provinciale*. Some of the introductions go considerably further, offering a brief general history of the organization of the officialities in the country or area in question, general bibliography (Switzerland), a list of all known officialities in the provinces (Hungary), etc. It seemed better to include such information where we had it, rather than omitting because we did not have it for all areas. The introduction to the German report differs from the others, in that it provides a bibliography accompanying the diocese list — the editor's attempt to make up for his inability to obtain more reports from Germany.

The chapters are arranged in alphabetical order by the English name of the countries. Within the chapters, officialities are listed in alphabetical order, first by the name of the province in which they were located, then by the diocese, if any, and finally by the name of the subordinate area, in the case of officialities subordinate to the diocesan officiality. This arrangement means that provincial officialities and officialities exempt from diocesan, but not provincial, jurisdiction are listed under the name of the province alone. However logical this arrangement may be, it has created some practical difficulties because jurisdiction over exempt officialities was often controverted, and even where it was not controverted, it is sometimes not known. Before concluding that we have found no records from a given exempt officiality, it is best to look both under the province and under the diocese in which most or all of its territory was located, or in the Index of Persons and Places.

The individual reports are written in the language in which they were submitted. This seemed better than trying to translate the archival terminology that these reports employ. It gives, however, a macaronic quality to some of the chapters. Country names are given in the language in which the author is writing; place-names (including place-names used for ecclesiastical jurisdictions) other than country names are the "official" names, i.e., they are given in the official language of the place that bears the name.

Each report is divided into three or four numbered parts. The first part gives the province, diocese (if any), and name of the officiality and occasionally brief remarks on the history of the officiality. The names of the officialities have been standardized, so that the only time in which the form "officiality of (the bishop, archdeacon, cathedral chapter, abbey, etc.)" is not used is where it is known that there was no officer of the court who was called "official". The second part gives the name, address, and, where available, the telephone number of the archive(s) (or library) whose contents are the subject of the report. This is normally accompanied by a bibliography of the finding lists that the archive uses and sometimes by a brief history of the archive. Where the author of the report has visited the archive, the name of the archive is marked by an asterisk (*). This part also gives the abbreviation, if any, used for the archive in the report. (A complete listing of these abbreviations is found in the Index of Archives.) The country within which the archive is located is given only if differs from that in the title of the chapter. The third part gives a description of the documents, also marked with asterisks to indicate the ones which the author has examined personally (in situ, on film, or, in the case of France, by transfer to the AN). These descriptions are frequently divided into subsections, set off with numbered headings in italics. Where the list is long, it is given in the order of the archive classification. The first line of the description is standard: archive classification, physical description of quantity (in fols, pp, number of docs, etc), date or range of dates, and a brief indication of the contents. More elaborate descriptions are given in the smaller type that follows. The fourth part, where it is present, offers general comments on the surviving records of the officiality and/or general bibliography.

The contents of each chapter are listed at the front of the book. A table of general abbreviations follows the table of contents. All books or articles cited more than once have bibliographical short forms that are expanded in the table of bibliographical abbreviations that follows the table of general abbreviations.

OTHMAR HAGENEDER,
CHRISTOPH HAIDACHER, KLAUS LINDNER und HERWIG WEIGL

I. Österreich (Kirchenprovinz Salzburg)

Editor's Introduction

Most of the territory of modern Austria was in the medieval ecclesiastical province of Salzburg. Tangl's *Provinciale* offers the following for this province:

Salzburg (Salzeburgensis)
[Passau] (Patavensis)
[Regensburg] (Ratisponensis)
[Freising] (Frisingensis)
Gurk (Gurcensis)
[Bressanone (Brixen)] (Brixinensis)
Seckau (Secoviensis)
[Chiemsee] (Kimensis)
Lavant (Laventinensis)

Wien became a see before the council of Trent and was exempt from metropolitical jurisdiction. This report includes Wien and all the sees in the province of Salzburg. It thus includes what we know of the records of the officialities not only in modern Austria but also in the medieval sees of Bressanone (ITA), Chiemsee (BRD), Freising (BRD), Passau (BRD) and Regensburg (BRD).

Ecclesiastical jurisdiction in the province of Salzburg was complicated. In some areas claims to exemption were contested over long periods of time. Suffice it say here that the Salzburg archive (01/2) contains *acta* and *processus* in cases held before the Salzburg official in which the parties come from the suffragan sees of Bressanone, Chiemsee, Freising, Lavant, Passau, Regensburg and Seckau, and from the subordinate or exempt jurisidictions of the archdeacon of Baumburg and of the provost of Berchtesgaden. In some of these documents the case seems to have come to the official of Salzburg by way of appeal from the lower court; in others the case seems to have been brought before the official of Salzburg directly as a matter of first instance; in still others it is unclear which is involved. Rather than trying to assign these documents to what is in many cases an uncertain jurisdiction of origin, it seemed better to leave them in the description of the Salzburg archive and to refer the reader to the Index of Persons and Places for a complete listing.

The report was prepared under the general direction of Prof. Hageneder. Dr. Weigl prepared the report on the Salzburg archive, Dr. Haidacher that on the archive at Bressanone, and Mr. Lindner those on the archives in Regensburg and München (Freising holdings). (The Bressanone holdings are almost all post-Tridentine, but since we had the information about them it seemed useful to publish it.) For the rest, the information was provided to Prof. Hageneder by the archivists of the various archives. In this regard, we should particularly like to thank Dr. Walter Jaroschka, Generaldirektor der staatlichen Archive Bayerns; Dr. Hans Spatzenegger, E.B. Konsistorialarchiv Salzburg; Dr. Peter Tropper, Diözesanarchiv Gurk-Klagenfurt; and Dr. Johann Weißensteiner, Diözesanarchiv Wien. The following archivists reported that they had no holdings of medieval records concerning the church courts: Univ. Dozent Dr. Karl Heinz Burmeister, Vorarlberger Landesarchiv Bregenz; Dr. Heinz Moser, Tiroler Landesarchiv Innsbruck; Hofrat Dr. Alfred Ogris, Kärntner Landesarchiv Klagenfurt; Hofrat Dr. Gerhard Pferschy, Steiermärkisches Landesarchiv Graz; Hofrat Dr. Franz Stundner, Niederösterreichisches Landesarchiv Wien; Hofrat Dr. Alois Zauner, Oberösterreichisches Landesarchiv Linz; and Dr. Hans Peter Zelfel, Diözesanarchiv Eisenstadt.

[01.]

1. Salzburg, Offizialat des Erzbischofs.

Salzburg war der Gerichtshof für seine Diözese sowie Appellationsinstanz der Suffragan- und Eigenbistümer. Allerdings wurden auch Fälle aus deren Gebiet behandelt, ohne daß ein direkter Bezug zu Salzburg oder eine Appellation erkennbar wäre.

2. *E.B. Konsistorialarchiv, Kapitelplatz 2, A-5010 Salzburg, Tel. (0662) 42 5 91/49 [KAS].

Die Bestände betreffen grundsätzlich geistliche Belange *(res ecclesiasticae)*, im Bereich der geistlichen Gerichtsbarkeit aber alle ihre möglichen Aspekte. Die Archivalien der Erzbischöfe als Landesfürsten *(res status, res camerae)* wurden nach der Säkularisation des Erzstifts 1806 ins Haus-, Hof- und Staatsarchiv in Wien gebracht. Siehe:

Ludwig Bittner ed., *Inventar österreichischer staatlicher Archive* 5: *Inventar des Wiener Haus-, Hof- und Staatarchivs* 7 (Wien 1938) 29-32.

*Archiv des Erzbistums München und Freising, Maxburgstraße 2, D-8000 München 33, Postfach 360, Tel. (089) 2137 345 [AEMF].

Die Angaben über dieses Archiv werden von Herrn Lindner mitgeteilt. Siehe unten 03/2.

3. *1. KAS – Konsistorial- bzw. Offizialatsprotokolle*:

Die Papierbände in Kasten 2 ("liber actorum" bzw. "protocollum actorum consistorialium") haben keine eigene Signatur. Sie sind modern gebunden, wobei mehrere der ehemals getrennten Jahrgänge zusammengefaßt wurden und gelegentlich die Deckblätter verloren gingen. Sie habe schmales Quartformat (halbbrüchig), die Paginierung ist modern. Sie wurden meist von mehreren Schreibern kontinuierlich geführt.

Sie enthalten Verzeichnisse der Gerichtspersonen und streng chronologisch knappe Eintragungen der gerichtlichen Vorgänge an den drei wöchentlich stattfindenden Gerichtstagen unter Nennung einer oder beider Parteien, der Art des Falles und der Handlung des Prokurators bzw. seiner Ernennung, ohne inhaltliche Aufschlüsse über den Streitfall zu geben. Parteien sind Kleriker wie Laien. Behandelt sind Zehent-, Schulden-, Testaments-, Ehesachen und Versorgungsansprüche, häufig auch Appellationen. Es sind keine zugehörigen Dokumente eingebunden oder eingetragen.

Die Eintragungen beginnen in den ersten Jännertagen des Jahres und reichen in den ersten vier Jahrgängen noch in den Jänner des folgenden. Ab 1539 sind manche Eintragungen etwas ausführlicher, ihre Zahl geht jedoch zurück. Es werden auch weniger Gerichtstage gehalten und die Bände sind unvollständig, viele Seiten am Schluß und manchmal auch im Inneren sind leer. Der Umfang wächst erst im 17. und 18. Jahrhundert stark an.

*Kasten 2 [Vol. 1]. 167 + 163 pp. 1505, 1517.

*Kasten 2 [Vol. 2]. 91 + 171 pp. 1518, 1519.

*Kasten 2 [Vol. 3]. 69 + 68 + 67 + 78 pp. 1539, 1540, 1541, 1545.

*Kasten 2 [Vol. 4]. 87 + 97 + 74 + 62 pp. 1546, 1547, 1548, 1549.

*Kasten 2 [Vol. 5]. 1551, 1553-8.

1551: p 1-12 nur bis Februar 20, Rest leer.

1553: p 1-32 bis Mai 5, 16 pp leer, dann 3 pp für November/Dezember.

1555: p 1-12, 17-71. 1556: p 1-84, nach p 2 14 unpag. Seiten leer.

1557: p 1-13 bis März 31 und für Dezember 17, dazwischen Lagen verloren.

1558: p 1-22 bis März 16, p 1-35 Mai 20 bis Dezember 29.

*Kasten 2 [Vol. 6]. 1559-60, 1563-7.

1559: p 1-67.

1560: p 1-39 bis Oktober 2.

1563: p 1-56.

Weiters für die Jahre 1564-7.

Die Serie lauft mit Unterbrechungen weiter und ist ab 1611 vollständig.

2. *KAS – Registratura antiqua*:

Die sogenannte "Registratura antiqua" (KAS 11/102 für alle Bände) ist eine uneinheitliche Serie von Bänden aus Papier mit Pergamenteinbänden im Quartformat. Sie bestehen großteils aus in grob chronologischer Ordnung zusammengebundenen Prozeß"registern" ("registrum processus"), d.h. nach Ende der oft mehrjährigen Prozesse vor dem Salzburger Offizial angefertigten Niederschriften des Prozeßverlaufs, der dabei vorgelegten und ergangenen Schriftstücke und der Zeugenaussagen. Die ursprünglich getrennt liegenden Prozesse dürften, nach den Aufschriften — soweit vorhanden — der Einbände zu schließen, spätestens im 17. Jahrhundert zusammengebunden worden sein. Als Einbände wurden Offizialatsurkunden bzw. Notariatsinstrumente des 15. und 16. Jahrhunderts verwendet. Die wohl ehemals vorhandenen Einbände der einzelnen Prozesse (vgl. unten "Akten") gingen dabei verloren. Die durchlaufende Paginierung ist modern.

*KAS 11/102, Vol. 1. 324 pp. 1463-1474. *Registra processus.*

Benefizial-, Besitz-, Schulden-, Erbschafts- und Ehesachen, Appellationen. Parteien sind Kleriker und Laien. Auch die nicht als Appellationen bezeichneten Fälle gehen über den eigentlichen Salzburger Diözesanbereich in den der Suffragane (besonders Passaus) hinaus.

*KAS 11/102, Vol. 2. 482 (3-485) pp. 1404-1503 (Inserte ab 1318). *Registra processus, varia.*

Neben *registra processus* (wie vol. 1) auch einzelne Notariatsinstrumente, Transsumierungen, Zeugenaussagen, Mandate, Briefe, Instruktionen verschiedener Aussteller gerichtlichen und rechtssetzenden Inhalts; auch Streitigkeiten des Erzbischofs.

*KAS 11/102, Vol. 3bis. 535 pp. 1436-1510 (Inserte ab 1400). *Registra processus.*

Am Einband bezeichnet "Processus varii varia obiecta ... nec non transacta bullarum pontificum ... item diplomata imperatorum". *Registra processus*, Notariatsinstrumente, Urkundenabschriften, wie vol. 2.

*KAS 11/102, Vol. 5. 365 pp. 1511-1525. *Registra processus*, wie vol. 1.

*KAS 11/102, Vol. 6. 239 pp (alt foliiert 1-119, alter Pergamenteinband). 1516. "Registrum processus inquisicionis ..."

Prozeß zwischen zwei Geistlichen über Diebstahl, Betrug und Gefangenschaft, der vor den Offizialen von Passau und Salzburg geführt wurde.

*KAS 11/102, Vol. 7. 134 +70 pp (modern gebunden). 1498-1578. *Registra processus.*

Prozeß 1498 vor dem Archidiakon von Baumburg als iudex ordinarius in einer Ehesache; kurze Prozeß"register" (1512-1578) vor dem Salzburger Offizial.

*KAS 11/102, Vol. Passau (ohne Nummer). 185 fols (alt foliiert). 1508/1510. *Registrum processus.*

Prozeß über eine niederösterreichische Pfarre (Ochsenbach), der in zweiter Instanz an den Salzburger Offizial gelangte (1508); Transsumierung (1510) eines Vertrags (1419) zwischen österreichischen Adeligen (Maissau, Puchheim).

3. KAS – Akten:

Die in die umfangreichen Bestände eingestreuten Quellen zur geistlichen Gerichtsbarkeit betreffen Fälle aus den Suffraganbistümern, die auf dem Appellationsweg an den Salzburger Offizial gelangten. Es sind *registra processus* sowie "originale" Einzelakten. Die einzeln liegenden *registra processus* sind Quartbände aus Papier mit originalen Pergamenteinbänden, in die oft zugehörige Einzelakten eingelegt sind.

Die Aktenbestände reichen bis ins 20. Jahrhundert. Die Signaturen bezeichnen die Faszikel, in denen die zitierten Quellen enthalten sind, und nicht nur diese selbst.

*KAS Akten 4/19. 1519-1525. Seckau: *Registrum processus* und Einzelakten über eine steirische Pfarre.

*KAS Akten 4/29. 1520/21. Lavant: *Registrum processus* über Ehesache.

*KAS Akten 4/52. 1506-1570. Chiemsee: Einzelakten betreffend den Bischof von Chiemsee.

*KAS Akten 4/57. 1501ff. Berchtesgaden: Einzelakten zu verschiedenen Prozessen, Matrimonialsachen ab 1522, Testamentssachen ab 1543, vor dem Salzburger Offizial betreffend Berchtesgaden und Umgebung.

*KAS Akten 4/58. 1519-1521, 1563-1569. Bressanone: *Registrum processus* in Zehentsache, beiliegend zugehörige Einzelakten (1519-21); Einzelakten zu verschiedenen Appellationen (1563-9).

*KAS Akten 4/78. c1600. Freising: Verzeichnis der Appellationen aus dem Bistum Freising nach Salzburg unter Angabe von Partei und Betreff für die Jahre 1461-1591 (36 Fälle).

*KAS Akten 4/96. 1505/06, 1545, 1526-1576. Passau: *Registra processus* (1505, 1545); Einzelakten (1526-1576).

*KAS Akten 4/99. 1466-1468, 1516-1518. Regensburg: Einzelakten zu einem Inkorporationsstreit und einem Prozeß über Kircheneinkünfte.

*KAS Akten 4/101. 1443-1477. Regensburg: 5 *Registra processus* mit beiliegenden Originalakten über Zehent, Schulden, Injurien und Ehe.

*KAS Akten 4/102. 1476-1605. Regensburg: 17 *Registra processus*, wie oben. Zwei Verzeichnisse der Appellationen nach Salzburg (wie oben Freising) für die Jahre 1444-1674 bzw. 1694 (76 bzw. 77 Fälle).

Die im KAS vorhandenen Originalurkunden wurden für die Zeit von 1200-1500 von Adam Doppler in den *Mitteilungen der Gesellschaft für Salzburger Landeskunde* 10 (1870) - 16 (1876) publiziert.

4. AEMF:

*S 117. Actus Consistoriales et formulae Curiae Salisburgensis.

4. Literatur:

Andreas Mudrich, 'Das Salzburger Archivwesen', *Mitteilungen des k.k. Archivrats* 2 (1916) 1-32, 181-249

Archive im deutschsprachigen Raum, 2. Aufl., Minerva Handbücher (Berlin/ New York 1974) 2:864f

Hans Paarhammer, *Rechtsprechung und Verwaltung des Salzburger Offizialates (1300-1569)*, Dissertationen der Universität Salzburg 8 (Wien 1977)

Geschichte Salzburgs. Stadt and Land Heinz Dopsch und Hans Spatzenegger ed., 1.1, 2. Aufl. (Salzburg 1983), 1.2 (Salzburg 1983), 1.3 (Salzburg 1984).

Zur geistlichen Gerichtsbarkeit im heutigen Gebiet Österreichs in der Zeit vor dem Einsetzen der Quellenserien des KAS siehe:

Hageneder, *Geistliche Gerichtsbarkeit*

Winfried Stelzer, *Gelehrtes Recht in Österreich. Von den Anfängen bis zum frühen 14. Jahrhundert* MIÖG Ergänzunsband 26 (Wien/Köln/Graz 1982).

[02.]

1. Salzburg, Bressanone (Brixen), Offizialat des Bischofs.

Bressanone bildete den Gerichtshof für seine Diözese. Die geistliche Gerichtsbarkeit wurde seit dem 14. Jahrhundert von Generalvikaren in Vertretung des Bischofs ausgeübt. Im Jahre 1631 wurde dieses Generalvikariat durch die kollegiale Behörde des Konsistoriums ersetzt (Vorformen mit eingeschränkten Rechten sind in Bressanone schon seit c1600 bekannt).

2. *Diözesanarchiv, Hofburg, I-39024 Bressanone, Tel. (0472) 30505.

Das bischöfliche Archiv wurde in der 2. Hälfte des 18. Jahrhunderts systematisch geordnet und die Bestände in einem vierbändigen Repertorium verzeichnet. Die Säkularisation des Jahres 1803 brachte die Zerreißung des Archivs mit sich; ein beträchtlicher Teil der Archivalien wurde nach Innsbruck überstellt. Durch die bayerische Besatzung und die napoleonischen Kriege kamen Bestände nach München und Wien. Schließlich mußte nach dem 1. Weltkrieg der größte Teil der in Innsbruck und Wien lagernden Archivalien von Bressanone an Italien ausgeliefert werden. Somit verteilen sich die Bestände des alten Archivs von Bressanone heute auf folgende sechs Archive: Diözesanarchiv Bressanone, Staatsarchiv Bolzano (Bozen), Tiroler Landesarchiv Innsbruck, Haus-, Hof- und Staatsarchiv Wien, Hauptstaatsarchiv München, Landesarchiv Ljubljana (Laibach). Im Folgenden werden nur die Bestände des Diözesanarchivs behandelt.

E.B. Konsistorialarchiv, Salzburg.

Siehe oben 01/3/3: KAS Akten 4/58.

3. *1. Konsistorialprotokolle*:

Die jeweils mehrere Jahrgänge umfassenden Papierbände besitzen keine eigene Signatur. Die Bände weisen Quartformat auf, wurden zum Teil halbbrüchig geschrieben und besitzen eine zeitgenössische Paginierung. Sie wurden von mehreren Schreibern geführt, als Sprache fand sowohl Latein als auch Deutsch Verwendung, wobei letzteres überwog.

Die Bände beinhalten in chronologischer Reihenfolge (mit kleinen Ausnahmen) relativ ausführliche Eintragungen über die gerichtlichen Vorgänge, wobei das Datum der Verhandlung, die beiden Parteien, das Streitobjekt, die Argumentation der beiden Gegner und das Urteil angeführt werden; fallweise wurden den Fall betreffende Schriftstücke eingetragen beziehungsweise eingeheftet. Seit dem Jahre 1631 werden auch immer die anwesenden Konsistorialräte samt Vorsitzendem genannt. Als Parteien treten sowohl Kleriker als auch Laien in

Erscheinung. Fast alle Bereiche der geistlichen Gerichtsbarkeit sind anzutreffen, vor allem Ehesachen, Testamente, Zehentstreitigkeiten und Schuldenangelegenheiten.

Sämtliche Fälle spielen sich im Bereich der Diözese Bressanone ab. Die Form der Eintragungen variiert in den ersten Jahren, stabilisiert sich jedoch recht bald. Die Serie der Konsistorialprotokolle ist ab den 30-er Jahren des 17. Jahrhunderts vollständig.

*[Vol. 1]: 1601 (p 3, 4); 1602 (p 1, 2, 5-61); 1603 (p 61-96); 1604 (p 96-103); 1613 (p 119-141); 1614 (p 142-180); 1615 (p 181-207); 1616 (p 208-303); 1617 (p 304-312); 1618 (p 313-369); 1619 (p 370-484); 1620 (p 485-526); 1621 (p 527-562); 1622 (p 563-619); 1623 (p 620-700); 1624 (p 701-785); 1625 (p 786-833); 1626 (p 834-917).

*[Vol. 2]: 1630 (p 1-95); 1631 (p 96-562); 1632 (p 562-793); 1633 (p 794-915).

*[Vol. 3]: 1633 (p 1-38) (ab nun ist die Serie vollständig).

2. *Dispensen*:

Die in Quartformat geschriebenen Papierbände besitzen keine eigene Signatur, die Paginierung ist zeitgenössisch, mehrere Schreiber waren an der Abfassung der Bände gleichzeitig beteiligt.

Die Bände enthalten Ehedispensen, wobei im frühesten Dispensenband die Fälle sehr ausführlich behandelt sind, während die späteren Aufzeichnungen knapper abgefaßt sind. Genannt werden Datum, die beiden Partner, Ort, Heiratshindernis, sowie die Taxe. Als Sprache diente Latein.

*[Vol. 1]: "Investitur Protokoll II" enthält neben Investituren der Jahre 1571-1585 Ehedispensen der Jahre 1522-1529 (p 1-163).

*[Vol. 2]: 1690-1733: ab nun ist die Reihe vollständing.

3. *Akten*:

Unter den umfangreichen Aktenbeständen bilden die Konsistorialakten einen beträchtlichen Anteil. Dieser Bestand ist allerdings durch keinen Findbehelf erschlossen, sondern nur nach Orten geordnet.

4. Literatur:

Leo Santifaller, *Die Urkunden der Brixner Hochstifts- Archive 845-1295*, Schlernschriften 15 (Innsbruck 1929)

Leo Santifaller und Heinrich Appelt (ed.), *Die Urkunden der Brixner Hochstifsarchive 1295-1336* 1: *Die Urkunden*; 2: *Einleitung. Register. Siegelabbildungen* Brixner Urkunden 2 (Leipzig 1941-43)

Emil Ottenthal und Oswald Redlich, *Archivberichte aus Tirol* 2 (Wien-Leipzig 1896) 416-560

Franz Wieser, *Das bischöfliche Konsistorium und seine rechtliche Stellung in der Diözesanverwaltung* ungedruckte Dissertation, Rom, 1948. (Zusammenfassung im *Schematismus des Säkular- und Regularklerus der Diözese Brixen für das Jahr 1950* (Bressanone 1950)).

[03.]

1. Salzburg, Freising, officiality of the bishop.

2. *Archiv des Erzbistums München und Freising (see above 01/2).

The archive has a typed list of "Freisinger Offizialats protokolle," which has been compiled since my first visit to the archive in 1982.

The records are well kept, easily accessible and by-and-large very well preserved.

*Bayerisches Hauptstaatsarchiv, Schönfeldstraße 5, D-8000 München 22, Postfach 22 02 40, Tel. (089) 2198-482 [BHA].

This archive contains exactly the same type of consistory court records as the AEMF. The main difference is that the records in the BHA have a pigskin binding, which appears to be very old, if not original. The annual volumes in the episcopal archive, on the other hand, seem to have been provided with a hard-cover binding relatively recently.

Together the two archives seem to contain about seventy percent of the case material of the consistory court of Freising for the period from 1462 to 1526.

The archive contains a voluminous hand-written bound list of manuscripts in the order of their geographical origin, which, on closer examination, may turn up additional material on other courts.

3. *1. AEMF*:

*H 215. 138 fols. February 14 to November 24, 1424. Act book.

This act book contains business heard by the consistory court on a day-by-day basis. The arrangement is strictly chronological. For each date, the scribe started a new section, though not necessarily a new page. Matrimonial cases and cases involving church dues are not kept separate. Different parts of one case are often spead over several pages. A large majority of cases involved matrimonial matters.

*H 216. 249 fols. January 14 to December 20, 1471. Act book.

Same as above. This act book seems almost complete, although parts of the first four fols have been torn off. The time of day on which a witness was interrogated or on which a sentence was passed etc. was generally noted. Sentences were usually pronounced together at the end of the day. A number of letters from parish priests responding to court inquiries are bound with the case they concern. Quotations from this volume have been used in my Harvard dissertation.

*H 217. 319 fols. January 8, 1473 (appears to be original p 1) to February 25, 1474. Act book.

Same as above. Appears complete.

*H 218. 263 fols. January (p 1) to December 20, 1475. Act book.

This volume is divided into two sections. The first five fols contain *Constituciones procuratorum*. The second section contains the *Liber actorum*, same as above. The volume appears complete.

*H 219. 275 fols. 1477. Act book.

This volume includes a cover page quoting "In principio erat verbum etc." The *Constituciones procuratorum* and the *Liber actorum* follow as above. The volume appears complete and is in very good condition.

*H 220. c400 fols. January (p 1) to November 18, 1478. Act book.

This volume contains a brief section of *Constituciones procuratorum*. The main part is the *Liber actorum*, as above. The volume is in good condition.

*H 221. c300 fols. January (p 1) to December 20, 1480. Act book.

The volume contains two sections, as above. The volume appears complete and is in a very good condition.

*H 222. c200 fols. January (p 1) to December 19, 1483. Act book.

Some fols seem to be missing, because from August 25 to November 28 no cases are recorded. The volume contains two sections, as above.

*H 223. c350 fols. January, 1484 (p 1) to January 12, 1485. Act book.

The volume contains two sections, as above.

*H 224. 360 fols. January (p 1) to December 17, 1487. Act book.

Two sections, as above. The volume appears complete and is in good condition.

*H 225. c100 fols. 1489 to 1491. Act book.

The volume contains *Constituciones procuratorum*, but no case material.

*H 226. c300 fols. January (p 1) to December 19, 1492. Act book.

Two sections, i.e. *Constituciones procuratorum* and *Liber actorum*. The volume appears complete and is in good condition.

H 227. 1493. Act book, same type as above.

H 228. 1494. Act book, same type as above.

H 229. 1495. Act book, same type as above.

H 230. 1497. Act book, same type as above.

*H 231. c400 fols. 1501. Act book.

The volume contains *Constituciones procuratorum* (6 fols.) and the *Liber actorum*. It appears complete and is in good condition.

H 232. 1503. Act book, same type as above.

H 233. 1504. Act book, same type as above.

H 234. 1504. Act book, same type as above.

H 235. 1507. Act book, same type as above.

H 236. 1507. Act book, same type as above.

H 237. 1509. Act book, same type as above.

*H 238. 441 fols. 1501. Act book.

The volume contains *Constituciones procuratorum* (9 fols.) and the *Liber actorum*, as above.

H 239. April 29 to September 26, 1511. Act book (partial year).

H 240 (B 1205). 1520. Act book.

H 241 (B 1204). 1593-1596. Act book.

H 241a (B 1258). 1617-1618. Act book.

H 242. 1621-1623. Act book.

H 243. 1624-1630. Act book.

2. *BHA*:

HL Freising 93. 1462. Act book.

HL Freising 94. 1463. Act book.

HL Freising 95. 1465. Act book.

HL Freising 96. 1467. Act book.

HL Freising 97. 1468. Act book.

HL Freising 98. 1472. Act book.

*HL Freising 99. 184 fols. January (original p 1) to December 19, 1474. Act book.

The volume consists of two sections, a brief section of *Constituciones procuratorum* and the *Liber actorum*, exactly the same type of record as in the AEMF. The volume is very well preserved and appears to be complete.

HL Freising 100. 1476. Act book.

HL Freising 101. 1479. Act book.

*HL Freising 102. 338 fols. January (p 1) to December 19, 1481. Act book.

The volume consists of two sections, as above. The volume is very well preserved and appears to be complete.

*HL Freising 103. 292 fols. January (p 1) to December 31, 1482. Act book.

The volume consists of two sections, as above. It is very well preserved and appears to be complete.

HL Freising 104. 1486. Act book.

HL Freising 105. 1488. Act book.

HL Freising 106. 1490. Act book.

HL Freising 107. 1500. Act book.

HL Freising 108. 1502. Act book.

HL Freising 109. 1506. Act book.

*HL Freising 110. 292 fols. January 14 to December 1517. Act book.

The volume consists of two sections, as above. It is in good condition and appears to be near complete.

*HL Freising 111. 131 fols. 1526. Act book.

Same type as above. The volume is in good condition and appears to be near complete. A description of this volume, including quotations is provided in my Harvard Dissertation.

HL Freising 243. 1606ff. Consistory court records.

HL Freising 669. 1528. Fragments of an inquisitorial process concerning many people arrested for witchcraft.

4. The General Director of the BHA also reports: "Hingewiesen sei noch auf das in der Bayerischen Staatsbibliothek München unter der Signatur Clm 97 verwahrte Formularbuch des Freisinger Dompropstes Egloff Hornpeck ("Formulare ecclesiasticum secundum stilum ecclesiae Frisingensis") von ca. 1370-1419, dessen Inhalt sich hauptsächlich auf das kanonische Recht bezieht."

[04.]

1. Salzburg, Gurk, Offizialat des Bischofs.

2. Kärntner Landesarchiv, Sammelarchiv des Geschichtsvereins von Kärnten, Landhaus, A-9020 Klagenfurt.

Die Angaben über dieses Archiv werden vom Diözesanarchivar Tropper mitgeteilt.

3. MS 6/23. 12 fols, 225 X 150 mm. 1428-31. Liber citationum Gurcensis.

[05.]

1. Salzburg, Passau, Offizialat für Österreich unter der Enns mit Sitz Maria am Gestade in Wien.

2. Diözesanarchiv Wien, Wollzeile 2, 1010 Wien, Tel. (0222) 53 25 61 [DAW].

Die Angaben über dieses Archiv werden vom Diözesanarchivar Weißensteiner mitgeteilt.

Bayerisches Hauptstaatsarchiv [BHA] (siehe oben 03/2).

Die Angaben über dieses Archiv werden von Generaldirektor Jaroschka mitgeteilt.

3. *1. DAW*:

PP 1. 151 fols, 220 X 160 mm. 8. Jänner bis 10. November 1504. "Konsistorialprotokoll de Anno 1504".

Enthält in streng chronologischer Ordnung die Protokolle über die drei- bis viermal wöchentlich abgehaltenen Sitzungen des Konsistoriums. Rund 950 Einträge. Rechtsmaterien: *Actiones cridicae, causae matrimoniales, obligationes parochorum ad personalem residentiam, constitutiones procuratorum, causae iniuriarum, causae debiti* etc.; enthält kurzum alle Sachen, die in die Kompetenz des Offizials und seines Konsistoriums fielen.

PP 2. 319 fols (c150 leer), 330 X 215 mm. 8. Jänner 1526 bis 31. Juli 1536. "Acta Consistorialia de anno etc. vicesimo sexto conscripta".

Aufbau und Inhalt wie PP 1 (fol 307r: "Constitutiones Procuratorum et Obligationes partium 1526-1536").

PP 3. 245 fols, 220 X 165 mm. 10. Jänner 1541 bis 28. November 1547. "Konsistorialprotokoll 1541-1547".

Aufbau und Inhalt wie PP 1.

PP 4. 220 fols, 310 X 210 mm. 14. August 1550 bis 26. April 1556. "Acta Consistorii Pataviensis extra Ordinaria seu extra consistorium".

Stellt in der Hauptsache ein Ausgangsprotokoll des Konsistoriums dar; enthält als solches Aufzeichnungen über die Gewährung der *cura animarum*, Erlegung von Taxen, *citationes*; gelegentlich wurden auch Mandate der niederösterreichischen Regierung bzw. des Landesfürsten in vollem Wortlaut eingetragen. Auch Ansuchen um *litterae dimissoriales* wurden verzeichnet.

PP 76. 294 fols, 405 X 285 mm. 14. August 1550 bis 31. Jänner 1558. "Protocollum Consistoriale de Anno 1550 usque 1557".

Aufbau und Inhalt wie PP 1.

PP 77. 242 fols, 412 X 277 mm. 1. Feburar 1558 bis 9. Juli 1563. "Acta Consistorialia Curiae Pataviensis infra Onasum ab Anno Millesimo quingentesimo Octavo, Die vero prima mensis Februarii conscripta".

Aufbau und Inhalt wie PP 1.

PP 248. 117 fols, 303 X 202 mm. 1550 bis 27. Jänner 1559. "Liber testamentorum presbyterum et plebanorum defunctorum ab Anni Millesimi quingentesimi quinquagesimi die Augusti feria sexta inscriptorum".

Enthält die Abschriften von Testamenten von 51 Geistlichen aus dem Offizialat Österreich unter der Enns; die Testamente wurden jeweils vor das Konsistorium gebracht und zur Approbation vorgelegt.

PP 249. 118 fols, 375 X 271 mm. 1560 bis 1618. "Liber seu Protocollum Testamentorum demortuorum Parochorum de Anno 1560".

Enthält die Abschriften von Testamenten von 70 Geistlichen aus dem Offizialat unter der Enns bis 1618.

PP 233. 34 fols, 305 X 221 mm. "Inventarium aller Acten und Sachen des fürstlichen Passauerischen Offiziallat Ambts in Österreich under Enns in Wienn de Anno 1580".

Das Inventar verzeichnet auch die Prozeßakten der Offiziale Glüngl (1556-1560), Hillinger (1560-1565), Zadesius (1565-1566), Haldenberger (1567-1572), Ruf (1572-1574), Palderstein (1574) und Raidel (1574-1580). Dabei finden sich folgende Rubriken: *Causae Matrimoniales; Causae Testamentales; Causae iniuriarum, debitorum et fiscales; Causae Variae; Litterae Compassus.* Die *causae* wurden jeweils in *expeditae et pendentes* unterteilt. Die Parteien und die *causa* werden in Stichworten angegeben.

PP 265. 190 fols, 305 X 206 mm. "Weyland Herrn Mathaei Rott gewestn Hochstift Passauischen Unterennserischen Offizialats-Notarii in Wienn über hiesiges Officium mit sonderlichen Vleiß zusammengetragene Notata".

Mathäus Rott (auch Roth) war von c1605 bis etwa 1617 Notar des Offizialats unter der Enns. In der vorliegenden Handschrift trug er aus den Konsistorialprotokollen Präzedenzfälle aus dem 16. Jahrhundert zur Klärung von Jurisdiktionsstreitigkeiten zwischen Bischof (bzw. Offizial) und Landesfürst bzw. Bischof (bzw. Offizial) und (exemten) Klöstern zusammen.

Die Reihe der Passauer Konsistorialprotokolle reicht im Diözesanarchiv Wien bis 1785 (Abtretung des Viertels unter dem Manhartsberg an die Erzdiözese Wien und der Viertel Ober dem Manhartsberg und Ober dem Wienerwald an die neugegründete Diözese St. Pölten).

2. *BHA*:

HL Passau 927. 1580-1592. "Liber causarum consistorialium curiae episcopalis Passavensis per Austriam infra Onasum".

Konsistorialprotokoll. Wie HL Passau 927: HL Passau 927a (1595), 927b (1613-1618), 927c (1618-1622), 927d (1622-1627).

4. Für die Jurisdiktion dieses Offizialats, siehe die Ausführungen zu PP 1 und PP 233 (oben 05/3/1) und:

Annemarie Fenzl, 'Kirchliche Archive in Wien — Aufgaben und Probleme', *Scrinium* 19 (1978) 26-47

Hageneder, *Geistliche Gerichtsbarkeit*

Josef Oswald, 'Der organisatorische Aufbau des Bistums Passau im Mittelalter und in der Reformationszeit', ZRG KA 30 (1941) 131-64

Henriette Peters, 'Passau in Wien', *Wiener Diözesankalender* (1969) 24-26

Willibald Plöchl, 'Zur Rechtsgeschichte der Wiener geistlichen Konsistorien', MIÖG 63 (1955) 323-37

Johann Weißensteiner, 'Die "Passauer Protokolle" im Diözesanarchiv Wien', *Beiträge zur Wiener Diözesangeschichte* 23 (1982) 17-19

Theodor Wiedemann, *Geschichte der Reformation und Gegenreformation im Lande unter der Enns* 5 (Prag-Leipzig 1886) 484ff

Gerhard Winner, *Das Diözesanarchiv St. Pölten; Behörden und Institutionen, ihre Geschichte und Bestände* (1962) 21ff

Rudolf Zinnhobler, *Die Passauer Bistumsmatrikeln* 1, Neue Veröffentlichung des Institutes für Ostbayrische Heimatforschung 31a (1978) 57ff.

[06.]

1. Salzburg, Regensburg, officiality of the bishop ("consistorium ecclesiae Ratisponensis").

2. * Bischöfliches Zentralarchiv, St. Petersweg 11, 8400 Regensburg, Tel. (0941) 58 813.

3. * No class. 4 vols. Act books

The pre-seventeenth century holdings of this archive are largely uncatalogued. The archivists referred to some of the court records as "Acta Judicialia" and to others as "Konsistorialprotokolle." There are four large bound volumes containing the court records of the years 1480, 1489, 1490, and 1500. Each volume is divided into six sections and the sections are arranged chronologically. The titles of the sections and the numbers of entries are as follows (based on the volume for 1490):

"Registrum citacionum de a.d. 1490", 159 pages, c13 per page. "Obligaciones de ...", 150 pages, c4 entries per page. "Constituciones de ...", 28 pages, c5 entries per page. "Registrum prophanarum causarum de ...", 78 pages, 65 cases. "Registrum attestacionum de ...", 57 pages, c2 witnesses per page. "Matrimoniales cause de ...", 394 pages. At least one full page is alloted to each profane and matrimonial case, although this means that many pages are half empty. Some pages contain less than fifteen lines, others more than fifty. A few cases required two or three pages. When a case lasted for a long time, additional entries were always made on the same page. The last entries in the volume of 1490 date from 1495 and 1496. The volumes of 1489 and 1490 seem to be essentially complete. In the volume of 1500 as many as 20 pages from December seem to be missing and the matrimonial cases of 1480 break off after the first 23 pages.

The "Matrimoniales causae" of 1536 seem to be the only section of such an annual register that survives for the period between 1500 and the mid-seventeenth century. This section is unbound, but very well preserved. It covers the period from February 4, 1536 till January 31, 1537 and there are 98 cases on c200 pages.

* No class. 21 vols. 1531 X 1554. "Manuale consistorii."

These cover most of the period from February 3, 1531 till January 31, 1554. In these books the court actions are listed together with the fees that were charged in the "matrimoniales causae" and apparently also in the "prophanae causae." They seem to have been used for accounting purposes, because very little effort was made to describe what the cases were actually about. The most significant of these seems to be the "Manuale consistorii" of 1536, which covers the same period and the same cases as the register of "matrimoniales causae" of that year.

One similar volume containing the "citaciones" and the fees charged for them covers the years 1535 till 1537.

4. See:

R. Wiegand, 'Die Rechtsprechung des Regensburger Gerichts in Ehesachen unter besonderer Berücksichtigung der bedingten Eheschließung nach Gerichtsbüchern aus dem Ende des 15. Jahrhunderts', AKKR 107 (1968) 403-63.

[07.]

1. Salzburg, Salzburg, Gericht des Archidiakons von Baumburg.

2. Bayerisches Hauptstaatsarchiv [BHA] (siehe oben 03/2).

Die Angaben über dieses Archiv werden von Generaldirektor Jaroschka mitgeteilt.

E.B. Konsistorialarchiv, Salzburg.

Siehe oben 01/3/2: KAS 11/102, Vol. 7.

3. *1. BHA*:

HL Salzburg 1079. 1442-1454. Gerichtsprotokoll des geistlichen Gerichts des Archidiakons von Baumburg.

[08.]

1. Salzburg, Salzburg, court of the archdeacon of Chiemsee.

2. *Archiv des Erzbistums München und Freising (see above 01/2).

3. *S 61. c100 fols. 1501 to 1537. "Protocollum consistoriale".

Consistory court records from the court of the archdeacon of Chiemsee.

[09.]

1. Salzburg, Salzburg, court of the archdeacon of Gars.

2. *Archiv des Erzbistums München und Freising (see above 01/2).

3. *S 118. c200 fols. 1470-1481. "Protocollum Consistoriale Goar. Archidiac."

The entries are not case by case, but strictly chronological as in Freising (above 03/3/1). They are not divided into sections, and there are only about 40 pages per year. The sentences are not in this volume. See also S 119.

[10.]

1. Salzburg, Salzburg, Gericht des Archidiakons von Gmünd.

2. Archiv der Diözese Gurk, Mariannengasse 2, A-9010 Klagenfurt, Postfach 58, Tel. (0 42 22) 57 7 70.

Die Angaben über dieses Archiv werden vom Diözesanarchivar Tropper mitgeteilt.

3. Alte Salzburger Akten K131. 40 fols. 1475. Protokoll eines Prozesses um die Pfarre St. Leonhard in Weißenstein.

Archidiakonatsarchiv Gmünd, 26 fol., 1561. Fragment eines Gerichtsprotokolls des Archidiakons, Eheangelegenheiten betr.

4. Von dem Archivar: "Da wir bei den Ordnungsarbeiten des Gmünder Archidiakonatsarchives noch nicht sehr weit sind ... sind weitere Funde nicht auszuschließen." Siehe auch unten 11/3/1.

[11.]

1. Salzburg, Salzburg, Gericht des Archidiakons von Unterkärnten.

2. Archiv der Diözese Gurk [ADG] (siehe oben 10/2).

Kärntner Landesarchiv [KLA] (siehe oben 04/2).

3. *1. KLA*:

MS 5/4, 173 fols, 345 X 220 mm. s16/in. Sammelhandschrift mit Akten aus den Archidiakonaten St. Michael/Lungau, Gmünd und Unterkärnten, besonders Friesach, und aus Passau.

Inc. "Honorabilis domine decane. Salutem. Nuper in causa vestra." Betrifft viele Friesacher Angelegenheiten.

4. Von dem Archivar des ADG: "Da wir ... die Arbeiten am Friesacher Archidiakonatsarchiv noch nicht begonnen haben, sind weitere Funde nicht auszuschliessen."

[12.]

1. Wien (exemt), Offizialat des Bischofs.

2. Diözesanarchiv Wien (siehe oben 05/2).

3. WP 1. 200 fols, 290 X 220 mm. 1491-1517. "Consistorial Protocol des Bisthumbs Wienn, darin die Testamentsachen begriffen ab Anno 1491".

Enthält rund 140 Testamentsabschriften, die jeweils vom Offizial oder vom Notar des Konsistoriums approbiert wurden. (Die eigentlichen *Konsistorialprotokolle* beginnen erst 1597.)

4. Siehe die Ausführungen zu Passau (oben 05/3/1) und die genannte Literatur (oben 05/4). Siehe auch:

Viktor Flieder, *Stephansdom und Wiener Bistumsgründung: Eine diözesan- und rechtsgeschichtliche Untersuchung* Veröffentlichungen des Kirchenhistorischen Instituts der katholisch-theologischen Fakultät der Universität Wien 6 (Wien 1968)

Karl Fischer, *Verwaltung und Hofhaltung unter dem Wiener Bischof Nausea (1541-1552)* geisteswiss. Diss. Univ. Wien 1981.

MONIQUE VLEESCHOUWERS-VAN MELKEBEEK

II. Belgium

Editor's Introduction

Tangl's *Provinciale* lists the following sees, all or part of the territories of which lie within the boundaries of modern Belgium:

[Reims] (Remensis)
Cambrai (Cameracensis)
Tournai (Tornacensis)
Thérouanne (Morinensis)

[Köln] (Coloniensis)
Liège (Leodiensis)

Time has not been kind to the ecclesiastical archives in Belgium. One important court book survives of the officiality of the bishop of Cambrai at Brussel:

> Brussel, Algemeen Rijksarchief, *Officialiteit van Brussel* 1. 296 fols. 1448-1459. Ed. Vleeschouwers/Van Melkebeek, *Liber sentenciarum*.

The material listed in the report on the Cambrai officiality contains further material that has reference to modern Belgium. See below III/43.

For the rest, it is a sad story: Most of the records of Thérouanne were probably lost when the city was sacked by Charles V in 1553. Liège suffered badly in the First World War, Tournai in the Second.

As Dr. Vleeschouwers's report shows, all is not lost. A small group of Tournai records managed to find their way to the Archives départementales du Nord in Lille, and there are scattered Tournai records in Belgian local archives. Some material has survived at Liège. See:

> Émile Brouette et Paulette Pieyns-Rigo, 'Regestes des officiaux des évêques de Liège, 1214-1300', *Bulletin de la Société d'histoire du diocèse de Liège* 46 (1966) 1-139
>
> Paulette Pieyns-Rigo, 'Notaires d'officialité et notaires publics au service de l'officialité liégeoise 1252-1337', *Bulletin de la Commission Royale d'histoire* 132 (1966) 297-332.

In correspondence Mme. Pieyns-Rigo has indicated that there is more than what is cited in the article. This was confirmed by correspondence from Prof. Michael Lejeune who reports that there is "at the Archives de L'État at Liège a relatively important fonds of the diocesan officiality between 1430 and 1797."

In 1975, I visited the archiepiscopal archive in Mechelen. (The see was founded in 1559 as part of a general reorganization of ecclesiastical jurisdiction in the Low Countries; we are using 1559 as a terminal date for purposes of these reports, so far as the Low Countries are concerned.) While most of the material there postdates the creation of the see, there are a few documents concerning ecclesiastical jurisdiction that date from before the creation of the see. My notes of the visit did not survive a transatlantic shipment, but through the kindness of Dr. Vleeschouwers I was able to refresh my recollection on the basis of the only printed description of the contents of the archive:

> 'Inventaire sommaire des archives de l'Archevêché', *Annuaire du clergé de l'archevêché de Malines* 16 (1912) vi-xvii; 17 (1913) vi-xviii.

There is a manuscript handlist at the archive, and my recollection is that it does not use the numbering system employed in the *Inventaire*. The *inventaire* lists 13 registers of accounts of the officiality of Liège at Leuven, dating from 1473 to 1577, together with three registers of miscellaneous docs from the same officiality, mostly dating from the s16/1, one formulary of episcopal and one of archidiaconal acts from the s15, and a *liasse* of correspondance concerning the creation of the new sees in 1560. I cannot recall having seen any of these documents. The *inventaire* also lists 23 registers of material concerning the "vicariat de Bruxelles dans l'église de Cambrai". Some of these I recall quite clearly, and they almost certainly pertain to some sort of court, perhaps that of the official of Cambrai at Brussel. In particular, I recall that the three registers described in the *inventaire* as "procès-verbaux des séances du vicariat" (1508-1552) contain depositions in Flemish from what must be contentious matters. The same series also contains synodal statutes, various formularies, accounts, episcopal acts, and documents concerning the holders of benefices and conflicts concerning jurisdiction. In addition, the *Inventaire* describes a small groups of docs and a single doc, dated 1447-1472 and 1549, respectively, from the *fonds* of the archdeacon of Antwerpen, which may concern contentious matters.

There may be individual docs in other modern archives, but Dr. Vleeschouwers believes that with the exceptions noted above she has examined every record in a class devoted to "officialities" in the archives in modern Belgium and at the Archives du Nord at Lille, and in some cases she has gone considerably further than that.

No attempt is made here to list all the individual docs (charters, correspondence, etc) that have reference to these officialities. A full listing of those prior to 1300 may be found in Vleeschouwers-Van Melkebeek, *Officialiteit van Doornik* and the most interesting of them are printed in:

Monique Vleeschouwers-Van Melkebeek, *Documenten uit de praktijk van de gedingbeslissende rechtspraak van de officialiteit van Doornik: oorsprong en vroege ontwikkeling (1192–1300)*, Koninklijke Academie voor Wetenschappen, Letteren en Schone Kunsten van België, Iuris Scripta Historica 1 (Brussel 1985).

For the post-Tridentine ecclesiastical courts in Belgium, the major study is:

Jozef de Brouwer, *De kerkelijke rechtspraak en haar evolutie in de bisdommen Antwerpen, Gent en Mechelen tussen 1570 en 1795*, 2 banden (Tielt 1971-2)

Like many such books, it contains clues as to the possible location of pre-Tridentine records.

[01.]

1. Reims, Tournai, officiality of the bishop.

For the history of this officiality, see below 01/4.

2. *Archives départementales du Nord, 22, rue Saint Bernard, F-59045 Lille [ADN].

A small *fonds* of the records of the officiality was formed at the time of the establishment of the Archives départementales du Nord in the early s19. It probably goes back to the documents which were classified at Lille in the s17 at the request of the bishop of Tournai by Denis Godefroy, archivist of the *Chambre des Comptes*. The *fonds* is articles 14 G 87 through 14 G 110 in the *inventaire*:

A.-M. Piétresson de Saint-Aubin, *Archives Départementales du Nord. Répertoire numérique. Série G.*, 1.1 (Lille 1960).

Most of the records of the officiality were deposited in the Archives de l'État at Mons and in the Palais épiscopal at Tournai. Both repositories were destroyed by bombing in May 1940.

M. Vleeschouwers-Van Melkebeek, 'Officialité de Tournai: archives détruites, archives conservées', *Archief- en Bibliotheekwezen in België*, 48 (1977) 199-214.

*Rijksarchief, Duivelsteen, Gerard de Duivelstraat 1, B-9000 Gent.

*Archives de l'État, Place du Parc 2, B-7000 Mons.

Stadsarchief, Breidelstraat 3, B-8000 Brugge.

For these archives see below 01/3/4. Unless otherwise indicated references are to the ADN.

3. *1. Accounts of the bishop's courts*:

*14 G 105. 13 fols. 1.7.1429-30.6.1430. Register of accounts by Nicholas de Sancto Elario, Keeper of the Seal (fragment).

Contains a comprehensive view of the annual income and expenses of the bishop of Tournai so far as the exercise of his ecclesiastical jurisdiction is concerned. Key to the study of the competence of the officiality in criminal matters. See:

M. Vleeschouwers-Van Melkebeek, 'Aperçu typologique des principales sortes de registres produits par l'officialité de Tournai au moyen âge, avec notes sur le registre de sentences de Bruxelles (1448-1459)', *Sources de l'histoire des institutions de la Belgique. Actes du Colloque de Bruxelles 15.-18.IV.1975* (Bruxelles 1977) 423-442.

*14 G 91. 151 fol, parchment binding. 1.7.1446-30.6.1447. *Id.* by Peter de Vlenke, Keeper of the Seal.

*14 G 92. 165 fol, parchment binding. 1.7.1447-30.6.1448. *Id.* by Peter de Vlenke, Keeper of the Seal.

*14 G 93. 160 fol, parchment binding. 1.7.1461-30.6.1462. *Id.* by Peter de Vlenke, Keeper of the Seal.

*14 G 94. 165 fol, parchment binding. 1.7.1470-30.6.1471. *Id.* by John Pavonis, Keeper of the Seal.

*14 G 95. 80 fol, parchment binding. 24.11.1473-30.6.1474. *Id.* by John Pavonis, Keeper of the Seal.

*14 G 96. 131 fol, parchment binding. 1.7.1474-30.6.1475. *Id.* by John Pavonis, Keeper of the Seal.

*14 G 97. 103 fol, parchment binding. 1.7.1476-30.6.1477. *Id.* by John Pavonis, Keeper of the Seal.

*14 G 98. 95 fol, parchment binding. 1.7.1479-30.6.1480. *Id.* by John Pavonis, Keeper of the Seal.

*14 G 99. 83 fol, parchment binding. 1.7.1480-30.6.1481. *Id.* by John Pavonis, Keeper of the Seal.

*14 G 100. 185 fol, parchment binding. 1.7.1511-30.6.1512. *Id.* by William Bernard, Keeper of the Seal.

*14 G 101. 220 fol, parchment binding. 1.7.1519-30.6.1520. *Id.* by William Bernard, Keeper of the Seal.

*14 G 103. 236 fol, parchment binding. 1.7.1528-30.6.1529. *Id.* by William Bernard, Keeper of the Seal.

*14 G 104. 211 fol, parchment binding. 1.7.1530-30.6.1531. *Id.* by William Bernard, Keeper of the Seal.

*14 G 102. 92 fol. 1.7.1520-30.6.1521. Draft of register of accounts by William Bernard, Keeper of the Seal.

2. *Other accounts*:

*B 20038/19887. 18 fol. 10.5.1432-27.4.1433. Register of accounts of Michael Amici, Keeper of the Seal of the subordinate court of Brugge.

*14 G 107bis. 45 fol. 6.5.1441-16.4.1442. *Id.* by Henry Clapdorp, Keeper of the Seal of the subordinate court of Brugge.

*14 G 106. 37 fol. 1520-1536. Lists of receipts of arrears of fines imposed by the officiality of Tournai, 1501-1513.

3. *Other documents*:

*14 G 1. 85 fol. 1477. Inventory of the episcopal archives.

Ed. Vleeschouwers-Van Melkebeek, 'Archief'. Contains ample analyses of evidence in cases of conflict between episcopal and lay jurisdiction in the s14 and s15.

*14 G 88. 1 doc. 1458. Urban vs. episcopal jurisdiction in Brugge.

*14 G 89. 1 doc. 22.8.1455. Appointment of a new Keeper of the Seal at the subordinate court of Brugge with stipulation of limits of judicial power.

*14 G 90, pièce 111. 1 doc. 28.4.1461. Financial discharge of the Keeper of the Seal of Brugge by his superior in Tournai.

14 G 108. 5 docs. 1458-1712. Various ecclesiastical criminal cases.

14 G 109. 5 docs. 1560-1781. Matrimonial cases.

14 G 110. 7 docs. 1524-1746. Various ecclesiastical cases, civil and criminal.

4. *Documents in other archives*:

*Gent, Rijksarchief, *Gedeponeerd Fonds Bisdom en Sint-Baafs*, B 3295. 63 fol. 1443-1447. Copy by Osto Osts, *promotor curie Tornacensis*, of letters, many written by the official of Tournai to his absent lord, the bishop of Tournai, asking for counsel in judicial cases.

*Mons, Archives de l'État, *Archives de la famille Errembault de Dudzeele*, n° 487. 86 fol. 21.3.1393-5.12.1393. Register containing the names of the parishioners from the deaneries of Brugge and Oudenburg who were excommunicated or placed under interdict.

*Gent, Rijksarchief, *Gedeponeerd Fonds Bisdom en Sint-Baafs*, K 2563. 128 fol. 12.3.1451-25.11.1451. *Id.* from the deanery of Oudenburg.

Brugge, Stadsarchief, Politieke charters, 1e reeks, nrs. 9-13, 24-25, 38, 50, 53, 56, 88-89, 218-219, 272-273. 1269-c1301. Numerous docs and rolls (nr 219 alone contains 34 rolls) in a lawsuit between Brugge, Damme and Het Vrije van Brugge, *actores*, and the bishop of Tournai, *reus*, in the court of the archbishop of Reims and later, on appeal, before the papal court, concerning the bishop's exercise of synodal jurisdiction over the *actores*.

Ed. Daniël Lambrecht, *Een proces tussen de bisschop van Doornik enerzijds, Brugge, Damme en het Vrije anderzijds betreffende de synodale jurisdictie.*

1269–ca.1301, Koninklijke Commissie van de Oude Wetten en Verordeningen van België, Versameling van de Oude Rechtspraak in België 7.3 (Brussel forthcoming).

4. *1. General*:

The history of the officialities of the bishops of Tournai is complicated and is probably not completely recoverable granted the loss of so much material. No medieval court books survived the bombing of Mons and Tournai in May 1940. Only dispersed records throw light on the extent of the jurisdiction and application of Romano-canonic procedure.

Bishop Stephen of Tournai (1192–1203) introduced the officiality and its specific procedure. See generally Vleeschouwers-Van Melkebeek, *Officialiteit van Doornik*. A long-standing controversy (beginning in the s12) as to the competence of the ecclesiastical court over the inhabitants of towns (viz. Gent, Brugge, Kortrijk) in purely lay matters was ended in the s15/ex in favour of urban jurisdiction. Up to the time of Duke Charles the Bold of Burgundy († 1477), the counts of Flanders and the dukes of Burgundy were eager to protect and maintain the extensive competence of the church courts, even to the detriment of their lay courts. Prior to Charles's time Flemish towns which tried to resist by issuing edicts in which their inhabitants were perpetually banished for summoning each other before an ecclesiastical court were forced, under ducal pressure, to withdraw the edicts and to placate the bishop by fitting penance. At the end of the s15 the ecclesiastical court was, so far as laymen were concerned, competent only for purely sacramental matters.

2. Brugge:

From about 1259, the dean of Brugge mentions a *sigillum curie nostre*, distinct from the *sigillum christianitatis Brugensis*. In 1255 and 1256 this ecclesiastical court of Brugge knew an *auditor causarum*. From 1291 onwards a *sigillifer curie Brugensis* is known by name.

Beginning in the s13/ex, the bishop of Tournai was able to shift the business of the *curia Brugensis* from the local dean to the keeper of the seal of the bishop's subordinate court of Brugge. The latter was qualified to exercise a limited (up to fines of 60 Paris shillings in Flanders currency), but real, jurisdiction in civil cases. His territorial jurisdiction covered the three deaneries (Brugge, Oudenburg and Aardenburg) within the archdeaconry of Brugge. See above ADN, B20038/19887; 14 G 107bis; 14 G 89; 14 G 90, pièce 111.

In May of 1477, Ferry of Clugny, bishop of Tournai, was forced by Louis XI of France to leave the city of Tournai. A fully staffed officiality remained in Tournai, but its jurisdiction was limited to the town and the deanery of Tournai. From as early as June 1477, jurisdiction in the rest of the diocese was exercised by an equally fully staffed officiality in Brugge. This court had its own *sigillum sedis Tornacensis in Brugis* and functioned until at least

February of 1483. After the death of Ferry of Clugny in Rome on 7 October 1483, a schism broke out in the diocese of Tournai. Competing claimants to the see attempted to exercise jurisdiction over the see from courts established in Brugge, Gent and Tournai. See:

Vleeschouwers-Van Melkebeek, 'Archief', 131-7, 157-8, 174-5

Monique Vleeschouwers-Van Melkebeek, 'Un compte de la recette générale de l'évêché de Tournai (1507-1508) (Londres, P.R.O., E 36/82)', *Handelingen van de Koninklijke Commissie voor Geschiedenis* 151 (1985) 153-261, esp. 183, 189.

3. *Oudenaarde*:

In 1297, an *officialis Tornacensis in Flandria* operated from Oudenaarde in order to allow the count of Flanders to defend "as a free man" a case brought against him by the bishop of Tournai. The court was evidently very short-lived. See Vleeschouwers-Van Melkebeek, *Officialiteit van Doornik* 85.

4. *Lille*:

Around 1480-1481, Ferry of Clugny may have instituted three simultaneous officialities: Tournai, Brugge and Lille. See Vleeschouwers-Van Melkebeek, 'Archief', 157&n141. Lille had an officiality in 1493 during the schism. About 1488, this officiality is said to have made a ruling in a case between a parish priest in Brugge and the hospital of Sint-Jan in Brugge. See Brugge, Rijksarchief, Aanwinsten, nr. 1902, ff. 15r and 18v.

5. *Gent*:

Apart from the schismatic double and triple courts within the diocese of Tournai (s14/ex, and s15/ex to s16/in), William Filastre, bishop of Tournai is said to have removed the officiality of Tournai from Tournai to Gent in opposition to Charles VII of France in 1461-1462. See Vleeschouwers-Van Melkebeek, 'Archief', 145&n100.

In all periods, the way in which the various jurisdictions in Gent (town, deanery, archdeaconry) were integrated into the jurisdiction of the episcopal officiality of Tournai remains quite mysterious. We know that in 1266 the archdeacon of Tournai lost a large part of his jurisdiction to the officiality of the bishop and that from 1336 he had no jurisdiction left. See Vleeschouwers-Van Melkebeek, *Officialiteit van Doornik* 131, 133-4. We also know that very soon after 1266 (from March, 1272), the archdeaconry of Flanders was divided into two archdeaconries: Brugge (deaneries of Brugge, Aardenburg, Oudenburg) and Gent (deaneries of Gent, Land van Waas, Oudenaarde, Roeselare). *Id.* at 132.

No record of a jurisdictional settlement between the bishop and the newly-created archdeacons of Gent and Brugge has come to light. It is improbable that their jurisdiction would have surpassed that of their recently-limited colleague at Tournai.

The registers of accounts by the keepers of the seal of the officiality of Tournai all mention receipts of fines imposed upon subordinates living in the three archdeaconries. Gent is not excepted from these documents. In the s19, much was made of the privileges granted by Alexander III to the city of Gent (Jaffe-Löwenfeld n° 12449, 23 March 1175), but no historian has been able to fill in the picture. If the dean of Gent represented the officiality of Tournai from the s12/ex, either with respect to the deanery of Gent or with respect to the other deaneries within the archdeaconry, no account books or books of sentences of this "important" dean of Gent have emerged. No continuity, no evolution, no landmarks have ever been critically shown.

CHARLES DONAHUE, JR., and ANNE LEFEBVRE-TEILLARD

III. France

Introduction

In the French archival world the received wisdom is that the Revolution was largely responsible for the destruction of the records of the French officialities. While the Revolution is certainly to blame for some of the destruction, its effects can be exaggerated. The fact that so little survives from before 1450 in places that have quite impressive holdings after that date suggests that the Hundred Years' War was probably more destructive than was the Revolution. Then too, random fires, the religous wars of the seventeenth century (particularly in the east), and two wars in our century have all taken their toll.

The notion that the Revolution destroyed most of the records of *ancien régime* officialities has had ill effects. Not much archival research has been done on the French officialities since the pioneering work of Paul Fournier:

> *Les officialités au moyen âge* (Paris 1880, repr. Aalen 1984).

This is a shame, because, as the following reports show, quite an extensive body of records survives. Of 129 medieval dioceses the seats of which lay within the boundaries of modern France, 53 have left records from one or more of their officialities. Altogether 73 officialities are represented in the reports below. Not only do these records exist, but the French archival tradition has seen to it that they are, by and large, well-housed, well-preserved and accessible to the user.

We are reasonably confident that most of the relevant docs in the AD that have printed *inventaires* or *répertoires* are covered here. Material in municipal libraries is listed where it came to our attention. Material in other archives (e.g. diocesan archives) may be extensive and is not covered here. (In principle, all *ancien régime* records should be in public hands, but recent research in other areas, e.g. visitations, has shown that this is not always the case.)

Our subject-matter reach has been somewhat less extensive than that in some of the other reports. The existence of the CNRS, *Répertoire des visites* has meant that we have made no effort to include visitation records of any kind. We have also made no effort to include inquistion records, though in a few instances we have listed them when they came to our attention.

Like many series of books running over a long period of time, the great French series of *répertoires* and *inventaires* of the AD has become a bibliographical problem. Unless a contrary indication is given, our listings give the author(s) of the volume as they appear on the title page of the book; the title (omitting indication of the archive in question) up to the indication of authorship as it appears on the title page; volume or fascicle numbers in Arabic numerals without distinguishing between the two; an indication of the articles covered, if less than the whole series indicated in the title (in square brackets if it is not on the the title page), and place and date of publication. If the volume is not published, "dact" or "ms" is substituted for the place of publication, and the list is available at the archives. Thus a title page that gives us: "Inventaire-Sommaire/ des/ Archives Départementales/ du département de Vaucluse/ par/ L. Duhamel, L. Imbert, J. de Font-Réaulx/ Archivistes du Département/ Série G/ Tome II/ Archevêché (Suite), Chapitre, Cathédrale, Seminaire/ et Inquisition d'Avignon/ Avignon/ Archives de Vaucluse/ 1954" is rendered as "L. Duhamel, L. Imbert, J. de Font-Réaulx, *Inventaire sommaire* [*de la*] *Série G*. 2: [*Arts. 422-829*] (Avignon 1954)."

The preparation of these reports has been a collaborative effort between the two authors, beginning with the work that Prof. Lefebvre did for her *thèse* (Lefebvre-Teillard, *Officialités*) and the list given in Petit, *Registre*. While each of us has commented on and edited the work of the other, those reports written in French were written by Prof. Lefebvre and those in English by Prof. Donahue. Where a French description is given in the English, it is taken from the archive list being used.

The diocese list given below begins with that in Tangl's *Provinciale*. Dates of creation and change are given only when they concern the period from 1200 to 1500. Hence, new s16 foundations are ignored even if they fall within our period. Most of these changes were connected with the major reorganization of the dioceses in the Low Countries just before or just after the end of our period. The CNRS, *Répertoire des visites* includes all dioceses that have or had territory within the national boundaries of modern France. We have been more restrictive, including only those officialities whose seats lay within the boundaries of modern France. In addition, we have excluded Corsica, the medieval ecclesiastical history of which is quite different from that of the dioceses listed below.

Diocese List

† = A description of records from this diocese (though not necessarily from the diocesan officiality) will be found in what follows.

† Lyon (Lugdunensis)
† Autun (Eduensis)
Mâcon (Matisconensis)
Chalon-sur-Sâone (Cabilonensis)
† Langres (Lingonensis)

† Sens (Senonensis)
† Paris (Parisiensis)
† Chartres (Carnotensis)
† Orléans (Aurelainensis)
Nevers (Nivernensis)
Auxerre (Autisiodorensis)
† Troyes (Trecensis)
Meaux (Meldensis)

Reims (Remensis)
Soissons (Suessionensis)
† Châlons-sur-Marne (Cathalaunensis)
† Cambrai (Cameracensis)
[Tournai] (Tornacensis) — see II/01
Thérouanne (Morinensis)
Arras (Atrebatensis)
† Amiens (Ambianensis)
Noyon (Noviomensis)
† Senlis (Silvanectensis)
† Beauvais (Belvacensis)
Laon (Laudunensis)

† Rouen (Rothomagensis)
† Bayeux (Baiocensis)
Avranches (Abricensis)
Évreux (Ebroicensis)
† Sées (Sagiensis)
Lisieux (Lexoviensis)
Coutances (Constanciensis)

Tours (Turonensis)
† Le Mans (Cenomanensis)
Rennes (Redonensis)
Angers (Andegavensis)
† Nantes (Nanetensis)
Quimper (Corisopitensis)
Vannes (Vanetensis)
Saint-Malo (Macloviensis)
† Saint-Brieuc (Briocensis)
† Tréguier (Trecorensis)
Saint-Pol-de-Leon (Leonensis)
Dol (Dolensis)

† Bourges (Bituricensis)
† Clermont (Claromontensis)
† Saint-Flour (Sancti Flori) (cr. 1317)
† Rodez (Ruthenensis)
Vabres (Vabrensis) (cr. 1317)
Cahors (Caturcensis)
† Limoges (Lemovicensis)
Tulle (Tutellensis) (cr. 1318)
† Mende (Mimatensis)
Albi (Albiensis)
Castres (Castrensis) (cr. 1317)
† Le Puy (Aniciensis sive Podiensis) (exempt)

† Bordeaux (Burdegalensis)
† Poitiers (Pictaviensis)
† Maillezais (Malleacensis) (cr. 1317, La Rochelle after 1648)
Luçon (Lucionensis) (cr. 1317)
Saintes (Xanctonensis)
† Angoulême (Englolismensis)
† Périgeux (Petragoricensis)
Sarlat (Sarlatensis) (cr. 1318)
Agen (Agennensis)
Condom (Condomiensis) (cr. 1317)

Auch (Auxitanus)
Dax (Aquensis)
Lectoure (Lectorensis)
Comminges (i.e. Saint-Bertrand) (Convenarum)
Conserans (i.e. Saint-Lizier) (Consuranus)
Tarbes (Bigorritanus vel Tarinensis)

Oloron (Olorensis)
Lescar (Lascurrensis)
Bazas (Vasatensis)
Bayonne (Baionensis)
Aire (Adurensis)

Narbonne (Narbonensis)
Carcassonne (Carcasonnensis)
Béziers (Bitterensis)
Agde (Agathensis)
Lodève (Lotevensis)
Maguelonne (Magalonensis) (Montpellier from 1536)
† Nîmes (Nemausensis)
Uzès (Uticensis)
† Elne (Elnensis)
Alet (Electensis) (cr. 1318)
Saint-Pons de Tomières (Sancti Poncii Thomeriarum)

† Toulouse (Tholosanus) (cr. abp 1317)
Montauban (Montisalbanum) (cr. 1317)
Rieux (Rivensis) (cr. 1317)
Saint-Papoul (Sancti Papuli) (cr. 1317)
Lombez (Lomberiensis) (cr. 1317)
Mirepoix (Mirapiscensis) (cr. 1317)
Lavaur (Vaurensis) (cr. 1317)
† Pamiers (Appamiarum) (cr. 1295)

† Aix-en-Provence (Aquensis)
† Apt (Aptensis)
Riez (Regensis)
Riez (Regensis)
† Fréjus (Foroiuliensis)
Gap (Vapincensis)
† Sisteron (Sistericensis)

† Arles (Arlelatensis)
† Marseille (Massiliensis)
† Avignon (Avinionensis) (became abp in 1475 with suffragans: Carpentras, Cavaillon, Vaison)
† Orange (Aurasicensis)
† Vaison (Vasionensis)
† Cavaillon (Cavalicensis)
Saint-Paul-Trois-Chateaux (Tricastrinum)
† Carpentras (Carpentoracensis)
Toulon (Tolonensis)

Vienne (Viennensis)
Valence (Valentinum)
Viviers (Vivariensis)
† Die (Diensis)
† Grenoble (Gracionopolitanum)
[Genève] (Gebbensis) — see X/13

Tarentaise (Tarentasiensis)
[Sion] Sedunensis — see X/11
[Aosta] Augustensis

Besançon (Bisuntinus) — see X/01
[Basel] (Basiliensis) — see X/02
[Lausanne] (Lausanensis) — see X/04
Belley (Bellicensis)

Embrun (Ebredunensis)
† Digne (Dignensis)
Nice (Niciensis)
Grasse (i.e. Antibes) (Antipolitanus qui hodie dicitur Grassensis)
Glandève (Glandatensis)
Senez (Senecensis)
Vence (Venciensis)

[Trier] (Treverensis)
Metz (Metensis)
† Toul (Tullensis)
† Toul (Tullensis)
Verdun (Virdunensis)

[Mainz] (Maguntina)
Strasbourg (Argentinensis)

[01.]

1. Aix, officiality of the archbishop.

2. * Archives départementales des Bouches-du-Rhône, 66b rue Saint-Sebastian, 13000 Marseille [ADBR].

   * Dépôt annexe des ADBR, 23 rue Gaston de Sporta, Aix-en-Provence [ADBRA].

The material in these archives is rich but difficult to control. The best published guide is:

Hildesheimer/Giordanengo, *Guide.*

Broader in scope, but still useful is:

Bautier/Sornay, *Sources.*

The *fonds* proper of this officiality is now in the subseries 1 G. Most of the material in this subseries was apparently in the episcopal archives at the time of its deposit in the AD. Except for scattered docs, it all dates from after the s16/m (e.g. ten volumes of civil sentences, 1560 X 1788 (1 G 1145-54), six volumes of *audiences* 1597 X 1790 (1 G 1130-36)). The material at Marseille is listed in:

Maurice Rambault, *Répertoire numérique de la série G.* 1: *Arts.* [*1*] *G 1-503* (Marseille 1910)

Id., 2: *Arts.* [*1*] *G 504-1123* (Marseille 1911).

That at Aix (1 G 1130-1366) is listed in:

Répertoire de l'officialité d'Aix (dact sd)

found at Aix.

A considerable amount of medieval material concerning the officiality of Aix is in notarial archives located at Aix and still kept as such. It is listed in:

Aubenas, *Recueil* 1:xxi-xxii.

See also Bautier/Sornay, *Sources* 2:699.

In particular, material may be found in the *fonds Laucagne* (306 E), the *fonds Muraire* (308 E) and the *fonds Lombard* (309 E).

3. *1. ADBRA*:

   * 309 E 1510. 81 fols. s14/ex X s15/2. Formulary.

The volume is noted and summarized by Aubenas, *Recueil,* 1:xxi, 2:119-20. A number of different hands are at work here; hence the expansive dating. The formulary proper begins on fol 26. The intiial fols contain a miscellaneous series of docs bearing dates from 1397 to 1441 and also notes on legal matters. Legal notes are also found in the formulary proper.

308 E 1559A. 30 fols. s15/m (one doc dated 1465). Formulary.

The volume is noted and summarized by Aubenas, *Recueil,* 1:xxi, 2:120-1. It contains, among others, a *forma littere ad redendum debitum coniugale* (fol 25r).

* 306 E 17. Fols 46-53. 1419-21. Judicial acts contained in a notary's formulary.

308 E 1543. 1419-21. Procédures civiles.

This doc could not be located when I visited the archive in the autumn of 1981.

*306 E 1048. c150 fols. 1426-42. *Matricula* of cases.

Includes at least one set of depositions in a marriage case.

306 E 1062. 1442-45. Matricule de causes civiles.

This doc could not be located when I visited the archive in the autumn of 1981.

*306 E 1049. 184 fols. 1453-55. *Matricula* of cases.

The intial (unnumbered) fols contain a summary of business in the court at the beginning of the year.

*308 E 1048. 3 bound half-quires of c30 fols each. s15/m (one date of 1467). Register.

The first quire contains a register of expenses of various proctors; the other quires look like a register of proctors.

*308 E 1552. 9 large bound quires. 1478-81. Day-by-day account of cases before the court.

To note: a large number of appeal cases. (Difficult to read.)

4. There probably is not enough material to reconstruct a full-scale history of the medieval officiality of Aix, but there is enough material here for a researcher with patience to draw some conclusions about the nature of the court's jurisdiction. The material is not unlike that at Marseille, except that the court also had metropolitical jurisdiction. Aubenas, *Receuil*, 1:xxi-xxii, 2:123-38 (transcriptions of sample docs), shows the way into the notarial archives from which the history of this officiality can be written. See 07/3/3: 5 G 823, for further Aix material.

[02.]

1. Aix, Apt, officialité de l'évêque.

2. Bibliothèque municipale de Carpentras, 11 boulevard Albin - Durand, 84200 Carpentras [BMC].

   Archives départementales du Vaucluse, Palais des papes, 84000 Avignon [ADV].

   Voir Bautier/Sornay, *Sources* 2:739

   L. Duhamel, *Inventaire-sommaire de la série G.* 1: [*Arts. 1-421*] (Avignon 1914)

   L. Duhamel, L. Imbert et J. de Font-Réaulx, *Inventaire-sommaire* [*de la*] *série G.* 2: [*Arts. 422-829*] (Avignon 1954)

   Imbert/Font-Réaux, *Répertoire*.

3. *1. BMC*:

Ms 1655. Fols 58, 59, 65. 1277, 1278, 1320. Sentences de l'official d'Apt.

Voir Petit, *Registre*, p x.

2. ADV:

Étude Pondicq divers 31. 1430. Registre de la cour spirituelle d'Apt.

4. Le grand nombre des registres dans l'étude Pondicq (voir Bautier/Sornay, *Sources*, 2:1282-9), suggère que la découverte d'autres registres de l'officialité d'Apt est possible.

[03.]

1. Aix, Fréjus, officiality of the bishop.

2. Archivio Segreto Vaticano, 00120 Città del Vaticano.

See Bautier/Sornay, *Sources* 2:708, from which the following description was taken.

3. Introitus et Exitus 163. Fols 1-184. 1318-1340. Compte de l'officialité.

Condamnations prononcées par les juges.

Introitus et Exitus 4. 98 fols. 1300-1302. Registre de sentences de la cour épiscopale.

Sentences de l'officialité et à Fayence et à Fréjus; registre détaillé, intéressant pour l'histoire des moeurs.

Collectorie 104. Fols 5-41. 1303. Condamnations de la cour épiscopale.

Introitus et Exitus 7. 145 fols. 1303-1307. *Id.*

Introitus et Exitus 7bis. 1305-1306. *Id.*

Instrumenta Miscellanea 379. 1303-1305. Pièces.

Introitus et Exitus 6. Fol 112. 1303-1309. Enquêtes et sentences de l'évêque contre quelques clercs et laïques.

[04.]

1. Aix, Sisteron, officialité de l'évêque.

2. Archives départementales des Alpes de Haute Provence, 2 rue des Archives, 04000 Digne.

L'inventaire numérique complet par R. Collier est en cours d'impression.

3. 6 G 11. 1551-1556. Audiences de l'officialité de Sisteron.

4. Les sous-séries 2 G à 6 G concernent les officialités. L'inventaire complet méritera un examen plus approfondi.

[05.]

1. Arles, officialité de l'archevêque.

2. Archives départementales des Bouches-du-Rhône (voir 01/2).

Voir Bautier/Sornay, *Sources* 2:717

Aubenas, *Recueil*, 1:xxiii-xxiv

R. Busquet et P. Giraud, *Répertoire numérique de la série G. 3: Sous série III G* (Marseille 1935).

3. 3 G 209. Fols 1051-1165. 1491-1500. Procédure entre Benoît Cras, marchand d'Arles, et Guillaume Aycard, marchand de Martigues.

3 G 368. 1331 fols. 1542-1546, 1552. Matricule des causes civiles et criminelles et d'appel.

3 G 369. 1163 fols. 1547-1552. Matricule des causes civiles et criminelles et d'appel.

3 G 370. 1249 fols. 1553-1559. Matricule des causes civiles et criminelles et d'appel.

[06.]

1. Arles, Avignon, officialité de l'évêque (jusqu'en 1475).

Pour l'officialité d'Avignon depuis 1475 voir 07.

2. Archivio Segreto Vaticano [ASV] (voir 03/2).

Archives départementales du Vaucluse [ADV] (voir 02/2).

3. *1. ASV*:

Collectorie 40. Fols 1-270. 1387-1388. Trois comptes des recettes et dépenses du clavaire de l'officialité d'Avignon.

Collectorie 42. Fols 195-255; 256-356 [double]. 1389-1390. Comptes des recettes et dépenses du clavaire de l'officialité d'Avignon.

Regesta Avenionensia 268. Fols 501-532. Janv.-mars 1391. Idem.

Collectorie 43. Fols 188-321. Nov. 1391-nov. 1392. Idem.

2. ADV:

G I 9. Fols 274-307. 1368. Enquête sur les usuriers des diocèses de Provence faite par l'official d'Avignon sur ordre du pape Urbain V.

[07.]

1. Arles, Marseille, officiality of the bishop.

2. *Archives départementales des Bouches-du-Rhône (see 01/2).

Hildesheimer/Giordanengo, *Guide*, notes that most of the material concerning this officiality is now in the series 5 G. Some of the material was apparently in the episcopal archives at the time of its deposit in the departmental archives, but a large portion of it comes from notarial archives and was originally kept in separate notarial *fonds*. This was the situation at the time that Roger Aubenas published his *Recueil*, pp xxi-xxvi of which still contains the best printed description of the material. What follows employs the current numbering system and is based on a typewritten inventory available at the archive:

Répertoires numériques des sous-séries 1 G suppl. à 18 G (dact 1975)

from which the French titles of docs are taken. The *Répertoire* contains the following note:

> Les fonds notariaux peuvent encore conserver quelques registres concernant l'officialité, par ex.: 300 E 54, formulaire de l'officialité de Marseille par Mr. Raphael de Aquis, notaire de Marseille à la fin du XVe siècle (table edité par Aubenas, op. cit., t.2, p. 139-43) dont les registres sont conservés sous la cote 389 E (Bautier, op. cit., t.2, p. 1230) — 355 E 169, registres de dépositions de témoins, Hughes Laurent, notaire, 1479-1480.

3. *1. Registers (principally of* processus*) s14/ex-s15/in*:

*5 G 769. 18 fols. 1381. Registre de brèves de Étienne Venaissini, notaire de la cour épiscopale.

For Venaissini's registers see 351 E 3-13, 642-46; Bautier/Sornay, *Sources* 2:1217. A series of miscellaneous entries not arranged by date, some of which seem to have nothing to do with the business of the court. Confession of debt, constitution of a *cens*, note about a cleric accused of theft, entry concerning a man jailed for having engaged in a fraudulent sale.

*5 G 770. 8 fols. 1389. Same as 5 G 769.

*5 G 771. 215 fols. 1396-1400. Enquêtes et sentences — actes diverses. Guillaume Barban, notaire.

For Barban's registers see 351 E 86-121, 657-84; Bautier/Sornay, *Sources* 2:1219. Mostly docs in various cases arranged by the case, in many cases running over several fols. A sampling of the contents reveals: Fol 8r: constitution of two spiritual vicars by the bishop-elect. Fol 9r: constitution of a fiscal proctor. Fols 10r-16v: docs in a breach of faith case against a priest. Fols 17r-28v: depositions in a testamentary case concerning a vineyard. Fol 29v: criminal sentence against a clerk for theft. Fols 31r-38v: collations to and resignations of offices and benefices. Fols 39r-54v: witnesses, depostitions and docs in a testamentary case. Fols 56-57: another testamentary case. Fols 59r-79r: another testamentary case involving a religious house. Fol 81: grant of a chaplain. Fols 83r-87r: inventory of the goods of a deceased priest. Fols 88r-91v: absolution by inquest of a clerk suspected of murder. Fols 95-101: an inquest into the finances of a church. Fols 106r-108v: various gracious acts including one from the bishop for the benefit of the Jews of Marseille. Fols 117r-118r: sentence against a woman for engaging in divination. Fols 120v-121r: advowson case with a sentence. Fol 146r: married clerk who is a merchant absolved of charge of forging a notarial doc. Fol 149r: rendering of account by a tutor. Fol 153r: quittance of a tutor; repudiation of goods of an inheritance bound in. Fols 174r-182r: large inventory of goods. At this point the fols are torn with the tear getting progressively worse until the end.

*5 G 772. 133 fols. 1400-02. Procédures et sentences. Guillaume Barban.

Similar in style and contents to 5 G 771. Sampling of the contents reveals: Fol 2ff: proceedings against a man for stealing from the bishop's castle, long set of depositions. Fol 10r: assault case against a married clerk. Fol 14r: case against a clerk for beating his parents, depositions attached. Fol 24r: conspiracy of violence engaged in by a clerk, depositions. Fol 31r-52r: case against a clerk for selling Christians to the Saracens. Fol 56r: criminal proceeding against a layman for impeding the execution of a will. Fols 69r-82: concern Sardinia and the Saracens, may be related to fols 31-52. The final quire is all brief criminal cases mostly against clerks and mostly confessed. Having knives beyond the legal length and using them seems to be the most common offense. Other offenses include concubinage (fol 115r), theft of a fish *vocatum Ragadu alias dictum peyregoza* (fol 121r), rape of another man's wife (fol 129r).

*5 G 773. 192 fols. 1400-02. Same as 5 G 772.

Sampling of the contents reveals: Fols 1-8: a collection of criminal cases (usury, case against a priest for consorting with women in his cure). Fols 8-13: articles and testimony taken at the request of the papal court concerning the sale of a tavern. Fols 14-22: articles and testimony tending to show that a man imprisoned in the bishop's prison for debt is a clerk. Fols 24-26: another debt case concerning a group of Franciscans and a nun. Fols 37-40: "Causa universitatis hominum Massillie contra dominos officiales regios dicte civitatis super quodam naufragio cuiusdam navis naufragate in gargata portus Massilie." Fols 43-52: various gracious acts. Fols 53-56: case concerning ?clerical status. Fols. 64-67: absolution of a priest. Fols 77-93: *processus* in a case delegated from the appeals court at Arles in which one Catherine wife of Jacques Gomberti is attempting to clear herself from charges of usury by attacking the witnesses against her on the ground that they are her enemies. Fols 97-102: absolution of a clerk from a charge of fraud. Fols 103-06: sentence in favor of a priest in case involving maladministration of a will. Fols 110-32: probate of a will in Provençal and examination of witnesses about it. Fols 134-37: another will. Fols 138-41: a *cessio bonorum*. Fols 142-56: suit by a nunnery against the chapter of Marseille. Fols 162-78: inventories of the goods of a ?number of deceased. Fols 179-81: gracious acts. Fols 186-88: more of the case of city against the royal officials.

*5 G 774. 68 fols. 1406-08. Same as 5 G 772.

Most, if not all, of this doc is taken up with the proceedings in the case of Guillaume Fabran c. Frères et couvent de Saint-Louis (O.F.M.), Marseille. The brothers had sold land to Guillaume, which land the brothers claimed to have received as a legacy from one Catherine Girande. Guillaume then lost the land in the royal court of Marseille to one Gérard Girande who said that Catherine had devised the land to him.

*5 G 775. 249 fols. 1407-10. Same as 5 G 772.

A sampling of the contents reveals: Fols 1-14: testamentary proceedings (including inventory) involving a deceased priest. Fols 18-20: criminal sentence in favor of a clerk accused of assault. Fols 34-54: long *processus* involving the elemosynary of Saint-Victor. Fols 55-100: testamentary case, the bishop of Glandève c. the heirs of Pierre Alan, chevalier de Marseille, includes estate accounts. Fols 131-32: sentence against a clerk for housebreaking and rape. Fols 133-37: absolution of clerk for involvement in what may have been the same event. Fols 143-58: proceedings against a priest for seduction and keeping a concubine. Fols 161-62: grant of tutelage to a widow. Fols 167-168: *de presenti* marriage case, sentence for the plaintiff. Fols 171-98: testamentary *processus*. Fols 199-230: another testament case concluded by arbitration. Fols 231-36: *de presenti* marriage case with an unusually long libel, sentence for the defendant. Fols 240-43: bigamy case, current marriage annulled. Fol 246: sentence for a woman in a testament case.

*5 G 776. 200 fols. 1407-10. Same as 5 G 772.

A sampling: Fols 1-33: more on Fabran c. Saint-Louis (above 5 G 774); the case is one of delegated papal jurisdiction. Fols 62-97: proceedings in a case of the abbey of Saint-Victor against the Cistercian house at Vallis. Fols 98-116: another case (papal delegation) involving the same Cistercian house. Fols 117-125: another delegated case involving Saint-Victor. Fols 126-48: another delegated case involving the Carmelites at Marseille. Fols 149-65: another delegated case involving Saint-Victor. Fols 166-83: another. Fols 184-200: another.

2. *Later registers and* matriculae:

*5 G 778. 62 fols. 1465-72. Registre du greffe de l'officialité.

Apparently a register of gracious acts, e.g., fol 41v a constitution of dowry.

*5 G 779. 236 fols. 1473-75. Matricule des causes civiles.

Day-by-day account of proceedings before the court.

*5 G 780. One quire (?42 fols.) 1473-75. Registre de dépositions de témoins.

Not easy to read. Two sets concern wills; the rest seem to involve clerics.

355 E 169. 1479-80. Same as 5 G 780.

See above 07/2.

5 G 784. 1407-88. Matricule de la cour épiscopale.

5 G 790. 1489. Matricule des causes.

*5 G 794. 107 fols (numbered 107-213). 1489-89/90. Matricule de la cour épiscopale.

The system of the Marseille *matriculae* is complicated and is not made easier by the facts that some of the volumes have been bound together wrong and that the hand-list gives only an approximate indication of the contents and dates. The *rubrica* is an index to the contents of the book arranged alphabetically by the name of the party and giving references to the original foliation on which entries concerning the case appear. Sometimes it is bound in with the book that it rubricates, sometimes it is bound separately. The researcher who can straighten it all out will find the *rubricae* of some use in tracking down cases, since the references are usually accurate. This book contains fols 107-213 of book A for the year, the rubric for which is found at the beginning of 5 G 795. The entries give the procedural steps in the case and sometimes the depositions, but there do not seem to be any sentences.

*5 G 795. 213 fols. 1489-89/90. Matricule A rubriqué.

The rubric seems to cover both books A and ?B. Fols 107-213 seem to be from book B. A number of cases concern marriage and family matters.

*5 G 796. 1489-89/90. Matricule rubriqué.

Book C from the same year; it has its own rubric.

*5 G 798. 1490. Matricule rubriqué.

This appears to be book C for the year 1490-90/91. It has its own rubric.

*5 G 799. 1490. Rubrique des causes.

This appears to be the rubric for books A and B of 1490-90/91, but the books themselves seem to be missing. Perhaps, however, one of them is 5 G 800, which was not examined.

5 G 800. 1491. Matricule (1er vol.).

5 G 801. 1492. Matricule (2e vol.).

5 G 803. 1491-92. Matricule (1er vol.).

5 G 804. 1491-92. Matricule (2e vol.).

5 G 807. 1492-93. Matricule.

5 G 808. 1492-93. Matricule rubriqué.

5 G 810. 1493-94. Matricule.

5 G 812. 1494-95. Matricule (1er vol.) rubriqué.

5 G 813. 1494-95. Matricule (2e vol.) rubriqué.

5 G 814. 1495-96. Matricule A rubriqué.

5 G 815. 1495-96. Matricule B rubriqué.

5 G 817/1. 1496. Matricule.

5 G 817/2. 1496. Matricule.

5 G 819. 1496-97. Matricule rubriqué.

5 G 820. 1497. Matricule rubriqué.

5 G 821. 1497-98. Registre des dépens compensés entre les parties.

5 G 824. 1502-03. Matricule.

5 G 826. 1503-04. Matricule rubriqué.

5 G 828. 1504-05. Matricule rubriqué.

5 G 830. 1505. Matricule.

5 G 831. 1505-06. Matricule rubriqué.

5 G 832. 4 quires. 1519-28. Comptes de greffe pour les années 1519, 1521, 1525, 1527.

5 G 833/1. 1527. Matricule tenu a Roquevaire pendant la peste, juin 1527.

5 G 833/2. 1527-28. Greffe de l'évêché.

5 G 834/1. 1528-29. Matricule G.

5 G 834/2. 1529-30. Matricule E.

5 G 835. 1535-39. Comptes de greffe.

5 G 836. 1552-55. Carnet journal des recettes de la cour épiscopale.

3. Miscellaneous docs, formularies, etc:

*5 G 768. 2 docs. 1375, 1481. Deux lettres d'attache de l'official.

5 G 777. 1441-43. Two *processus*.

No. 1 (1443) concerns the receipt of a benefice. No. 2 (1441) concerns stolen jewels at the abbey of Saint-Victor.

5 G 781. 1480-92. Procès entre Franquette Bontillerie et Hugone Milliere de Marseille.

5 G 782. 1486-87. Procédures diverses.

5 G 783. 1487. Ordonnances rendues par l'officialité de Marseille.

5 G 785. 1489-90. Procédures diverses.

5 G 786. 1488. Procès de l'abbaye de Saint-Victor contre Jean et Guibert Laget d'Aurial.

5 G 787. 1489. Procès du cellerier de Saint-Victor contre Catherine Vivaud de Marseille.

5 G 788. 1489-90. Procédures diverses.

5 G 789. 1489. Procès du monastère de Sainte-Paule contre Nicolas Spirola, marchand à Marseille.

5 G 791. 1489. Procès de Louis Saure et Marguerite des Baux contre Pierre des Baux.

5 G 792. 1489. Procès de A. Massel contre Jean Lombard de Marseille.

5 G 793. 1489. Procès de l'hôpital du Saint-Esprit contre G. Aymeric.

*5 G 797. 5 unbound quires. 1489-90. Procédures diverses.

The first quire appears to be the *processus* in a debt case, perhaps testamentary debt. The second may be a debt case. The third appears to be a miscellaneous collection of criminal cases (violence to a clerk, violation of jurisdiction, proceedings against a religious for celebrating a parish mass, ?defamation). The fourth is a piece of a long *processus* that orginally had more than 300 fols.

5 G 802. 1490-91. Procédures diverses.

5 G 805. 1491-92. Procédures diverses.

5 G 806. 1492. Procédures diverses.

5 G 809. 1492-93. Procédures diverses.

5 G 811. 1492-93. Procédures diverses.

5 G 816. 1495-96. Procédures diverses.

5 G 818. 1496. Procédures diverses.

5 G 822. 1499. Procédures diverses.

5 G 823 (ex 380 E 1085). 171 fols. s15/ex. Formulaire d'actes et pièces jointes.

Ed. Aubenas, *Recueil* 1:1-117, 2:7-118. The formulae on the first 122 fols concern the officiality of Marseille those on the remaining fols (pp 2:66-116), the officiality of Aix. The last two fols return to Marseille (pp 2:116-17).

300 E 54. Fols 1r-36v. s15/ex. Formulaire d'actes et pièces jointes.

Table ed. Aubenas, *Recueil* 2:139-43.

5 G 825. 1502-03. Procédures diverses.

5 G 827. 1502-03. Procédures diverses.

5 G 829. 1504-05. Procédures diverses.

5 G 837 to 5 G 839. 1521-31. Enquêtes 1521-23, 1526-27, 1530-31.

5 G 840. 1531-32. Sentences, ordonnances et procédures.

5 G 841. 1537-41. Depositions, interrogatoires.

5 G 842 to 5 G 848. 1538-62. Enquêtes 1538, 1543-45, 1544-48, 1545-50 1550-53, 1553-54, 1560-62.

5 G 849 to 5 G 851. Miscellaneous material post-1550. Very skimpy.

4. Some use of the Marseille material has been made in Lefebvre-Teillard, *Officialités*, particularly in the section on procedure, and Aubenas, *Recueil*, has published one formulary and has given us the contents of a number more. Clearly, however, the history of this officiality has not yet been written. The documentation, though difficult to follow, is particularly rich in civil cases, and the court seems to have had an unusually broad testamentary jurisdiction.

[08.]

1. Arles, Orange, officialité de l'évêque.

2. Biblioteca Apostolica Vaticana, 00120 Città del Vaticano [BAV].

A. de Boüard, 'Les fonds des notaires d'Orange à la Bibliothèque du Vatican', MEFR 30 (1910)

Archives départementales du Vaucluse [ADV] (voir 02/2).

3. *1. BAV*:

Fonds des notaires d'Orange 359. Mars 1460 - Mars 1461. Registres du greffe de l'officialité.

Id. 360. 1455-1466. *Id.*

Id. 402. 1466-1467. *Id.*

Id. 361, 402. 1467. *Id.*

Id. 363. 1470-1471. *Id.*

Id. 364. 1471-1472. *Id.*

Id. 365, 403. 1473-1474. *Id.*

Id. 366. 1474-1475. *Id.* incomplet.

Id. 404. 1475-1476. *Id.* incomplet.

2. ADV:

G V 120. 1521. Manuel des causes civiles.

G V 121. 1521. Manuel des causes civiles.

G V 160. 1555-1559. Brevets ou brouillards.

G V 161. 1524-1727. Brevets ou brouillards.

[09.]

1. Avignon, officialité de l'archevêque (depuis 1475).

2. Archives départementales du Vaucluse (voir 02/2).

Voir Imbert/Font-Réaux, *Répertoire* p 59.

3. G I 125. Fol 48-145. 1551-1560. Compte des amendes et condamnations prononcées en la Cour archiépiscopale d'Avignon.

Sans grand intérêt, car la nature des condamnations n'est pas spécifiée, sauf en deux occasions.

G I 800bis. 1518. Manuel de la Cour archiépiscopale.

[10.]

1. Avignon, Carpentras, officialité de l'évêque.

2. Archives départementales du Vaucluse [ADV] (voir 02/2).

Voir Imbert/Font-Réaux, *Répertoire* pp 20-23.

3. G IIIbis 1 à 12. 1516-1568. Brevets ou brouillards:

01: 1516-1520	07: 1541
02: 1524	08: 1542-1543
03: 1531-1533	09: 1543-1545
04: 1534-1536	10: 154?
05: 1538	11: 1554-1564
06: 1539-1540	12: 1557-1568

G IIIbis 81 à 180. 1427-1563. Manuels des causes civiles et criminelles:

081: 1427	098: 1491-1492
082: 1428	099: 1492-1493
083: 1433	100: 1492-1494
084: 1433-1435	101: 1495-1496
085: 1435	102: 1497-1498
086: 1436-1437	103: 1499
087: 1437	104: 1499-1500
088: 1440	105: 1501
089: 1441	106: 1504-1555
090: 1442	107: 1506-1507
091: 1443	108: 1508
092: 1445	109: 1508
093: 1486-1487	110: 1511
094: 1487-1488	111: 1513
095: 1488	112: 1514
096: 1489-1490	113: 1515
097: 1490-1491	114: 1516

115: 1518
116: 1519
117: 1520
118: 1521
119: 1523
120: 1524
121: 1524
122: 1525
123: 1526
124: 1528
125: 1529
126: 1530
127: 1530
128: 1530
129: 1531
130: 1531
131: 1532
132: 1533
133: 1534
134: 1534
135: 1535
136: 1535-1536
137: 1536
138: 1537
139: 1538
140: 1539
141: 1540
142: 1540
143: 1541
144: 1541
145: 1541
146: 1542
147: 1542
148: 1543
149: 1544
150: 1544-1545
151: 1545
152: 1545-1546
153: 1546-1547
154: 1547
155: 1547
156: 1548
157: 1549
158: 1549
159: 1550
160: 1551
161: 1552
162: 1552
163: 1552-1557
164: 1554
165: 1556
166: 1555
167: 1556
168: 1557
169: 1558
170: 1558
171: 1558
172: 1557-1560
173: 1559
174: 1559
175: 1560
176: 1561
177: 1561
178: 1562
179: 1562
180: 1563

G IIIbis 283. 1549. Matricule.

4. Ces registres cotés G IIIbis sont en fait conservés actuellement sous les cotes B Rectorie 3293 à 3299 et 3319 à 3425 aux ADV. C'est une série exceptionnelle de registres, qui s'étend du s14 au s18 et mériterait une étude particulière.

[11.]

1. Avignon, Cavaillon, officialité de l'évêque.

2. Archives départementales du Vaucluse (voir 02/2).

   Voir Bautier/Sornay, *Sources* 2:748, 1316
   Imbert/Font-Réaux, *Répertoire* p 63.

3. Étude Rousset 45. 1351-1355. Registre du notaire P. Chabaud contenant des actes pour la cour épiscopale.

G IV 101. 32 fols. 1508. Manuel des *judicata.*

G IV 135. 406 fols. 1538-1540. Livre des dépens de la cour spirituelle.

[12.]

1. Avignon, Vaison, officialité de l'évêque.

2. Archives départementales du Vaucluse (voir 02/2).

   Voir Imbert/Font-Réaulx, *Répertoire* pp 33, 65.

3. G VI 200. 1377-1378. Registre des causes.

   G VI 201. 1521-1526. Registre des causes.

4. De plus, une série de brevets ou brouillards allant de 1471 au s18 est en cours d'inventorisation. Elle est coté B Rectorie 2955-2970 et 2978-2995 pour notre période, mais n'ayant pas encore fait l'objet d'un répertoire détaillé, juridiction spirituelle et juridiction temporelle y sont peu distinguées.

[13.]

1. Bordeaux, officialité de l'archevêque (diocésaine et métropolitaine).

2. Archives départementales de la Gironde, 13-25 rue d'Aviau, 33081 Bordeaux cedex.

   A. Gouget, C. Ducannès-Duval et E. Allain, *Inventaire sommaire* [*de la*] *série G.* 1: *Nos 1 à 920* (Bordeaux 1892)

   J.A. Brutails, *Id.* 2: *Nos 921-3156* (Bordeaux 1901)

   A. d'Anglade, *Supplément au répertoire numérique de la série G* (ms 1950)

3. G 73. 29 fols. 1377. Officialité métropolitaine de Bordeaux — copie d'actes à caractère patrimonial relevant de la juridiction gracieuse de l'official.

   Le G 73 a été utilisé par A.J. Boyé pour son étude:

   'Une vente de biens dotaux devant l'officialité de Bordeaux en 1377', *Revue Historique de Bordeaux* 17 (1924) 113-122.

   G 74. 530 fols. Fragments de registres d'audience de l'officialité diocésaine:

   1° registre 1382-1383

   2° registre 1438-1443

   3° registre 1459-1463

   4° registre 1468-1471

   5° registre 1465-1474.

[14.]

1. Bordeaux, Angoulême, officialité de l'évêque.

2. Archives départementales de la Charente, 24 rue Gambetta, 16000 Angoulême.

   L. Burias, *Inventaire sommaire [de la] série G. 2: De 339 à 993* (Angoulême 1961)

3. *G 660 (ex G 451). 187 fols. 1554-1555. Registre d'audience de l'officialité diocésaine.

   Ce registre ne contient pas toutes les audiences, mais presque exclusivement celles concernant trois d'affaires: les affaires de dettes (nombreuses monitions et quelques monitoires); les affaires matrimoniales (surtout des actions en reconnaissance ou des oppositions aux bans, mais pas de séparations) et enfin les injures verbales. Il est intéressant surtout sous l'angle de la procédure.

[15.]

1. Bordeaux, Maillezais, officialité de l'évêque.

   Créé en 1317, le siège de Maillezais a été transféré à La Rochelle en 1648.

2. Bibliothèque municipale, rue Gargoulleau, 17000 La Rochelle.

3. *Ms 241. 1545-1552. Registre des causes de l'officialité.

   Voir Petit, *Registre*, p xiv. Registre intéressant, utilisé dans Lefebvre-Teillard, *Officialités*.

[16.]

1. Bordeaux, Périgueux, officiality of the bishop.

2. *Archives départementales de la Dordogne, 2 place Hoche, 24000 Périgueux.

   Noël Becquart, *Guide des archives de la Dordogne* (Périgueux 1970)

3. *5 G 1. 3 docs and 1 roll of 10 mm. 1355-1400. Various case docs.

   The roll is a rather full *processus* of 1369 in a case involving the bailiffs of the city claiming a customary payment. The docs are an appeal from an arbitral sentence in a case of beating and outrage (1359) and two other appeal docs (1355, 1400).

   *5 G 2. 184 fols. s15. Formulary and style of the court.

   *5 G 3. 107 fols. 1447-1515. Formulary with a number of original docs folded in.

4. Although the documentation for the court of Périgueux is disappointingly skimpy, there is enough here for a small study of its jurisdiction and operation.

[17.]

1. Bordeaux, Poitiers, officialité de l'évêque.

2. Archives départementales de la Vienne, 14 rue E. Grimaux, 86000 Poitiers.

L. Redet, *Répertoire numérique de la série G supplément* (dact sd)

3. *G suppl. 57. s15-s17. Registres, etc.

Sous cette cote sont conservés de nombreux docs, parmi lesquels:

Un fragment de registre des causes d'office de l'année 1459 (12 Sep - 10 Dec), 34 fols (forme la fin du registre suivant).

Un registre des causes d'office de 1473, 138 fols. Ce registre s'apparente à un registre de greffe mais contient quelques indications concernant les sentences rendues.

Un fragment de registre de 1463, 9 fols. "Expleta registri emendarum causarum officii in venerabili curia officialatus pictavensis pagiatarum ...."

Un fragment de registre de 1464, 6 fols. "Expleta emendarum in venerabili curia officialatus pictavensis gagiatarum instantiam venerabili viro magistro J. Petit in lege licenciato causarum officii dicte curie promotore."

Un registre de greffe de 1473, 253 fols.

Un registre des causes de 1547, 316 fols. "Actum in curia officialatus pictavensis ...." C'est plutôt un registre de greffe qu'un registre de causes: les sentences y sont extrêmement rares. Une grande partie de la procédure est en français.

4. Le registre de 1547 a été utilisé dans Lefebvre-Teillard, *Officialités*. Le lot d'archives concernant l'année 1473 devrait pouvoir alimenter une étude ponctuelle de cette officialité à la fin du Moyen Age.

[18.]

1. Bourges, officialité de l'archevêque (métropolitaine).

2. *Bibliothèque Nationale, 58 rue de Richelieu, 75002 Paris [BN].

Nous ne citons ici que le catalogue pour le munuscrit décrit ci-dessous:

Catalogus codicum manuscriptorum Bibliothecae Regiae, Pars Tertia, 4 (Paris 1744).

3. *Ms. latin 5233. Fols. 13-20. s14/ex X s15/in. Formulaire de l'officialité.

Formulaire de 30 formules. Le fol 36 contient une sentence arbitrale.

[19.]

1. Bourges, Bourges, officialité du chapitre métropolitain Saint-Étienne.

2. Archives départementales du Cher, 9 rue Fernault, 18022 Bourges cedex.

   P. Gravayat, *Série G: Répertoire numérique* (Bourges 1981)

3. *8 G 261. 1538-1546. Registre du greffe.

   *8 G 262. 1546-1555. Registre du greffe.

   *8 G 274. s15/ex X s16/in. Formulaire de l'officialité.

   *8 G 292. 1511-1512. Registre des causes d'officialité.

   *8 G 293. 1512-1513. Registre des causes d'officialité.

   *8 G 294. 1519-1520. Registre des causes d'officialité.

   *8 G 295. 1520-1521. Registre des causes d'officialité.

4. Un petit mais bon lot d'archives. Ces archives ont été utilisées dans Lefebvre-Teillard, *Officialités*.

[20.]

1. Bourges, Clermont, officialité de l'évêque.

2. Archives départementales du Puy-de-Dôme, 18 boulevard Desaix, 63033 Clermont-Ferrand.

   L. Welter, *Répertoire numérique de la série G* (ms 1943)

3. *1 G 1806. 277 fols. 1503-1504. Registre des causes.

   "Hoc est papirus causarum vertentium coram domino officiali claromontensi in quibus magister Vincentius Ribier notarius curie iuratus, scripsit ...." Ce registre s'apparente plus à un registre de greffe qu'à un véritable registre de causes.

[21.]

1. Bourges, Limoges, officialité de l'évêque.

2. Archives départementales de la Haute-Vienne, square A. Leroux, 87032 Limoges.

   A. Petit, *Répertoire numérique de la série G* (Limoges 1931)

3. *4 G 1. 165 fols. 1532-1541. Extrait des registres des causes criminelles: condamnations à des amendes pécuniaires applicables à l'édification de l'église cathédrale.

   4 G 2. 1548-1554. Amendes payables à l'évêque ou applicable à de pieux usages.

4 G 3. 1541-1699. Citations, enquêtes, informations, sentences et autres pièces de procédures concernant ecclésiastiques et religieux.

4. Le premier de ces registres a été utilisé dans Lefebvre-Teillard, *Officialités*. Le dernier ne concerne pratiquement pas notre période.

[22.]

1. Bourges, Limoges, officialité du chapitre.

2. Archives départementales de la Haute-Vienne (voir 21/2).

3. 5 G 1. Fragment. 1459. Auditeurs et official du chapitre: enquête sur leur compétence.

5 G 2. 1559-1567. Cour des auditeurs et de l'official: registre des audiences.

5 G 3. 1535-1568. Cour des auditeurs des causes du chapitre: affaires ecclésiastiques.

5 G 5. 1500-1510. Procédure.

5 G 6. 1513-1514. Procédure concernant une affaire de meurtre.

5 G 7. 1513-1514. Procédure concernant une affaire d'injures.

5 G 6. 1544-1582. Procédures diverses concernant des ecclésiastiques.

4. Docs de trop peu d'importance pour permettre une étude exhaustive de cette officialité.

[23.]

1. Bourges, Mende, officiality of the bishop.

2. *Archives départementales de la Lozère, 7, place Urbain V, 48005 Mende.

The records of the officiality seem to have been acquired at the time of the establishment of the departmental archives in the early s19. A fire in that century destroyed substantial parts of the *ancien régime* holdings.

Ferd[inand] André, *Inventaire sommaire* [*de la*] *série G.* 1: *Nos. 1-1451* (Mende 1882)

lists all docs from the court known to me. It is quite detailed and accurate. The *fonds* of the officiality are articles G 922 through G 968 in the *Inventaire.*

H. Latour, *Guide des archives de la Lozère* (Mende 1979)

is a model of its kind.

3. *1. Chronological records*:

*G 963. 186 fols (12 quires), 15 loose docs. 1268-1272. Register of cases.

The ms. is bound in wood and leather in a style that suggests the s15. At that time the original fols 1 and 188 may have been used in the binding, for the first is now clearly missing and the last seems to be. The fifteen loose docs (correspondence, positions, interrogatories, articles, etc.) are now in an envelope within the book. They all seem to concern cases within the book. The first 7 fols have entries arranged by date. On fol 10r the clerk begins a new style in which he attempts to gather together the *processus* from a single case (including, at least in some cases, the libel, positions, depositions, etc.) before going on to the next one. The effort is not notably successful. A number of blank fols indicates that he sometimes overestimated how much space he would need, and frequent cross-references indicate that he also frequently underestimated. The cases are both criminal and civil, largely secular. Debts and assaults predominate, but there are cases of rights in land, inheritance, and at least one marriage case.

*G 934. 126 fols., parchment binding, 3 large quires. 1340-1345. Register of cases.

The book is largely, though not exclusively, made up of inquests in criminal cases and depositions of witnesses in civil ones. The criminal cases involve a large variety of offenses, mostly by clerics. The civil cases include marriage, testaments, marital property, and debt.

2. *Individual docs*:

*G 944. 116 fols. 1443. *Processus* in a case between the cathedral chapter and a layman about a *cens*.

*G 945. 72 fols. 1448. Doc concerning jurisdiction.

A doc made up on the basis of a search of nine registers of the court from 1283 to 1448, extracting cases concerning royal and episcopal jurisdiction. Neither of the surviving registers is mentioned, suggesting that they were not part of the normal run of registers.

*G 960. 48 fols. s14. Formulary.

Most of the items concern noncontentious jurisdiction (institutions, inductions, etc.) but some judicial matters.

*G 961. 15 fols. s15. Formulary.

Sample orders to absolve excommunicates, etc.

G 922. 6 docs. 1307-1322. Royal letters concerning jurisdiction.

G 923. 5 docs. 1291-1320. Concerning jurisdiction.

Including a letter of Nicholas IV to Bishop William Durantis (1286-1296).

G 924. 2 docs. 1322-1325. Jurisdiction over married clerks.

G 925. 3 docs. 1325-1328. Royal and secular jurisdiction.

G 926. 5 docs. 1132-1340. *Id.*

G 927. 3 docs. 1351-1357. *Id.*

G 928. 3 docs. 1354-1381. Seignorial vs. episcopal jurisdiction.

G 929. 6 docs. 1390-1400. Royal and episcopal jurisdiction.

G 930-932. 1503-1729. Royal and episcopal jurisdiction.

G 933. 2 docs. 1283-1339. One roll of condemnations of clerks by the official. Commission by Durantis to judges in a murder case.

G 935. Quire of 4 fols. 1344. Clerical defamation case.

G 936. Quire of 24 fols. 1347. A case of black magic attempted against the bishop of one Sir Pepin (priest).

G 937. Copy of G 936.

G 938. Quire of 34 fols. 1347. Case (with depositions) of assault during mass by a canon; appeal to Rome.

G 939. Quire of 14 fols. 1347. Copy of G 938.

G 940. 3 docs. 1353-1361. Case docs (including a sentence in a testament case).

G 941. 3 docs. 1373-1397. Two jurisdictional and one testament case.

G 942. Quire of 38 fols. 1377. *Cens* case, involving the clergy of the church of Mende and a husband and wife.

G 943. Quire of 35 fols. 1427-1430. Complex case of murder of a clerk with depositions.

G 946-957. 1503-1791. Various ecclesiastical cases, civil and criminal.

A couple of clerical fornication and adultery cases. The last is from the officiality of Uzès.

G 958. Quire of 14 fols. 1440-s17. *Monitoria* and some s17 depositions.

G 959. 22 docs. 1341-1525. Miscellaneous orders including orders involving debts.

G 964. 40 docs. 1264-1326. Miscellany of both secular and ecclesiastical jurisdiction.

G 965. Roll. 1390. A death sentence from the ?city court.

G 966. 4 docs. 1484 to 1786. Nominations of judges.

G 967 to G968. 5 docs. 1353 to 1354. Jurisdictional case against a royal official.

4. This small, mountainous diocese possesses one of the oldest court books that survives from any European ecclesiastical court. It was, of course, the see of

William Durantis, the great proceduralist of the late s13 (and of his nephew). Prior to 1306 the seignorial jurisdiction of the bishop and his spiritual jurisdiction seem to have been exercised by the same court, which employed Romano-canonic procedure. After the establishment of a secular royal court in the area, the bishop's court continued to exercise a wider range of jurisdiction than was normal in France in this period. The number of surviving docs concerning the jurisdiction of the court suggest a continual controversy during the s14 and s15 over the extent of the jurisdiction of the court.

[24.]

1. Bourges, Le Puy, officialité de l'évêque.

2. Archives départementales de la Haute-Loire, rue Étienne Delcambre, 43012 Le Puy.

   A. Jacotin, *Inventaire sommaire de la série G.* 1: *Arts. 1-730* (Le Puy 1903)

   E. Delcambre, *Id.* 2: *G 731 à 1172* (Le Puy 1948)

   P. Thilliez et Y. Soulingeas, *Répertoire numérique supplémentaire* (dact 1969-1975)

3. *G 259. 156 fols. 1444-1445. Registre des excommunications.

   Ne peut éventuellement servir que pour l'établissement d'une statistique du nombre des excommuniés.

4. Outre ce registre il existe aussi sous les cotes G 260-1 deux registres de la cour épiscopale datants de 1270 à 1284. Probablement il s'agit de la cour féodale de l'évêque, mais ces registres mériteraient un examen plus approfondi.

[25.]

1. Bourges, Rodez, officialité de l'évêque.

2. *Bibliothèque Sainte-Geneviève, place du Panthéon, 75005 Paris [BSG].

   Ch. Kohler, in *Catalogue général des Manuscrits des Bibliothèques publiques de France: Bibliothèque Sainte-Geneviève*, 2 vols. (Paris 1893-8)

   Archives départementales de l'Aveyron, 11 rue Louis Oustry 12000 Rodez [ADA].

   C. Estienne et L. Lempereur, *Inventaire sommaire de la série G.* 1: *G 1 à 942* (Rodez 1934)

   L. Lempereur, B. de Gaulejac et J. Bousquet, *Inventaire sommaire de la série G.* 2: *G 942 à 1205* (1958).

3. *1. BSG*:

Ms 863. 1467. Un procés pour hérésie devant l'officialité de Rodez.

2. ADA:

G 53. 18 fols. s15. Statuts et ordonnances de l'officialité de Rodez ou réglementation par l'official des attributions et devoirs tant des officiers de sa Cour que des avocats et procureurs appelés à y exercer leur ministère.

4. Outre cette pièce émanant directement de l'officialité, les ADA conservent plusieurs pièces relatives à la juridiction ecclésiastique du s13 au s16 et se rapportant pour la plupart à des conflits avec la juridiction laïque (G 10, G 24, G 26, G 27, G 475 et G 476).

[26.]

1. Bourges, St Flour, officialité de l'évêque (diocésaine).
2. Archives départementales du Cantal, rue de 139e R.I., 15006 Aurillac.

   L. Bouyssou, *Répertoire de la série G* (Aurillac 1972)

3. *1 G 35. 190 fols. 1558-1560. Registre des causes de l'officialité de St Flour.

   Contient essentiellement des procédures concernant des affaires de dettes, des monitoires et quelques rares affaires matrimoniales (moins d'une dizaine) sans que l'on soit presque jamais fixé sur l'issu du procès.

[27.]

1. Bourges, St Flour, officialité de l'évêque (officialité foraine d'Arpajon).
2. Archives départementales du Cantal (voir 26/2).
3. *1 G 34. 1545. Registre des causes de l'officialité foraine d'Arpajon.

   C'est un registre d'audience contenant de brèves notes sur le suivi des affaires. Sans grand intérêt. Écriture extrêmement difficile à déchiffrer.

[28.]

1. Embrun, Digne, officialité de l'évêque.
2. Archives Départementales des Alpes de Haute Provence (voir 04/2).
3. *1 G 12. 2 cahiers. 1458-1527, 1498. Registre de causes.

   *1 G 13. 2 cahiers. 1500-1510. Registre de causes.

   1 G 14. 1503-1504. Plumitifs d'audience.

   1 G 15. 1507-1508. Plumitifs d'audience.

1 G 16. 1508-1509. Plumitifs d'audience.

1 G 17. 1492-1493. Matricules de la cour.

1 G 18. 1503-1505, 1518. Matricules de la cour.

1 G 19. 1526. Matricules de la cour.

1 G 20. 1527. Matricules de la cour.

4. Certains de ces registres, les plumitifs en particulier, sont en mauvais état. Les registres de causes ont été utilisés dans Lefebvre-Teillard, *Officialités*.

[29.]

1. Lyon, officialité de l'archevêque (primatiale).

2. *BN (voir 18/2).

Archives départementales du Rhône, 2 chemin du Montauban, 69005 Lyon [ADR].

P. Lemoine, P.F. Gauthier, M.C. Guigue, G. Guigue, C. Faure et H. Hours, *Répertoire numérique de la série G: 1 G à 10 G* (Lyon 1959)

R. Lacour, *Répertoire numérique de la série G: 11 G à 29 G* (Lyon 1968)

Staatsarchiv des Kantons Bern, Falkenplatz 4, CH-3012 Bern, Suisse [STABE].

Les renseignements sur cet archive ont été donnés par Dr. Andreas Meyer.

3. *1. BN*:

*Ms lat 5187. Regestrum de certis gestis super administrationem sedis archiepiscopalis lugduni.

Contient des renseignements intéressants sur le personnel des officialités lyonnaises dans la s14/2 (1365-1375).

2. ADR:

2 G 4. 1488-1687. Causes d'appel des sentences rendues aux officialités de Sens, Tours, Paris et métropolitaine de Lyon.

10 G 1391 à 1405. Pièces concernant la primatie parmi lesquelles on signalera tout particulièrement:

10 G 1394. 1406-1476. Procès entre l'archevêque de Lyon et l'archevêque de Tours au sujet de la primatie de Lyon avec une réglementation des appels.

10 G 1396. 1458-1701. Copies de sentences rendues par les officiaux des

évêques de Bretagne, dont il y a eu appel aux délégués à Rennes de l'archevêque de Tours, puis à l'official primatial.

3. STABE:

A V 1461 (= U.P. 85). 1 vol, 436 pp. 1534. "Process inquisitorial faict et forme par autorite du siege archiepiscopal de Lyon en cas d'heresie: instance du procuratur fiscal dudit siege contre Baudichon de la maison neufve marchant de lieu de genefve" (en français).

4. Très peu d'affaires concernent notre période (une seule par ex. dans le 2 G 4). On trouve dans le ms 977 conservé à la BML (voir 30/3/1 infra) des renseignements concernant l'officialité primatiale.

[30.]

1. Lyon, officialité de l'archevêque (métropolitaine et diocésaine).

La dignité d'official métropolitain et diocésain étant souvent réunies sur une même tête, plusieurs docs sont répertoriés sous la rubrique officialité métropolitaine et diocésaine.

2. Bibliothèque municipale de Lyon, 30 boulevard Vivier Merle, 69431 Lyon cedex 03 [BML].

A. Molinier et Desvernay, in *Catalogue général des Manuscrits des Bibliothèques publiques de France*, 30 (2 vols.) (Paris 1900)

Archives départementales du Rhône [ADR](voir 29/2).

3. *1. BML*:

*Ms 977. 418 fols. 1485-1502. Registre du Conseil de l'archevêque de Lyon.

Le Ms 977 a été étudié par Lefebvre-Teillard, 'Une institution inconnue'.

2. ADR:

10 G 1450. 1512-1520. Registre du Conseil de l'archevêque de Lyon.

10 G 1399 et 1400. 1485. Pièces concernant un procès entre l'archevêque de Lyon et l'évêque de Chalon, devant l'official de Vienne, juge délégué.

10 G 1439. 1343-1694. Pièces diverses.

Contient entre autres un procès d'hérésie (1523-1524).

10 G 1440. 1455. Procédure contre des particuliers accusés d'escroquerie.

10 G 1441. 1476. Procédure menée par les greffiers de l'officialité et de la cour séculière de l'archevêque contre ce dernier.

10 G 1442. 1488. Procédure contre deux femmes accusées d'hérésie.

Sur cette affaire, voir également 2 G 4 et surtout le Ms 977, fol. 130v et seq.

10 G 1457. 1502. Appel par l'archevêque d'une ordonnance du bailliage de Beaujolais, interdissant aux laïcs de passer aucun contrat devant des ecclésiastiques.

[31.]

1. Lyon, Autun, officialité de l'évêque.

2. Archives départementales de Saône-et-Loire, place des Carmélites, 71025 Mâcon.

   L. Michon, A. Benet, L. Leux et A. Morgand, *Inventaire sommaire [de la] Série G (Arts. 1 à 941)* (Mâcon 1933)

3. G 718. Liasse de 76 pièces. 1335-1516. Quelques pièces concernant le privilège du for (1335, 1337, 1365, 1405 et 1466); des excommunications et des appels comme d'abus (1508-1511 et 1516).

   G 720. Liasse de 16 pièces. 1378. Accord entre l'évêque d'Autun et le chapitre au sujet de l'exemption.

   G 722. Sentence de l'official reconnaissant l'exemption de l'abbaye St Martin.

   G 723. 1488. Enquête sur l'élection de l'abbé de St Léonard de Corbigny.

   G 725 à 732. s13-s18. Pièces diverses relatives aux conflits soulevés par l'exercice du droit de bâtardise à l'égard de prêtres et l'inventaire des biens de prêtres morts intestats.

4. L'official d'Autun en 1523, le chanoine Jean Blondel a publié: *Statuta Curiae sedis episcopalis Eduensis* ... (Lugduni 1535), un livre assez rare (pas d'exemplaires dans le *National Union Catalogue*), dont il y a deux exemplaires à la BN (Rés E 4202 et 4203) et un dans la réserve de la Bibliothéque Sainte-Geneviève (voir 25/2). À part les *Statuta curie sedis eduensis* fort utiles, le reste ne peut guère servir que d'appoint pour des études particulières portant sur le privilège du for ou le droit successoral.

[32.]

1. Lyon, Langres, officiality of the bishop.

2. *BN (see 18/2).

3. *Ms lat. 5190. 180 fols. 1337-1343. Register of the officiality of Langres.

   The description is somewhat misleading. Most of the volume (fols 8r-173v) is taken up with docs concerning an appeal from the official of Langres to papal judges delegate from the abbey of Cavaillon in what begins as a routine case of disciplining a clerk for violence and turns into a full-scale attack on the official's jurisdiction. The beginning and ending fols are occupied by a series of unrelated entries, mostly in a very difficult script.

[33.]

1. Lyon, Lyon, officialité de l'archevêque (diocésaine).

2. Archives départementales du Rhône (voir 29/2).

3. 4 G 1. s15. Liber de decimis.

   4 G 2. s16. Formulaire (attribution douteuse).

   4 G 3. 1351-1366. Minutes de notaire Pierre de Valle.

   4 G 4. 1363-1376. Minutes de notaire J. Belli.

   4 G 5. 1379-1399. Minutes de notaire J. Avunculi.

   4 G 6. 1434-1435. Minutes de notaire C. Thomasset.

   4 G 6bis. 1529-1554. Minutes de notaire L. Dupuys.

   4 G 22. 1457-1580. Plaintes contre des ecclésiastiques.

   4 G 31. 1392-1667. Requêtes, ordonnances, sentences.

4. Le Ms 977 de la BML (voir 30/3/1) contient également des renseignements intéressants sur l'officialité diocésaine.

[34.]

1. Lyon, Lyon, officialité de l'archevêque (Cour des excès).

   La Cour des excès exerce la compétence pénale normalement dévolue à l'officalité diocésaine. Le Ms lat 5187 de la BN (voir 29/3/1) atteste l'existence d'un official des excès en 1365.

2. Archives départementales du Rhône (voir 29/2).

3. 10 G 1443. 1481, 1508-1511. Comptes d'amendes et émoluments de la Cour des excès du diocèse de Lyon.

   10 G 1452. 1511-1512. Compte rendu par B. Patrasson, receveur des amendes et compositions de la Cour des excès.

   10 G 663. 1485-1486, 1499. Compte des émoluments de la Cour des excès; rôles des causes appelées devant la Cour.

[35.]

1. Lyon, Lyon, officialité de l'archevêque et du chapitre de la cathédrale (Cour commune).

   La Cour commune est une institution originale et particulière à Lyon. Il s'agit d'une cour commune entre l'archevêque et le chapitre, chargée de juger les clercs délinquants dans la ville de Lyon, au sujet de laquelle le Ms 977 (voir 30/3/1) donne de nombreuses explications. Voir Lefebvre-Teillard, 'Une institution inconnue', 223.

2. Archives départementales du Rhône (voir 29/2).

3. 10 G 660-661. 1274-1280. Différend entre l'archevêque et le chapitre au sujet de la Cour commune.

   10 G 662. 1286-1402. Pièces concernant la Cour commune.

[36.]

1. Lyon, Lyon, officialité du chapitre Saint-Jean (justice du glaive spirituel).

2. Archives départementales du Rhône (voir 29/2).

3. 10 G 641. 1270-1377. Partage entre l'archevêque et le chapitre de la juridiction spirituelle et diverses excommunications.

   10 G 642. 1380-1477. Procédures contre des "prêtres habitués" et des clercs.

   10 G 643. 1514-1525. Procédures contre des "prêtres habitués" et des clercs.

   10 G 647. 1470-1472. Registre de greffe de la Cour du glaive spirituel.

   10 G 642. 1359-1516. Droit du chapitre de succéder aux bénéficiers morts ab intestat.

   10 G 579 à 586. Franchises et immunités du cloître (à la fois spirituelles et temporelles).

[37.]

1. Lyon, Lyon, officialité du chapitre Saint-Just.

2. Archives départementales du Rhône (voir 29/2).

3. 12 G 341. 1465. Sentence arbitrale sur le conflit opposant l'archevêque au chapitre Saint-Just au sujet de son exemption.

   12 G 342. Titres produits par le chapitre au sujet du conflit précédent.

12 G 362. 1511-1725. Informations faites par le promoteur contre des clercs de Saint-Just accusés de crimes ou de délits.

12 G 363. 1408-1429. Registre des audiences en matière civile.

12 G 364. 1430-1441. Registre des audiences en matière civile.

12 G 365. 1456-1493. Registre des audiences en matière civile.

12 G 366. 1499-1500. Registre des audiences en matière civile.

12 G 367. 1500-1602. Registre des audiences en matière civile.

12 G 377. 1430-1604. Sentences, ordonnances, expéditions.

12 G 383. 1529-1668. Actes divers de procédure.

12 G 386. 1400-1598. Plaintes, informations, interrogations, sentences, pièces diverses en matière criminelle.

[38.]

1. Narbonne, Elne, officiality of the bishop at Elne and at Perpignan.

2. Archives départementales des Pyrénées-Orientales, 11 rue du Bastion Saint-Dominique, 66020 Perpignan.

J.A. Brutails, Desplanque, et Palustre, *Inventaire sommaire* [*de la*] *Série G* (Perpignan 1904)

Pp 54-60 give an adequate description of those items that they cover, but they are not quite complete. In correspondence in 1981 the archivist mentioned that there were a dozen bundles of docs in Series G that had not been inventoried and that a typed alphabetical index of Series B (1951) contained a number of references to matters that seemed to concern various officialities. Unfortunately, I did not have time at Perpignan to pursue these matters further.

3. *G145. 28 fols. 1408. Register.

Mostly day-by-day entries in cases. Some marriage material, probate of a will, debt transactions, much procedural material.

*G 145bis (not inventoried). 41 fols. 1413-14. Register of the bishop's official at Perpignan.

The entries are long, sometimes taking up 2 fols. Docs in the cases are folded into the binding. A number of marriage cases, a case claiming a chaplain for a church, a number of pledges for the payment of debts, case involving spoliation of ecclesiastical revenues, various criminal cases involving clerical status, long doc registered with the court that looks like the ordination of a vicarage.

*G 146. 6 fols. 1427. Part of the register of the bishop's official at Perpignan, *sede vacante*.

Confession of debt by a whole village, another, publication of a will.

*G 147. 150 fols. 1536-37. Register.

Day-by-day account of proceedings. The vernacular now predominates.

G 148-152. 1559 X 1669. Broken series of five registers.

*G 142. 53 docs. and 1 quire of 18 fols. 1354-1499. Style and court docs.

The quire is a s14 style of the court. Incipit: "Si aliquis voluerit causas procurare in Curia spirituali debet sequentem practicum tenere secundum stilum curie vicariatus officialatus Elien'." The docs include: notarized will by a priest whose church was to benefit (1401), mandate to cite a woman who failed to inventory her husband's estate (sd), inhibition and citation mandates by the official of Narbonne in appeal cases (1417, 1462, 1476), warnings to a number of people to pay debts with acta on the dorse (1380, 1397, 1402, 1405, 1406, 1425, 1463), citation mandates with acta on the dorse (1431, 1463), citation mandate in a *de presenti* marriage case (1449), same in a testament case (1469), same in a case of deposit (1369), notarial doc appointing a proctor with acta (1354), libel, excommunication and other docs in a jactitation of marriage case (1397), various docs in criminal cases (1440, 1494).

G 143. 51 docs. s15/ex X s16/in. Similar to G 142.

G 144. 43 docs. 1535 X 1564. Similar to G 142.

G 153. 91 docs. 1372 X 1408. Similar to G 142.

G 154. 28 docs. 1474 X 1504. Similar to G 142.

G 155. 52 docs. 1537 X 1699. Similar to G 142.

G 156. 2 quires (122 fols and 93 fols). 1536. Procès.

Processus before the official of Perpignan concerning a young woman who had agreed to renounce her inheritance rights for an agreed sum. She asks to be released from the agreement on the ground that she was under 25.

G 157-58. Post-Tridentine material. Not much.

G 159-66. Fonds de l'inquisition.

Includes some pre-1500 docs, e.g., G 159, 165, 166.

4. There probably is not enough material to reconstruct a full-scale history of the medieval officiality, but there is enough material here for a researcher with patience to draw some conclusions about the nature of the court's jurisdiction.

[39.]

1. Narbonne, Nîmes, officialité de l'évêque.

2. Archives départementales du Gard, 20 rue des Chassaintes 30040 Nîmes.

A. de Lamothe, *Inventaire-sommaire [de la] Série G [Arts. 1-1559]* (Paris 1876)

E. Bligny-Bondurand, *Inventaire sommaire supplément à la série G [arts. 1560-1660]* (Nîmes 1916).

M. Gouron, *Inventaire sommaire de la série G [arts. 1661-1763]* (dact sd)

3. *G 945. 490 fols. 1525-1527. Manuel de la Cour spirituelle de Nîmes (causes civiles).

Le G 945 a été utilisé dans Lefebvre-Teillard, *Officialités*. C'est un registre qui concerne les affaires civiles *stricto sensu* (obligations surtout) et qui contient fort peu de sentences.

*G 946. 67 fols. 1549. Registre de causes.

Le G 946 contient surtout des causes beneficiales et matrimoniales.

[40.]

1. Reims, officialité de l'abbaye de Corbie.

2. *BN (voir 18/2).

Voir Léopold Delisle, 'Inventaire des Mss. latins et d'autres fonds conservés à la Bibliothèque Nationale sous les Nos. 16719-18613', *Bibliothèque de l'école des chartes* 31 (1870) 463 ff.

3. *Ms lat 17766 (ex Corbie 56). 86 fols. s15/in. Formulaire de l'officialité de Corbie.

Les formules datées portent des dates de 1380 à 1410 et concernent l'abbé Raoul. Les docs concernant la juridiction gracieuse sont mélangés avec ceux qui concernent la juridiction contentieuse ou les relations de l'abbaye avec d'autres juridictions. Quelques extraits concernent l'abbaye de Saint-Lucien de Beauvais.

*Ms lat 18371. 193 fols. s16/in. Style de l'officialité.

Mieux organisé que les autres formulaires de Corbie. Les formules portent des dates de 1497 à 1518. Utilisé dans Lefebvre-Teillard, *Officialités*.

*Ms lat 17145: 145 fols. 1521-1584. Registre de l'officialité de Corbie.

Un registre très disparate, qui contient l'enregistrement de testaments et concessions d'administration des biens des décédés (fols 1-42), enregistrements des dettes (fols 42-58, en français), quelques sentences des années 1581, 1522-1524 et 1530 (fols 64-95), des listes d'excommuniés (fols 96-144). Ce registre a été utilisé, dans Lefebvre-Teillard, *Officialités*.

[41.]

1. Reims, Amiens, officialité de l'évêque.

2. Archives départementales de la Somme, 88 bis rue Gauthier de Rumilly, 80000 Amiens [ADS].

Georges Durand, *Inventaire sommaire. 5: Série G (nos 1 à 1169)* (Amiens 1902)

Id. 6: *Série G (nos 1170 à 3044)* (Amiens 1910)

J. Estienne, *Répertoire numérique de la série G* (Amiens 1925)

3. G 482. 1253. Bulle d'Innocent IV qui interdit aux religieux, privilégiés, clercs séculiers et autres de la ville d'Amiens, de recourir à la juridiction séculière dans les lieux soumis à la juridiction de l'évêque.

   G 487. 1403. 1 doc. Affaire concernant un clerc criminel.

   G 528. 1444. 1 pièce. Transaction entre l'évêque et les notaires de l'officialitié.

   G 725. 1531. 1 pièce. Information sur un prêtre de mauvaise vie.

   G 739. 1444. 1 doc. Procès.

4. Outre ces minces épaves, les ADS conservent quelques docs intéressants sur des conflits de juridiction entre l'évêque et divers chapitres (G 451, G 480, G 656, G 788) et entre l'évêque et les juridictions laïques (G 483 à G 486 et G 488 à G 494), s13-s16.

[42.]

1. Reims, Beauvais, officiality of the bishop.

2. *Archives départementales de l'Oise, 58 avenue Victor-Hugo, 60030 Beauvais.

   J. Estienne, *Répertoire numérique de la série G.* 1: *G 1 à 7887* (Ameins 1948)

   Arts. 2819-4813 describes all the surviving records known to me. The post-Tridentine holdings are extensive; the pre-Tridentine holdings are skimpy.

3. *G 4591. 15 fols. 1 Nov. 1382 to 29 Nov. 1383. Register of fines.

   Receipts of fines, giving names, parishes, amounts, but not cause.

   *G 4592. 8 fols. 1445. *Id.*

   Fines taxed in the court, giving names, amounts, and cause.

   *G 4593. 10 fols. 1446. *Id.*

   *G 4594. 3 quires (of what was once a bound register). 1453-1455. *Id.*

   The style has changed again; there is more accounting and less information.

   *G 4595. 1 large quire. 1474-1479. *Id.*

   More substantive information in this one.

   G 4596. 1480-1482. *Id.*

   G 4597. 1523-1524. *Id.*

   G 4598. 1529-1530. *Id.*

   *G 4599. 1401-1402. Account of the keeper of the seal.

Written in half-size, minute-book style, listing fees paid for gracious acts mostly for the benefit of clergy but containing a number of licenses to husbands and wives relieving them from debts.

*G 4600. 2 quires. 1444-1445. *Id.*

This one, however, gives no indication of the nature of the act for which the fee was received.

*G 4601. 1470-1471. *Id.*

Some indication of the type of act.

*G 4602. 1475. *Id.*

*G 4603 to G 4675. 1476-1584. *Id.*

A fairly complete series.

4. There is enough here for a small-scale study.

[43.]

1. Reims, Cambrai, officiality of the bishop.

2. *Archives départementales du Nord, 22 rue Saint-Bernard, 59045 Lille [ADN].

The *fonds* of the officiality of Cambrai has been at Lille at least since the early s19. It has only recently been classified:

Pierre Piétresson de Saint-Aubin, *Répertoire numérique* [*de la*] *Série G*. 2.1: *3 G à 5 G* (Lille 1968)

gives the numbers and a brief but accurate description of what follows. There is also a hand-list (shelf mark: Fol. 27) at the Archives which lists cause papers *(procédures)* by name of party and date, with a system of reference that does not correspond to the *Répertoire*, e.g., "23.117 Anchin—Fragment de requête de l'abbaye (1293)." I was informed that this material is not in the modern classification. There are literally hundreds of docs, at least some of which date from the medieval period. The modern classification for the officiality is in Subseries 5 G and comprises 622 articles of which those listed in what follows antedate 1600.

See also II/00; II/01.

3. 5 G 24. 1588-s18. Fragmentary formularies of acts.

5 G 25. 1568-1569. Register of cases or roll of audience.

5 G 47. s16/ex. *Id.*

5 G 48. s16/ex. *Id.*

*5 G 148. 98 fols. 1438-1447. Register of sentences of the officiality.

Sentences of the Cambrai official are fuller than those of many officials and give a reasonably clear picture of what the case was about. The register is probably not complete and seems to have been compiled on a term-by-term basis. Both civil and criminal cases are included, along with a number of cases denominated "civil" which seem to pertain to the bishop's secular jurisdiction. The cases include marriage, divorce, sexual offenses, debt, wills, and church property. For another sentence book from the same diocese with a similar style, see II/00.

*5 G 149. 52 fols. 1442-1455. *Id.*

See above 5 G 148. Dr. Vleeschouwers-Van Melkebeek informs us that sentences from January, 1442, through June, 1443, are bound into this volume, rather than into 5 G 148.

*5 G 150. 174 fols. 1543-1551. *Id.*

The passage of almost a century has produced a few obvious changes in the style of sentences or their subject matter. There is, however, a notable increase in their number.

5 G 151. 1569-1580. *Id.*

5 G 152. 1588-1599. *Id.*

5 G 189. 1275-1565. Orders and notes of sentences.

5 G 353. s15-1697. Various civil cases.

5 G 372. 1542-1548. Cause papers in a case of seduction and breach of promise.

5 G 451. 1462-1649. Dispensations to marry.

5 G 496. 1558-1680. Criminal matters, mostly involving sexual offenses.

5 G 596. 1347-1739. Appeals to the Holy See.

5 G 599. 1 roll. 1323. Delegations from the Holy See.

5 G 601. Statutes of 1565.

5 G 605. 1435-1436. Account of the chapel of the officiality.

5 G 607. 1560-1563. Book of excommunicates.

Chronological list with sanctions and names.

5 G 608. 1569-1580. *Id.*

4. The Cambrai records deserve more attention than they have received. They are particularly rich in early modern material, but a considerable amount survives from the later Middle Ages as well. As an imperial city Cambrai and its bishop seem not to have been subjected to as much secular control in the late Middle Ages as were the officialities in the north of France. Considerable use is made of 5 G 150 in Lefebvre-Teillard, *Officialités*. See especially her consideration of the relatively loose standard for separation of

goods (*morum incompatibilitas*) at pp 201-03. Similar cases exist in 5 G 148 and 5 G 149. For a comparative study of sentences of the officiality of Cambrai at Brussel and those in ADN, see Monique Vleeschouwers-van Melkebeek, 'Aspects du lien matrimonial dans le *Liber Sentenciarum* de Bruxelles', TRG 53 (1985) 43-97. On the relationship between the official at Cambrai and that at Brussel, see *id.* at 45-7.

[44.]

1. Reims, Châlons-sur-Marne, officiality of the bishop.

2. *Archives départementales de la Marne, 1 rue Just Berland, 51000 Châlons-sur-Marne.

P. Pelicier, *Inventaire sommaire* [*de la*] *Série G.* 4: [*Arts. à Châlons*] (Châlons, 1900)

This volume of the *Inventaire* describes all the articles in Series G that are housed at Châlons (as opposed to Reims). They have separate numbers, beginning (again) with G 1. Arts. 895-950 concern the officiality of Châlons.

3. *G 895. 37 fols. 1430-1431. Annual account of the *sigillifer* of the court.

Divided according to sources of revenue: absolutions, dispensations, 'excesses' (including the type of crime), wills, testimonial letters, non-residents, residents.

G 896. 24 fols. 1435-1436. *Id.*

G 897. 28 fols. 1441-1442. *Id.*

G 898. 22 fols. 1446-1447. *Id.*

G 899. 115 fols. 1460-1461. *Id.*

G 900. 52 fols. 1464-1465. *Id.*

G 901. 52 fols. 1477-1478. *Id.*

*G 902. 66 fols. 1478-1479. *Id.*

G 903. 70 fols. 1479-1480. *Id.*

G 904. 59 fols. 1481-1482. *Id.*

G 905. 54 fols. 1489-1490. *Id.*

*G 906. 60 fols. 1496-1497. *Id.*

G 907. 94 fols. 1506-1507. *Id.*

G 908. 81 fols. 1507-1508. *Id.*

G 909. 55 fols. 1512-1513. *Id.*

G 910. 62 fols. 1514-1515. *Id.*

G 911. 54 fols. 1515-1516. *Id.*

G 912. 69 fols. 1516-1517. *Id.*

G 913. 58 fols. 1517-1518. *Id.*

G 914. 46 fols. 1520-1521. *Id.*

G 915. 59 fols. 1522-1523. *Id.*

G 916. 59 fols. 1524-1525. *Id.*

G 917. 67 fols. 1525-1526. *Id.*

G 918. 66 fols. 1528-1529. *Id.*

G 919. 66 fols. 1529-1530. *Id.*

G 920. 50 fols. 1539-1540. *Id.*

*G 921. 155 fols. 15 June 1471 — November 1475. Register of cases.

Arranged on a day-by-day basis. Criminal cases predominate if they are not the exclusive concern of the register.

*G 922. 136 fols. 15 April 1493 — 22 February 1494. 'Registrum causarum officii curie cath' '. *Id.*

G 923. 121 fols. 1502-1503. *Id.*

*G 924. 119 fols. January, 1508 — July, 1509. *Id.*

G 925. 189 fols. July, 1509 — May, 1511. *Id.*

*G 926. 266 fols. May, 1511 — 1513. *Id.*

G 927. 219 fols. 16 May, 1516 — October, 1517. *Id.*

G 928. 101 fols. 1520-1521. *Id.*

G 929 to G 934. 1521-1528. *Id.*

G 935 to G 950. s17 and s18 registers and case docs.

4. The criminal jurisdiction of the officiality of Châlons is probably the best documented in France after that of Troyes. The records are used to good effect in Lefebvre-Teillard, *Officialités* and in Gottlieb, *Getting Married.*

As in the case of the Troyes records there remains the question whether the records are typical of the whole jurisdiction of the court, and as in the case of the Troyes records we suspect that there was not much of a civil jurisdiction to complement this activity on the criminal side. The accounts are useful for statistical purposes. It would seem that over the course of the s15 the

Châlons court experienced a large growth in criminal business. The fines for particular offenses remained roughly the same, but the total revenue from such fines increased ten-fold.

[45.]

1. Reims, Senlis, officiality of the bishop.

2. *Archives départementales de l'Oise (see 42/2).

J. Estienne, *Répertoire numérique de la série G*. 1: *G 1 à 7887* (Ameins 1948)

Arts. 4882-3 describe all the surviving records known to me. The pre- and post-Tridentine holdings are skimpy.

3. *G 4882. 1494-1524. Miscellaneous single docs.

[46.]

1. Rouen, officialité de l'archevêque (métropolitaine et diocésaine).

2. *BN (voir 18/2; 40/2).

*Archives départementales de la Seine Maritime, Préfecture, cours Clemenceau, 76036 Rouen [ADSM].

C. de Robillard de Beaurepaire, *Inventaire sommaire* [*de la*] *série G*. 1: *Nos 1 à 1566* (Paris 1868); 2: *Nos 1567 à 3172* (Paris 1871); 3: *Nos 3173 à 4820* (Paris 1881); 4: *Nos 4821 à 6220* (Paris 1887); 5: *Nos 6221 à 7370* (Rouen 1892); 6: *Nos 7371 à 8514* (Rouen 1896); 7: *Nos 8515 à 8962* (Rouen 1900)

3. *1. BN*:

*Ms lat 18224. Fols 282r-283r. c1265. Formulary of the official.

A brief collection of forms, interesting for their antiquity, bound into what is basically a ms of Geoffrey of Trani.

2. ADSM:

*G 149 à 185. 1414-1473. Comptes des promoteurs de l'officialité de Rouen.

*G 249 à 271. 1424-1485. Registres des amendes, compositions et reconciliations des promoteurs de l'officialité de Rouen.

Présentés à l'appui de leurs comptes par les promoteurs, ces registres contiennent un résumé des faits qui ont conduit à la perception de l'amende. Ils constituent une très belle série couvrant la plus grande partie du s15.

*G 276. 1453-1529. Liasse, 18 pièces. "Recepta emolumenti registrorum excommunicatorum curie archiepiscopalis rothomagensis."

*G 278. 1425-1455. Liasse, 15 pièces. "Recepta emolumenti registri curie rothomagensis."

*G 279. 1409-1516. Liasse, 53 pièces. Comptes de recettes présentés à l'archevêque par les maitres des testats et intestats.

*G 280 à 312. 1432-1544. Registres "emolumenti officii testamentorum civitatis et diocesis rothomagensis."

*G 4900. 93 fols. Liste des noms des prisonniers dans la prison de l'archevêque avec leur libération et leurs dettes.

*G 4997. 1505-1544. Pièces diverses concernant des procès.

*G 9784 (pas inventorié). 1460-1461. 58 fols. Registre des amendes etc du promoteur de l'officialité.

4. Outre ces docs émanant directement de l'officialité, les ADSM conservent sous les cotes: G 1880, 1884, 1885-1888, 1890, 1893 et 1894, une série de docs concernant les conflits de juridictions qui ont opposés l'archevêque soit à la juridiction laïque, soit à son chapitre (s14/ex-s15). Il y a aussi une grande collection de plumitifs (G 4901-4933) datants du s17 et s18 et une grande collection de docs (G 4943-5181) datants pour la plupart de la période postérieure à la nôtre.

[47.]

1. Rouen, officiality of the abbey of Cerisy.

2. Archives départementales de la Manche, 103 rue Marechal-Juin, 50010 Saint-Lô.

3. H 1407. 87 fols. 1314-1457. Register of the court of the official of Cerisy.

Ed. G. Dupont [et L. Delisle], 'Le registre de l'officialité de Cerisy', *Mémoires de la société des antiquaires de Normandie*, 3e sér. 10 (30) (Caen 1880) 271-662.

One of the earliest of the French church court records, and certainly the earliest published. The transcript for the 1880 publication was done by Delisle, and the material was arranged in chronological order by Dupont. The register is by no means complete. There is a gap between 1346-1369 and another from 1414-1451, both of which probably reflect events of the Hundred Years' War. The purpose of the record seems to have varied over its long course of composition. Initially the doc seems to record both proceedings conducted at the monastery and those conducted by the official during his regular visitations of the twenty-five villages within the exempt jurisdiction of the monastery. As time goes on, visitation and criminal material seems more and more to predominate, although it is not clear whether this reflects a change in jurisdiction in fact or simply a change in record-keeping practices. Sexual offenses predominate throughout, although a wide variety of ecclesiastical offenses (defamation, witchcraft, striking a cleric, etc.) are found. Later material (1474-1480 and 1485) was edited by:

Paul Le Cacheux, 'Un fragment de registre de l'officialité de Cerisy', *Bulletin de la Société des antiquaires de Normandie* 43 (1935) 291-315. See also:

Jean-Luc Dufresne, 'Les comportements amoureux d'après le registre de l'officialité de Cerisy', *Bulletin philologique et historique du Comité des travaux historiques et scientifiques* (1973) 131-56.

4. One record, however important, can only tell a partial story, but the history of exempt monastic jurisdictions in the north of France could be reconstructed from this and other surviving records, e.g., Montivilliers, Corbie, Fécamp.

[48.]

1. Rouen, officialité de l'abbaye de Fécamp.

2. *Archives départementales de la Seine Maritime [ADSM] (voir 46/2).

3. *G 5185. 31 fols. 1539-1544. Modèles d'actes de nomination à diverses charges surtout temporelles de l'abbaye, plus une formule de citation.

*G 5187. 63 fols. 1404-1435. Registre de sentences.

L'enregistrement des sentences ne parait sérieusement fait que pour la première année. Il devient ensuite très épisodique et plutôt fantaisiste.

*G 5211. 16 docs. 1544-84. Pièces de procédure.

*G 5217. 107 docs. Pièces de procédure concernant des affaires matrimoniales, dont deux du s15.

*G 5233. 8 docs. 1242-1468. Actes passés devant l'official.

*G 5240. 88 docs. 1139-1693. Série de docs relatifs à l'exemption de l'abbaye de Fécamp.

Rassemblés par les moines en vue du conflit les opposant à l'archevêque, ces docs serviront à la confection d'un mémoire imprimé, conservé aux ADSM sous la cote G 5183.

*G 5242. 1428-1775. Nomination aux charges de l'officialité.

Un seul doc concerne notre période.

*G 5250. 1 doc. 1462-1463. Règlement pour les officiers de la cour.

*G 5251. 19 docs. s12-s18. Pièces diverses concernant notamment la juridiction.

*G 5252. 19 docs. 1408-1772. Pièces diverses.

Peu de choses concernant notre période.

*G 5253. 29 docs. 1352-1434. Sentences diverses.

*G 5254. 27 docs. 1451-1679. Sentences diverses.

*G 5255. 42 fols. s16/1. Formulaire.

Formules concernant les testaments, les affaires matrimoniales, etc.

4. Rapproché des docs de Montivilliers, ce lot d'archives devrait permettre une étude assez approfondie des juridictions exemptes dans cette province. Il y a aussi la documentation sous les cotes G 5182 à G 5267 qui permettrait la continuation de l'histoire jusqu'au s18. On peut ajouter les docs sous les mêmes cotes, datants de notre période, qui ne concernent pas l'officialité proprement dite, mais qui concernent l'administration des bénéfices de l'abbaye, les assemblées du chapitre, le vicaire général, etc.

[49.]

1. Rouen, officialité de l'abbaye de Montivilliers.

2. *Archives départementales de la Seine Maritime (voir 46/2).

3. *G 5268. 170 fols. 1406-1485. Registre du promoteur de l'officialité.

Assez proche d'un registre d'amendes, ce registre concerne essentiellement la période 1406-1411 (un seul acte de 1485 au fol 21, plutôt là par erreur).

G 5269. 285 fols. 1424-1464. Registre du promoteur.

G 5270. 119 fols. 1433-1484. Registre du promoteur.

G 5271. 418 fols. 1462-1513. Registre du promoteur.

G 5272. 142 fols. 1497-1511. Registre du promoteur.

G 5273. 270 fols. 1498-1528. Registre des excommuniés.

G 5274. 102 fols. 1517-1579. Registre de sentences en matière civile et spirituelle.

G 5280. 12 fols. 1433-1487. Fragment de registre.

G 5311. 5 fols. 1529-1531. Liste d'amendes.

G 5314. 1 doc. 1368. Pièce émanant de la juridiction royale concernant un clerc criminel.

*G 5315. 98 doc. 1386-1691. Procédures diverses.

Interesse surtout la période postérieure à la nôtre.

*G 5316. 118 docs. 1500-1724. Procédures criminelles.

Deux docs seulement concernent nôtre période.

G 5317. 100 docs. 1506-1519. Minutes de sentences (à rapprocher de G 5274).

G 5318. 29 docs. 1506-1709. Procédures criminelles.

G 5321. 1 doc. 1386. Mandat d'excommunication.

G 5325. 1 doc. 1445. Sentence dans une affaire de fiançailles.

G 5328. 17 docs. 1528-1694. Mandement du doyen de Montivilliers pour la publication des excommunications, aggraves et réaggraves, ainsi que pour la publication des monitoires.

G 5331. 14 docs. 1502-1573. Procédures diverses dont un procès porté devant le conseil de l'archevêque.

G 5357. 1 doc (entre 3). 1540. Sentence au sujet d'une inhumation en l'église St Sauveur.

G 5361. 1 doc. 1287. Sentence au sujet du droit de collation.

G 5362. 1 doc. 1344. Conflit au sujet du privilège du for.

G 5363. 1 doc. 1314. Composition au sujet de certaines évocations que l'archevêque de Rouen prétendait exercer à l'égard de Montivilliers.

G 5369. 1 doc. 1285. Copie d'un acte de 1285, concernant l'exemption de l'abbaye.

G 5386. 19 docs. 1444-1588. Procédures criminelles.

G 5388. 78 docs. 1535-1691. Procédures criminelles.

N'interesse pratiquement pas notre période.

4. La documentation concernant cette juridiction exempte est probablement la plus abondante pour ce type de juridiction et doit être rapprochée de celle de Fécamp et Cerisy. Certains de ces docs ont été utilisés dans Lefebvre-Teillard, *Officialités*.

[50.]

1. Rouen, officialité de l'archevêque à Pontoise.

Pontoise était une possession "extra diocésaine" de l'archevêque de Rouen qui y nomme un vicaire pour y rendre en son nom la justice. L'archevêque tient fermement en main son vicaire pour qu'il n'y ait pas de prétention à l'exemption.

2. *Archives départementales de la Seine Maritime (voir 46/2).

3. *G 317 à G 408. 1447-1554. Comptes du vicariat.

Belle série de comptes du vicariat de Pontoise. Certains registres explicitent mieux que d'autres la cause de l'amende, le G 373 par exemple. Le G 373 (17 fols, 1518-1519) s'intitule: "Registrum promotoris causarum officii venerabilis curie ecclesiastice Pontisare et ejusdem curie et totius vicarii secretarii de et super emendis et ceteris actibus secretarie." Les actes du secrétariat semblent être pour la plupart des dispenses pour non-résidence. Les amendes sont pour la plupart imposées aux clercs pour offenses mineures. Le registre donne aussi des indications sur les affaires pendantes devant la cour.

[51.]

1. Rouen, Bayeux, officialité de l'évêque.

2. *BN (voir 18/2; 40/2).

3. *Ms lat 11033. Fol 137v. 1288. Règlement des avocats exerçant près de l'officialité.

[52.]

1. Rouen, Sées, officialité de l'évêque.

2. Archives départementales de l'Orne, 6-10 av. de Basingstoke, 61013 Alençon.

3. *1 G 35. 126 fol. s15/ex. Formulaire.

Ce formulaire est intéressant, car il contient un nombre très varié de modèles, d'actes et de sentences.

*1 G 26. 171 fol. s16. Formulaire.

Ce formulaire ne contient presque exclusivement que des formules à l'usage du clergé et des affaires bénéficiales.

[53.]

1. Sens, officiality of the archbishop.

2. *BN (see 18/2).

*Archives départementales de l'Yonne, 37 rue Saint-Germain, 89000 Auxerre [ADY].

Claude Hohl, *Guide des archives de l'Yonne* (Auxerre 1974)

Michel Quantin, *Inventaire sommaire. 2: Série G* (Auxerre 1873)

Arts. 236-44 contain all the surviving records known to me.

3. *1. BN*:

*Ms lat 4812. Fols. 65r-67r. s16/m. Style of the officiality (in French).

2. ADY:

*G 236. 174 fols. 1480. "Registrum causarum venerabilis curie archiepiscopalis superioris et metropolitani Senonensis tam ordinariarum quam appellacionum".

Day-by-day entries in civil cases with perhaps some *ex officio* entries as well. The purpose of the book is to record steps in the procedure. Hence it is difficult to form a picture of the jurisdiction of the court. Many cases are appeal cases with the underlying substance not given; there are definitely cases concerning marriage and testaments.

G 237 to G 244. Miscellaneous registers and docs, mostly from s17 and s18.

4. The one surviving medieval court book from this important jurisdiction has received, so far as I know, no scholarly attention. It is difficult to read and when deciphered it reveals disappointingly little information, but with patience it could be made to yield up its secrets. It would probably reveal a jurisdiction not unlike that of the Paris consistory in the s14.

[54.]

1. Sens, Chartres, officiality of the ?great archdeacon and of the cathedral chapter.

2. *Archives départementales d'Eure et Loire, 9 rue du Cardinal-Pie, 28000 Chartres.

All that survives of the records of the medieval officialities at Chartres is contained in seven bound volumes that were classified by mistake among the 110 bound registers of contracts of cathedral chapter. The volumes were first noticed in:

Merlet, 'Registres'.

A description may be found in:

L. Merlet, *Inventaire sommaire*. 6.1: *Série G* [*Arts. 1-3620*] (Chartres 1890) 119-21.

Neither the notice nor the description is wholly accurate. As will appear below, Merlet's supposition in 1856 that we are dealing with four registers of the great archdeacon and three of the officiality of the chapter seems more likely to be correct than his supposition in 1890 that all seven registers were registers of the great archdeacon.

3. *G 811. 170 fols (not including the binding fols). December, 1380 to summer 1383. Register.

Day-by-day listing of *assignationes* and *emende* before what appears to be the officiality of the great archdeacon of Chartres. There are also a number of miscellaneous entries including some depositions in marriage cases.

*G 812. 149 fols. Easter, 1398 to Ascension, 1401. Register.

Same as above with more emphasis on *assignationes* and *emende*. Front cover suggests *Registrum curie belsie*.

*G 813. 116 fols. 29 Nov. 1400 to 1407. Sentence book.

Mostly *emende*, with notes of payment, arranged by years rather than days. Begins with a new *officialis curie belsie*. This is the source of the statistics for the year 1405 in Merlet, 'Registres'.

*G 814. 183 fols. January, 1403/4 to September, 1405. Register.

Assignationes and emende, like G 812.

*G 815. 191 fols. 20 June 1409 to 1 July 1415. Register.

Day-by-day accounts of proceedings probably before the official of the chapter, source of the quotations in Merlet, 'Registres'.

*G 816. 183 fols. 3 July 1415 to ?20 Oct. 1420. Register.

Continuation of the previous book.

*G 817. 193 fols. 1380 X 1434. Register.

Parish-by-parish list of ?debts, ?excommunications and *emende* probably for the officiality of the chapter. The book may not be complete; the alphabetical list of parishes stops at 'm'.

4. The Chartres records clearly deserve more attention than they have received. The earliest of them are among the earliest of the French ecclesaistical court records, among the very few that survived the Hundred Years War. G 811, in particular, contains, in addition to the usual run of criminal cases for sexual offenses, a number of relatively full *processus* in civil marriage and testament cases.

[55.]

1. Sens, Orléans, officialité de l'évêque.
2. Bibliothèque municipale de Tours, Place Anatole France, B.P. 232, Tours.
3. Ms 765. Fols. 133-290. s14/ex. Formulaire de l'officalité.

Ce formulaire a été partiellement édité:

J. Bry, 'Notice sur un formulaire du XIVe siècle à l'usage de l'officialité d'Orléans', NRHD 38 (1914) 417-60.

Le manuscrit a disparu pendant la guerre de 1940, dans l'incendie de la bibliothèque de Tours.

[56.]

1. Sens, Paris, officiality of the bishop.
2. *Archives Nationales, 60 rue des Francs-Bourgeois, 75141 Paris, France.

Of the many guides to the contents of the AN perhaps the best for our purposes is:

Guide aux fonds judiciares.

Considering the large number of s18 docs in this collection, the present collection in the AN probably represents the archives of the diocesan court which were taken over in mass at the time of the Revolution.

3. Z^{10} 26. 1384 to 1387. Register of civil cases.

Ed. Petit, *Registre*

The register concerns only civil cases and among these marriage cases predominate. See:

J.-Ph. Lévy, 'L'officialité de Paris et les questions familiales à la fin du XIVe siècle', in *Études d'histoire de droit canonique dédiées à Gabriel Le Bras* (Paris 1965) 2:1265-1299.

Z^{10} 11. 1509 to 1511. Register of the second auditor.

Day-by-day accounts of the proceedings before the second auditor of the officiality. Reports of witnesses predominate. See:

E. Fournier, 'Les auditeurs de l'officialité épiscopale parisienne au Moyen Age', *Le Canoniste* (April, 1927)

Fournier, *Origine* 191-95.

Z^{10} 91. 4 docs (among many more). s14. Acts of court.

Originally found in the binding of Z^{10} 26. Ed. Petit, *Registre* col. 525-36.

4. The Paris episcopal officiality has left us little, although the published register is of first importance. The lack is to some extent made up by the surviving records of the archdeacon's court (see no. 59).

[57.]

1. Sens, Paris, officiality of the cathedral chapter.
2. *AN (see 56/2).
3. *LL 29 (ex Z^{10} 27). 279 fols. 1486/7 to 1498. Day-by-day account of all business before the court.
4. The Paris chapter and four associated parishes depended directly on the Holy See. This appears to be the sole surviving doc from its court. It has been studied in Fournier, *Origine* pp 178-87.

[58.]

1. Sens, Paris, officiality of the archdeacon of Brie.
2. *AN (see 56/2).
3. *Z^{10} 27. 140 fols. 1499-1505. Day-by-day account of all business before the court.

Includes both civil and criminal cases. The book is much like the earlier registers of the Paris archdeacon's court and seems to reflect a similar jurisdictional reach. Some use of this book is made in Lefebvre-Teillard, *Officialités*.

[59.]

1. Sens, Paris, officiality of the archdeacon of Paris.

2. *AN (see 56/2).

Unlike the material for the diocesan court, the material for the archidiaconal court dates for the most part from the end of the s15 and the beginning of the s16. It may have been taken over into the *fonds* of the diocesan court when the archidiaconal court lost its importance in the s16. The following account of the docs is summary because an excellent account exists in:

Pommeray, *Officialité archidiaconale* pp iii–xxx.

3. *1. Mixed registers*:

*Z^{10} 1. 135 fols. 1460-1461.

Day-by-day of accounts of proceedings before the official in both civil and criminal cases. Cases involving marriage and sexual offenses probably constitute the single largest class of cases, and criminal cases greatly outnumber civil. The range of criminal jurisdiction is well described in Pommeray, *Officialité archidiaconale* pp 197–425. The cases include a wide range of offenses of the clergy and offenses against the clergy, profanation and other offenses against ecclesiastical property, clandestine marriage and engagement, adultery and fornication, and a miscellany of "spiritual" offenses (sabbath breaking, false miracles, etc.).

*Z^{10} 2. 230 fols. 1461-1463. *Id.*

*Z^{10} 3. 188 fols. 1463-1465. *Id.*

*LL 517, no. 74 (formerly no. 13, *ex* L 494, no. 76). 50 fols. 1493/4–1494/5. Annual account of the seal-bearer and receiver of the archdeaconry.

Full account of receipts of fines and fees and of expenses. Considerable detail. For the headings see Pommeray, *Officialité archidiaconale* pp ix–x. Total receipts c473 Paris pounds; total expenses c286 Paris pounds.

*Z^{10} 16. 50 fols. 1550. Same as above, LL 517, no. 74.

2. Civil registers:

*Z^{10} 4. 250 fols. 1477-1479.

Day-by-day account of proceeding before the official in civil cases. Much of the register is devoted to procedural matters, and the total number of cases is quite small. An original system of marginalia allows one to identify the more substantive entries reasonably quickly. There are some marriage cases. The rest is miscellany of cases usually involving clerics.

*Z^{10} 5. 198 fols. 1479-1480. *Id.*

*Z^{10} 6. 291 fols. 1483-1485. *Id.*

*Z^{10} 7. 321 fols. 1491-1495. *Id.*

*Z^{10} 8. 324 fols. 1499-1503. *Id.*

Z^{10} 9. 418 fols. 1503-1506. *Id.*

Z^{10} 10. 381 fols. 1506-1508. *Id.*

Z^{10} 12. 368 fols. 1513-1515. *Id.*

Z^{10} 13. 346 fols. 1515-1516. *Id.*

Z^{10} 14. 474 fols. 1517-1519. *Id.*

2. *Criminal registers*:

*Z^{10} 25. 134 fols. 1355-1366. Register of fines.

This register is considerably fuller than others of its type. It gives the name of the offender, the type of offense, and the date by which the fine is to be paid. Each entry is crossed out (apparently when the fine was paid) usually with the sign manual of the receiver in the margin. Ten to twelve entries per folio gives a total of 250-350 per annum. Cases of violence to clerks seem to predominate, but there are many other types of cases including a number of concubinage cases.

*Z^{10} 17. 102 fols. 1426-1439. List of excommunicates arranged on a parish-by-parish basis.

Gives the name of the excommunicate, the name of person who had obtained the excommunication, whether it was for contumacy, substantive offense *(re)*, and the name of the ? process-server. The last folio has miscellaneous entries including a list of officers of the court (see Pommeray, *Officialité archidiaconale* p 124).

*Z^{10} 18. 247 fols. 1484-1487. Day-by-day account of the criminal cases before the archdeacon's official.

Almost every entry results a separate disposition of a case. Thus, there are far more cases represented here than in the civil registers. The range of offenses is as noted above for Z^{10} 1.

Z^{10} 19. 295 fols. 1487-1493. *Id.*

Z^{10} 20. 217 fols. 1493-1497. *Id.*

Z^{10} 21. 399 fols. 1497-1505. *Id.*

Z^{10} 22. 251 fols. 1515-1518. *Id.*

Z^{10} 23. 263 fols. 1521-1526. *Id.*

*Z^{10} 24. 397 fols (fol 368 is the last one written on). 1518-1529. Register of fines.

The beginning of the register contains some criminal entries for the year 1521, but the doc soon turns into a register of fines in much the same style as Z^{10} 25, above.

4. The Paris archidiaconal records have been the subject of a solid study (Pommeray, *Officialité archidiaconale*) and considerable use of them is made in Lefebvre-Teillard, *Officialités*, particularly in the marriage section of the book. Z^{10} 25, because of its antiquity, deserves more attention than it has received as do the civil records.

[60.]

1. Sens, Paris, officiality of Saint-Germain.

2. *AN (voir 56/2).

3. *Z^{10} 242. Liasse of several hundred docs. 1407-1564.

A large unorganized group of miscellaneous docs concerning the court. Many of them parchment and notarized. A number seem to be docs actually used in litigation. Many seem to date from the second and third decades of the 16th century.

4. This somewhat-notorious exempt jurisdiction has left a considerable mass of material of which these seem to be earliest. Z^{10} 243 is a similar collection from a somewhat later date and there is further material for the 17th century in LL 1131 to LL 1142. See: *Guide aux fonds judiciaires* p 361.

[61.]

1. Sens, Sens, officialité du chapitre.

2. Archives départementales de l'Yonne (voir 53/2).

Arts. 663-675 sont le fonds de l'officialité.

3. G 663. 64 fols. 1527-1528. Registre des causes.

Un registre de sentences de l'officialité en affaires aussi bien civiles que criminelles. Les affaires des clercs forment la plus grande part.

G 664. 98 fols. 1533. Registre des causes.

G 665. 1534. Registre des causes.

Le contenu des registres change à ce moment pour donner plus de détail intéressant les causes criminelles. Les causes civiles semblent disparaître.

4. Petite série intéressante, utilisée dans Lefebvre-Teillard, *Officialités*.

[62.]

1. Sens, Sens, officiality of Saint-Julien-du-Sault.

2. *Archives départementales de l'Yonne (see 53/2).

3. *G 245. Roll of 3 mm. 1350-1351. "Compotus officialis sancti Juliani."

Account of receipts and expenses of the court. The dorse contains the detail of fines for *excessus*.

*G 246. Roll of 2 mm. 1351-1352. *Id.*

*G 247. Roll of 3 mm. 1355-1356. *Id.*

G 248. Roll. 1358-1359. *Id.*

G 249. Roll. 1363-1364. *Id.*

G 250. Roll. 1364-1366. *Id.*

*G 251. Roll. 1414-1415. *Id.*

This roll contains less information than the previous ones.

*G 252. 133 fols. 1414-1415. *Id.*

The change from rolls to registers has not produced much change in the information-content. The book remains basically an account of receipts and expenses rather than an account of proceedings in the court.

*G 253. 151 fols. 1490-1499. *Id.*

G 254 to G 255. 190 docs. 1391-1552. Miscellaneous docs of the officiality.

4. There is enough here for a small-scale study of this small exempt jurisdiction that was supressed in 1552. Criminal matters dominate. The subject-matter jurisdiction does not differ much from Troyes or Châlons.

[63.]

1. Sens, Troyes, officiality of the bishop.

2. *Archives départementales de l'Aube, 21 rue Étienne-Pedron, 10000 Troyes, France.

Gildas Bernard, *Guide des archives départementales de l'Aube* (Troyes 1967)

H. d'Arbois de Jubainville et Francisque André, *Inventaire sommaire [de la] Série G*. 2: *Arts. G 2545 à G 4253* (Paris/Troyes 1896)

Arts. 4170-4253 are the *fonds* of the officiality and are well-described in the *inventaire*.

3. *G 4170. 76 fols. 1389 to 1396. Register of the notary of the court.

Ed. Jean Breban, *Registre de l'officialité épiscopale de Troyes 1389-1396*, Thèse droit, Paris (dact 1954).

This volume is quite unlike the others in the series. It contains a large number of recognisances of debts, but also letters of execution of sentences of the official, mostly in criminal matters, but also some concerning the non-contentious jurisdiction (letters of tonsure, etc). Breban's edition is as accurate as such editions are likely to be, and his introduction and tables are useful.

*G 4171. 180 fols. 1423-1475. "Registrum assecuramentorum sentenciarum criminalium et plurium inhibicionum ac monicionum in curia trecensis factarum."

This register is most like G 4170 in the series, but the criminal matters predominate and the recognisances are correspondingly fewer.

*G 4172. 166 fols. 1427-1443. "Registrum causarum officii curie Trecensis."

The relationship between this register and G 4171 needs to be explored. It would seem that this is a day-by-day account of criminal proceedings in the court for the years stated. Sentences, warnings and inhibitions are recorded, along with some recognisances. There does not seem to be any overlap between the entries in this book and those in G 4171.

*G 4173. 174 fols. 19 May 1455 to 16 April 1456. Day-by-day account of proceedings, similar in content to G 4172.

*G 4174. 64 fols. April to 10 September ?1457. *Id.*

*G 4175. 137 fols. September 1457 to May 1458. *Id.*

*G 4176. 196 fols. 3 October 1460 to 30 December 1461. *Id.*

*G 4177. 176 fols. 2 January to 24 December 1462. *Id.*

*G 4178. 209 fols. 2 January to 22 December 1464. "Registrum causarum officii curie trecensis." *Id.*

*G 4179. 212 fols. 27 December 1464 to 23 December 1465. *Id.*

G 4180. 242 fols. 2 January to 8 November 1466. *Id.*

G 4181. 346 fols. June 1483 to 17 April 1484. *Id.*

G 4182. 24 fols. 15 April to 11 May 1493. "Registrum causarum officii Johannis de Garmoisia, clerici, curie trecensis tabellionis." *Id.*

G 4183. 293 fols. 8 April 1494 to 18 April 1495. *Id.*

G 4184. 157 fols. June 1498 to 29 March 1499. *Id.*

G 4185. 189 fols. 27 April 1500 to 3 April 1501. *Id.*

G 4186 to G 4203. 1502-1537. *Id.*

G 4204 to G 4214. s16/in. *Processus*, mostly criminal.

G 4216 to G 4218. 1483-1528. Registers of fines.

G 243 to G 248. 1400-1498. Accounts of fines.

G 4219 to G 4235. s16. Miscellaneous docs.

4. The criminal jurisdiction of the officiality of Troyes is probably the best documented for all of France. The records are used to good effect in Lefebvre-Teillard, *Officialités* and in Gottlieb, *Getting Married.*

There remain, however, many things that are puzzling about the Troyes records. Notable among these is the question whether the surviving records tell the whole story. Suffice it to say here that if they do not tell the whole story, they probably tell the largest part of it. It is hard to imagine that if the Troyes court had a civil jurisdiction as extensive as that of the Paris diocesan officiality or even as extensive as that of the Paris archdeacon's officiality, such jurisdiction would not have left more of a trace in the surviving material.

[64.]

1. Toulouse, officialité de l'archevêque (métropolitaine).

2. * BN (voir 18/2).

* Bibliothèque Sainte-Geneviève [BSG] (voir 25/2).

Bibliothèque Municipale de Toulouse, 1 rue de Périgord 31070 Toulouse cedex [BMT].

3. BN Ms lat 4462. Decisiones capellae Tholosanae.

* BSG Ms 1646. *Id.*

BMT Ms 377. *Id.*

Jean Corsier, official à la fin du s14, a fait un recueil de ses décisions. Il en existe plusieurs manuscrits. Ces *Decisiones capellae Tholosanae* ont été éditées par Étienne Aufrère, conseiller au parlement de Toulouse et membre du conseil de la curie archiépiscopale, au début du s16, avec un commentaire et une mise à jour fort interessants. À part quelques rares décisions éparses, c'est tout ce qu'il reste de connu pour la période médievale.

[65.]

1. Toulouse, Pamiers, officialité de l'évêque.

2. Archives départementales de l'Ariège, 28 avenue du Général de Gaulle, 09000 Foix.

G. Trouillard, J. Paix, E. Galabert, E. Pelissier, E. Laval, A. de Saint Blanquat, J.F. Le Nail et C. Pailhès, *Répertoire numérique de la série G: G 1-265* (Foix 1979)

A. de Saint Blanquat, *Id.: G 266-286* (dact 1970)

J.F. Le Nail, *Id.: G 287-345* (dact 1976)

Les répertoires ne sont pas encore complets et n'incluent pas nos articles.

3. G 372. 1313. Mémoire sur la juridiction des clercs de Pamiers.

G 373. 1338-1348. Registre des audiences de l'official de Pamiers.

[66.]

1. Tours, Saint-Brieuc, officialité de l'évêque.

2. *BN (voir 18/2).

3. *Ms lat 1458. Fols 112-133. s15/ex-s16/in. "Advisamenta stili curie ecclesiastice Briocensis".

Il est dit au fol 127 q'un ancien statut refusait d'excommunier pour dette, lorsque la somme était inférieure à 12 deniers "ne multitudo excommunicatorum amplietur."

[67.]

1. Tours, Le Mans, officialité de l'évêque.

2. *BN (voir 18/2; 40/2).

3. *Ms lat 10930. 1429. 60 fols. Formulaire de l'officialité.

[68.]

1. Tours, Nantes, officialité de l'évêque.

2. Archives départementales de la Loire Atlantique, 6 rue de Bouillé, 44000 Nantes.

L. Maitre, *Inventaire sommaire*. 4: *Séries G et H* (Nantes 1884)

3. *G 64. 75 fols. 1498-1529. Formulaire de 1529, suivi des statuts de la Cour en vigueur depuis.

Article interessant, utilisé dans Lefebvre-Teillard, *Officialités*. Les formules datent de 1498 à 1529.

[69.]

1. Tours, Nantes, officialité du chapitre St Pierre.

2. Archives départementales de la Loire Atlantique (voir 68/2).

3. G 65. 1509-1510. Registre de l'officialité du chapitre.

*G 66. 1526-1528. Livre du greffe de l'officialité du chapitre. Contient l'enregistrement sommaire des testaments.

[70.]

1. Tours, Tréguier, officialité de l'évêque.

2. *BN (voir 18/2).

3. *Ms nal. 426. 21 fols. s13/ex X s14/in. Formulaire.

Formules de toutes sortes dont les formules aux fols 2, 6, 10 et 12 concernent l'officialité. Voir L. Delisle, dans *L'histoire littéraire de la France* 31 (Paris 1893) 25-35, pour une notice et des extraits.

[71.]

1. Trier, Toul, officialité de l'évêque.

2. *BN (voir 18/2).

Archives départementales de la Meurthe et Moselle, 1 rue de la Monnaie, 54000 Nancy [ADMM].

H. Lepage, *Inventaire sommaire.* 4.1: *Série G* (Nancy 1880)

3. *1. BN*:

*Ms nal. 1519. 405 fols. s16/1. Recueil de pièces de procédures de l'officialité de Toul.

*Ms nal. 2617-2621. s15-s16. Pièces de l'officialité de Toul: comptes, procédures diverses.

2. ADMM:

G 1232. 27 fols. 1525-1548. Copies d'actes émanés de l'évêque et de l'official.

G 1233. 150 fols. 1544-1554. Registre de l'officialité. Lettres, plainte du duc de Lorraine sur la juridiction ecclesiastique, sentences etc.

4. La documentation parait suffisante pour faire une étude approfondie de cette officialité dans la première moitié du s16.

[72.]

1. Vienne, Die, officialité de l'évêque.

2. Archives départementales de la Drôme, 14 rue de la Manutention, 26007 Valence.

J. de Font-Réaulx, *Répertoire numérique de la série G* (dact 1950)

3. *7 G 2. 1527. Registre des causes.

Ce registre contient surtout des affaires de dîmes.

[73.]

1. Vienne, Grenoble, officiality of the bishop at Grenoble and at Chambéry.

2. Archives départementales de l'Isère, 2 boulevard des Adieux, 38000 Grenoble.

   See Bautier/Sornay, *Sources* 2:792 n1, 796.

3. IV G 117 *in fine*. 1380-1381. État des lettres délivrées (par le sceau de l'officialité de Grenoble).

   IV G 123. s14/ex, 1424-1427, 1441-1442. État des lettres délivrés. Comptes de ferme (du sceau).

   IV G 124^{5}. 1435-1436. Comptes de ferme.

   IV G 124^{7}. 1443ff. Comptes des sceaux de Grenoble, des écritures de celles de Chambéry et des cens et dîmes du décanat de Savoie (affermés ensemble).

   IV G 117. 1411-1415. Comptes du sceau (de l'officialité de Chambéry).

   IV G 124^{1} 1415-1419. *Id.* (ferme).

   IV G 124^{6} 1435-1436. *Id.* (pas à ferme).

   IV G 124^{2} 1415-1423. Comptes des bans, compositions et condamnations.

   IV G 124^{3} 1423-1428. *Id.*

   IV G 124^{4} 1429-1435. *Id.*

   IV G 298. Quire. 1469-1471. Ordinations, citations devant l'official et institutions canoniques des cures et bénéfices.

4. The officialities of Grenoble have been the object of at least two studies:

   V. Chomel, 'Notes sur l'activité disciplinaire des officialités du diocèse de Grenoble, 1418-1448', in *Études Noël Didier* (Paris 1960) 49-59

   J. Pilot, 'Sur quelques actes et procédures d'excommunication en Dauphiné (XIVe et XVe siècles)', *Bull. Soc. statist. Isère* 2e sér., 4 (1860) 204ff, 5 (1860) 408ff.

   For docs concerning episcopal judges acting in what is probably a secular capacity, see Bautier/Sornay, *Sources* 2:796 (registres judiciaires).

KLAUS LINDNER

IV. Germany

Editor's Introduction

We did not do quite so badly for Germany as the following lone report might suggest. Mr. Lindner was also able to furnish extensive reports on Freising and Regensburg, which are to be found in Chapter I, which covers the whole of the medieval province of Salzburg, and Dr. Meyer has some references to material in German archives in the Swiss report (Chapter X). Nonetheless, the results for Germany are disappointing, and we might ask why and what can be done to advance archival research on the German officialities.

In central Europe the political and ecclesiastical history of the region has separated, in many but not all instances, the archives from their original custodians without placing them under central control, as they have been in France. Thus medieval ecclesiastical court archives may be found in state archives, in city archives, in ecclesiastical archives, or in state, city or university libraries, each with its own system of classification and arrangement, systems which are frequently not published and sometimes not even written down. These systems are so diverse as to defy easy characterization, and most of them do not seem to have separate categories within which records of the officialities (as opposed to ecclesiastical records generally) are kept.

Obviously in such a situation one can not even begin writing to archives, much less visiting them, until one has some sense of what one is looking for. In order to give some sense of what may be there, we list below the medieval dioceses within the modern geographical limits of Germany (except those within the ecclesiastical province of Salzburg and including one that is now in France), the modern name of the see, and a select bibliography of published works concerning the officialities within the diocese. For a more complete bibliography of works prior to 1971, see:

> W. Trusen, 'Die gelehrte Gerichtsbarkeit der Kirche', in H. Coing (hg.), *Handbuch der Quellen und Literatur der Privatrechtsgeschichte* 1 (München 1973) 467-504, especially 499-501.

The order of the dioceses and the Latin spelling of names is taken from Tangl's *Provinciale*:

Maguntina (Mainz, BRD):

H. Fath, 'Das archidiakonale Gericht zu Aschaffenburg: Die iudices ecclesie Aschaffenburgensis', *Aschaffenburger Jahrbuch*, 5 (1972) 51-249 (contains a detailed *Verzeichnis* of 704 documents (1249 X 1555) in the Würzburg Staatsarchiv and the Aschaffenburg Stiftarchiv).

M. Hannappel, 'Mainzer Kommissare in Thüringen', *Zeitschrift des Vereins für thüringische Geschichte* n.F. 36 (1942) 146-209 (prints (176-209) the "Register Mainzer Generalkommissare von 1498, 1501 u. 1510" from Mss in the Erfurt Domarchiv).

B. Krusch, 'Studie zur Geschichte der geistlichen Jurisdiction und Verwaltung des Erzstiftes Mainz; Comissar Johann Bruns und die kirchliche Einteilung der Archidiakonate Nörten, Einbech und Heiligenstadt', *Zeitschrift des historischen Vereins für Niedersachsen* (1897) 112-277 (s16 focus; considerable use made of the Mainz *Ingroßaturbücher* said to be in the royal Kreisarchiv in Würzburg).

G. May, *Die geistliche Gerichtsbarkeit des Erzbischofs von Mainz im Thüringen des späten Mittelalters: Das Generalgericht zu Erfurt* Erfurter Theologische Studien 2 (Leipzig, 1956) (full-scale study with extensive bibliography of prior literature and much unpublished material from the Erfurt Domarchiv; to note: "Gerichtsbuch" (GG II 8), 1495-9).

Eistetensis (Eichstätt, BRD).

Dr. Ingeborg Johanek has written a doctoral thesis on this officiality.

Herbipolensis vel Wirzeburgensis (Würzburg, BRD):

A. Lhotsky, 'Ein Würzburger Formularbuch aus dem 13. Jahrhundert', MÖIG (Erg. Bd.) 12 (1933) 259-96.

W. Trusen, 'Auseinandersetzungen um die geistliche Gerichtsbarkeit im Hochstift Würzburg am Ende des Mittelalters', in *Festschrift für Ferdinand Elsener* (Sigmaringen 1977) 260-68 (considerable citation of unpublished material from the Würzburg Stadtarchiv).

Argentinensis (Strasbourg, FRA):

K. Stenzel, 'Die geistlichen Gerichte zu Straßburg im 15. Jahrhundert', *Zeitschrift für Geschichte des Oberrheins* 68 (n.F. 29) (1914) 365-466; 69 (n.F. 30) (1915) 52-95, 201-53, 343-85 (considerable material cited from the then-Stadtarchiv and Bezirksarchiv in Strasbourg, prints a s17 abstract of s14-s16 cases).

Spirensis (Speyer, BRD):

O. Riedner, *Die geistlichen Gerichtshöfe zu Speier im Mittelalter* Görres-Gesellschaft Sektion für Rechts- und Sozialwissenschaft, Veröffentlichungen 26 (Paderborn, 1915) (first vol. never appeared; to-date the most extensive publication of German church court documents (1224 X 1547) drawn from a wide range of archives of which those in Karlsruhe, Speyer and München provide the most material).

Idem, *Das Speirer Offizialatsgericht im 13. Jahrhundert* Jur. Diss. Erlangen (Speyer 1907) (relies on much the same sources as the above).

Wormaciensis (Worms, BRD).

Verdensis (Verden, BRD).

Hildeshemensis (Hildesheim, BRD):

G. Schrader, 'Die bischöflichen Offiziale Hildesheims und ihre Urkunden im späten Mittelalter (1300-1600)', *Archiv für Urkundenforschung* 13 (1935) 91-176 (a model study; numerous citations of documents in Hildesheim and Hannover archives).

Halberstadensis (Halberstadt, DDR):

A. Diestelkamp, 'Zur Geschichte der geistlichen Gerichtsbarkeit in der Diözese Halberstadt am Ausgang des Mittelalters', *Sachsen und Anhalt* 7 (1931) 277-340.

Idem, 'Die geistliche Gerichtsbarkeit in den zur Diözese Halberstadt gehörigen Teilen der Kurmark, der wettnischen Gebiete, der Grafschaft Mansfeld und des Herzogtums Braunschweig im 15. und in der ersten Hälfte des 16. Jahrhunderts', *Sachsen und Anhalt* 8 (1931) 163-276 (both studies are largely based on printed *Urkunden*).

N. Hilling, *Die Offiziale der Bischöfe von Halberstadt im Mittelalter* Kirchenrechtliche Abhandlungen 72 (Stuttgart 1911) (mostly published *Urkunden*).

Idem, 'Sechs Gerichtsordnungen für das Bistum Halberstadt', AKKR 122 (1947) 324-41; 125 (1951) 29-72.

J. Müller-Volbehr, *Die geistlichen Gerichte in den Brauschweig-Wolfenbüttelschen Landen* Göttinger Studien zur Rechtsgeschichte 3 (Frankfurt, 1973) (basically an institutional study, considerable unpublished material cited pp 307-8; to note: the account book of the last official of Braunschweig).

Padeburnensis (Paderborn, BRD) (see Halberstadt).

Bambergensis (exemptus) (Bamberg, BRD):

H. Straub, *Die geistliche Gerichtsbarkeit des Domdekans im alten Bistum Bamberg von den Anfängen bis zum Ende des 16. Jahrhunderts: eine rechtsgeschichtliche Untersuchung* Münchener theologische Studien KA 9 (München 1957) (excellent survey of the archival material; most of the case material is post-Tridentine).

Augustensis (Augsburg, BRD) (see below 01).

Coloniensis (Köln, BRD):

R. Bettgenhaeuser, 'Drei Jahresrechnungen des kölnischen Offizialatsgerichts in Werl: 1495-1516', *Annalen des historischen Vereins für den Niederrhein* 65 (1898) 151-201.

H. Förster, 'Die Organisation des erzbischöflichen Offizialgerichtes zu Köln bis auf Hermann von Wied', ZRG KA 11 (1921) 254-350 (based on statutes and printed *Urkunden*).

F. Gescher, 'Das älteste kölnische Offizialstatut (1306-1331)', ZRG (KA) 14 (1925) 475-85 (printed from the Stadtarchiv in Köln).

Idem, 'Das Offizialat der Erzbischöfe von Köln in 13. Jahrhundert', *Annalen des historischen Vereins für den Niederrhein* 115 (1929) 136-66 (like most of G's important work on the Köln diocesan administration, this is based largely on scattered early *Urkunden*).

J. Hansen, 'Jahresrechnung des kölnischen Offizialgerichtes in Soest vom 1. März 1438 bis zum 1. März 1439', *Westdeutsche Zeitung für Geschichte und Kunst* 7 (1888) 35-54.

H. Keußen, 'Kölner Prozeßakten', *Mitteilungen aus dem Kölner Stadtarchiv* 24 (1893) 61 (prints a list of 100 *processus* (1364-1550) which were, at least at that time, 'nur der Beginn einer großen Fülle gleichartigen Stoffes' in the Stadtarchiv).

J. Löhr, *Die Verwaltung des kölnischen Großarchidiakonates Xanten am Ausgange des Mittelalters* Kirchenrechtliche Abhandlungen 59/60 (Stuttgart, 1909) (cites an extraordinary amount of material from the Xanten Domarchiv including many late s15 *Protokolle* and s15 account books).

Monasteriensis (Münster, BRD):

F.-L. Knemeyer, 'Das Notariat im Fürstbistum Münster', *Westfälische Zeitschrift* 114 (1964) 1-142 (= Diss. jur. Münster).

Mindensis (Minden, BRD).

Osnaburgensis (Osnabrück, BRD):

J. Prinz, 'Aus dem Anschreibebuch des Osnabrücker Offizials Reiner Eissinck (1488-1509)', *Osnabrücker Mitteilungen* 67 (1956) 81-115.

Bremensis (Bremen, BRD):

A. Kühtmann, 'Geistliches Recht und geistliche Gerichtsbarkeit in Bremen', *Bremer Jahrbücher* 14 (1888) 86-128.

Sleswicensis (Schleswig, BRD):

A. Boockmann, *Geistliche und weltliche Gerichtsbarkeit im mittelalterlichen Bistum Schleswig* Quellen und Forschungen zur Geschichte Schleswig-Holsteins 52 (Neumünster 1967).

Razeburgensis (Ratzeburg, BRD).

Zwerinensis alias Michiliburgensis (Schwerin, DDR).

Lubicensis (Lübeck, BRD).

Magdeburgensis (Magdeburg, DDR).

Havelbergensis (Havelberg, DDR).

Brandeburgensis (Brandenburg, DDR).

Misnensis alias Misenensis (Meißen, DDR).

Cicensis vel Numburgensis (Naumburg, DDR).

Trevensis (Trier, BRD):

H.-J. Krüger, 'Zu den Anfängen des Offizialats in Trier', *Archiv für mittelrheinische Kirchengeschichte* 29 (1977) 39–74.

F. Michel, *Zur Geschichte der geistlichen Gerichtsbarkeit und Verwaltung der Trierer Erzbischöfe im Mittelalter* Veröffentlichungen des Bistumsarchivs Trier 3 (Trier, 1953) (prints (109–27) two accounts from the Koblenz officiality (1330, 1428–9) and one from the Trier officiality (1505–6), extensive citation of archival material in connection with lists of officials and advocates).

The following works concerning Romano-canonic procedure in the Middle Ages contain references to the practice of the officialities and hence to documents concerning them:

H. Budischin, *Der gelehrte Zivilprozeß in der Praxis geistlicher Gerichte des 13. und 14. Jahrhunderts im deutschen Raum* (Bonn, 1974) (based on published *Urkunden*).

N. Hilling, 'Kirchliche Gerichtsordnungen des 14-16 Jahrhunderts aus deutschen Bistümern: Eine Studie über die Quellen des Kirchenrechts', AKKR 109 (1929) 577–83 (lists all the *Gerichtsordungen*, mostly published, known at the time).

A. Steins, *Der ordentliche Zivilprozeß vor dem bischöflichen Offizial* Diss. Jur. München (München 1972).

A. Steins, 'Der ordentliche Zivilprozeß nach den Offizialatsstatuten: ein Beitrag zur Geschichte des gelehrten Prozesses in Deutschland im Spätmittelalter', ZRG KA 59 (1973) 191–262.

There is obviously a great deal there, and a considerable amount of good local work has been done. It is to be hoped that the publication of these reports will stimulate more.

[01.]

1. Mainz, Augsburg, officiality of the bishop.

2. Archiv des Bistums Augsburg, Hafnerberg 2, 8900 Augsburg, Tel. (0821) 3166 410 [ABA].

   Bayerisches Hauptstaatsarchiv [BHA] (see I/02/2).

   The information concerning the BHA comes from a letter to Prof. Hageneder from the Director General of the BHA.

3. *1. ABA*:

   The pre-seventeenth century holdings of this archive are largely uncatalogued. Under the title "Registrum principalium" (this seems to refer to the "partes principales" in the cases) the archive possesses records of the "matrimoniales causae" from December 28, 1532 onwards. There is about one case per page and there are 280 pages in 1533. In 1537 Augsburg turned Protestant, and the bishop and his court fled and established themselves in Dillingen. The number of cases declined to about 120 in 1537 and remained on this level for a number of years.

   In the same archive there is a volume containing only cases in which the defendant did not appear (i.e., there were no *partes principales*). All these cases dealt with petitions to dissolve *sponsalia de futuro.* All these petitions were granted, if it could be demonstrated that the defendant had not answered a citation to come to court. There were ca. twelve such cases per year from 1533 till 1563. The last entry in this volume was made on November 26, 1563, shortly after the Council of Trent, and the second half of the volume is left blank.

2. BHA:

Augsburg Hochstift, Münchener Bestand 514a. s14/2. Fragment of a register of the officiality.

Augsburg Hochstift, Münchener Bestand 1018. 1498-c1550. "Verzeichnis des Vogts Hans Regel zu Dinkelscherben über hingerichtete und gefangene Inquisiten".

4. See also:

F. Frensdorff, 'Ein Urtheilsbuch des geistlichen Gerichts zu Augsburg aus dem 14. Jahrhundert', *Zeitschrift für Kirchenrecht* 10 (1871) 1-37 (transcriptions of cases from Donaueschingen, Fürstlich-Fürstenbergischen Hofbibliotek Ms 772).

R. Maschke, 'Aus dem Urteilsbuch des geistlichen Gerichts Augsburg', in *Festgabe der Kieler Juristen-Fakultät* (Kiel, 1907) 215-53 (more transcriptions from the same Ms).

PÉTER ERDŐ

V. Ungarn
(Kirchenprovinzen von Esztergom und Kalocsa)

Editor's Preface

The first report of the group to be completed starkly presented a number of editorial problems that we had only partially addressed in planning our work. A recitation of the arguments favoring the resolutions that are reflected in what follows would only be tedious and would detract from the splendid achievement that this report represents. Suffice it to say here that this report contains what is known to us of the surviving records of the ecclesiastical courts of the medieval provinces of Esztergom and Kalocsa. Where those records are presently situated within the geographical boundaries of modern Hungary, Dr. Erdő is reasonably confident that the report is complete, or near to complete. Where the records are not so located, the author has provided indications as to where the records may be located and has also given descriptions of what is known to him.

On a more mechanical level, as in all our reports, place-names other than country-names are given in the language of the country. There are more than the usual number of linguistic variations represented here, and we have tried to give cross-references in the Index of Persons and Places to the more common variants.

For the reader beginning from the medieval papal chancery, we offer here the list of dioceses "in Ungaria" from Tangl's *Provinciale.* All of these dioceses are mentioned in Dr. Erdő's list of courts that follows his introduction, together with a number of other jurisdictions:

Esztergom (Strigoniensis)
Eger (Agriensis)
[Nitra] (Nitriensis)
Vác (W(V)aciensis)
Győr (Jauriensis)
Pécs (Quinqueecclesiensis)
Veszprém (Vesprimiensis)

Kalocsa (Colocensis)
[Alba Julia] (Ultrasilvanum, Albensis, Transsilvaniensis)

[Zagreb] (Zagrabiensis)
[Oradea] (W(V)aradiensis)
Csanád (Cenadiensis, Chanadiensis)
[Sremska Mitrovica] (i.e. Szerém) (Sirimiensis, Sirmiensis)
[Argeş] (Argensis)

Einleitung

1. *Institutionengeschichtliches*:

1. Das Verhältnis zwischen Archidiakonate und Offizialate war in Ungarn nicht gespannt. Die alten Archidiakonate üben ihre gerichtliche Funktionen in der ersten Hälfte des s14 ungestört aus. Gegen Mitte desselben Jahrhunderts unterzeichnen einige Archidiakone ihre Gerichtsakten als "vicevicarius" oder "delegatus".

2. Es kommt sehr häufig vor, daß einige kirchliche Würdenträger (Archidiakone, Kanoniker, Äbte, Pröpste) als Delegierte oder "vicevicarii" weit von ihrem Heimatgebiet gerichtliche Funktionen ausüben.

3. In einigen Perioden ist es auch sehr üblich, daß dieselben Personen (aber auch manche Bischöfe und ausländische Prälaten) die gerichtliche Tätigkeit aufgrund einer päpstlichen Delegation ausüben.

4. Die Form des Offizialats als ordentliche Institution der Gerichtsbarkeit — soweit sich aus den noch vorhandenen Dokumenten feststellen läßt — verbreitete sich nicht gleichzeitig im ganzen Land. In der ersten Hälfte des s14 sind die Gerichtsakten z.B. in Esztergom und Győr noch überwiegend im Namen des Bischofs (bzw. des Erzbischofs) verfaßt, während in Eger als herausgebende Behörde schon der Generalvikar bezeichnet wird.

5. Die Verbreitung des römisch-kanonischen Gerichtsverfahrens ist in Ungarn im Jahre 1279 praktisch schon abgeschlossen (Conc. Budense, a. 1279, c. 24, 39, 58, in Péterffy, *Sacra Concilia* 111, 114, 120-1). Die Offizialate aber als typische Gerichtsorgane werden erst in der ersten Hälfte des s14 charakteristisch.

2. *Archivistisches*:

1. Auf dem Gebiet des heutigen Ungarns gibt es kein einziges Offizialatsgericht, dessen Archiv die Periode der türkischen Herrschaft (1526-1686) ungestört überlebt hat. Es kommt also nur selten vor, daß sich die meisten Dokumente eines Gerichtes in einem bestimmten Archiv befinden und dort einen Fonds bilden. Die Urkunden sind vorhanden, aber sie sind in verschiedenen Archiven und gedruckten Ausgaben zerstreut.

2. In den kirchlichen Archiven Nordwestungarns findet man eine beträchtliche Zahl mittelalterlicher Dokumente. Der Fonds der kirchlichen Gerichtsakten der Diözesanarchive enthält aber Dokumente aus der Zeit vor 1563 nur im Prímási Levéltár, Esztergom (darüber siehe: 01/2).

3. Die meisten Dokumente der Vikariate des mittelalterlichen Ungarns sind im Magyar Országos Levéltár, Budapest (darüber siehe: 01/2) zu finden. In diesem Archiv hat man unter der Signatur "Oklevélkibocsátói mutató, 42. csoport (vikárius)" ["O.m., 42"] ein Verzeichnis über die von den verschiedenen Generalvikaren ausgestellten Urkunden. Dieses Verzeichnis war eine unentbehrliche Grundlage für die folgenden Listen. In Listen aufgrund des Registers O.m., 42, geben wir zuerst die Archivnummer und dann das Datum.

Offizialatsgerichte in Ungarn (1300-1563)

01. Ungarn, Esztergom, Offizialat des Erzbischofs (Primas)
02. Rumänien, Esztergom, Offizialat des Dekans von Braşov
03. Tschechoslowakei, Esztergom, Offizialat des Propstes von Bratislava
04. Ungarn, Esztergom, Offizialat des exemten Abtes von Pannonhalma
05. Rumänien, Esztergom, Offizialat des Dekans von Sibiu
06. Tschechoslowakei, Esztergom, Offizialat des Propstes von Spišská Kapitula
07. Ungarn, Esztergom, Eger, Offizialat des Bischofs
08. Ungarn, Esztergom, Győr, Offizialat des Bischofs
    Rumänien, Esztergom, Milcov, ? — siehe unten: Argeş[1]
09. Tschechoslowakei, Esztergom, Nitra, Offizialat des Bischofs
10. Ungarn, Esztergom, Pécs, Offizialat des Bischofs
11. Ungarn, Esztergom, Vác, Offizialat des Bischofs
12. Ungarn, Esztergom, Veszprém, Offizialat des Bischofs
13. Ungarn, Kalocsa, Offizialat des Erzbischofs
14. Rumänien, Kalocsa, Alba Julia (hinsichtlich der Gegend auch "Siebenbürgen" genannt), Offizialat des Bischofs
15. Rumänien, Kalocsa, Alba Julia, Offizialat des Vikars "extra Meszes"
    Rumänien, Kalocsa, Argeş, ?[3]
    Jugoslawien, Kalocsa, Beograd, Offizialat des Bischofs[1]
16. Ungarn, Kalocsa, Csanád, Offizialat des Bischofs
    Jugoslawien, Kalocsa, Đakovo (hinsichtlich der Gegend auch "Bosnien" genannt), Offizialat des Bischofs
    Jugoslawien, Kalocsa, Knin, Offizialat des Bischofs[2]
17. Rumänien, Kalocsa, Oradea, Offizialat des Bischofs
    Rumänien, Kalocsa, Severin, ?[1]
    Jugoslawien, Kalocsa, Sremska Mitrovica, Offizialat des Bischofs — siehe oben: Đakovo
18. Jugoslawien, Kalocsa, Zagreb, Offizialat des Bischofs
19. Jugoslawien, Kalocsa, Zagreb, Offizialat des Propstes von Čazma

[1] Bestand nur kurze Zeit, Gerichtsurkunden nicht bekannt.
[2] Gehörte kurze Zeit zu einer ungarischen Kirchenprovinz.
[3] Bestand kurze Zeit, Identität mit der Diözese Milcov ist umstritten.

Die Ergänzung dieser Liste mit Offizialaten von einigen Pröpsten ist noch möglich. Über Milcov, Argeş, Beograd, Đakovo, Knin, Severin, und Sremska Mitrovica, siehe: Gyetvai, *Egyházi szervezés* 50-69, 93-102.

[01.]

1. Esztergom, Offizialat des Erzbischofs (Primas).

2. *Esztergomi Prímási Levéltár, Berényi Zsigmond u. 2, H-2500 Esztergom, Ungarn [EPL].

*Magyar Országos Levéltár, Bécsikapu tér 2-4, H-1250 Budapest, Ungarn [MOL].

*Főkáptalani Levéltár, Berényi Zsigmond u. 2, H-2500 Esztergom, Ungarn [FKL].

Veszprémi Káptalani Levéltár, Tolbuhin u. 16, H-8201 Veszprém, Ungarn [VKL].

Veszprémi Püspöki Levéltár, Tolbuhin u. 16, H-8201 Veszprém, Ungarn [VPL].

Bibliotheca Batthyanyana, Alba Julia, Rumänien [BBAJ].

*Főszékesegyházi Könyvtár, Bajcsy Zsilinszky u. 28, H-2500 Esztergom, Ungarn [FKE].

Beschreibungen des Bestandes des EPL:

G. Bónis, *Útmutató az esztergomi Prímási Levéltárhoz* Levéltári leltárak 24 (Budapest 1964) (zu den Gerichtsakten siehe S. 235-6)

G. Prokopp, 'Az Esztergomi Prímási Levéltár', in Balázs, *Magyarország levéltárai* (Budapest 1983) 272-80.

Die Gerichtsurkunden sind in drei Fonds zu finden: (1) das "Archivum Ecclesiasticum Vetus" (AEV) — Urkunden bis 1778 — ist vor allem für die Dokumente bis 1526 und für die zweitinstanzlichen Prozesse (vor allem vor dem Erzbischof-Primas) zwischen 1526 und 1563 wichtig; (2) die "Acta Consistorialia" (Acta Consist.) sind für die Prozeßakten nach 1525 grundlegend; (3) das "Archivum Saeculare" enthält manche Urkunden aus der Zeit vor 1526 (die Abteilungen dieses Fonds werden mit den Buchstaben des lateinischen Alphabets bezeichnet, z.B., "F-2-24").

Einige Dokumente über die Tätigkeit dieses Offzialats sind in anderen Archiven zu finden, vor allem in MOL. Siehe:

Magyar Országos Levéltár.

Bibliographie der Publikationen über dieses Archiv:

G. Ember u. P. Balázs, 'Magyar Országos Levéltár', in Balázs, *Magyarország levéltárai* 33-50.

Einige Urkunden dieses Offizialats finden sich in dem Archiv des Kapitels von Esztergom, FKL. Über dieses Archiv siehe:

G. Prokopp, 'Az Esztergomi Főkáptalan Levéltára', in Balázs, *Magyarország levéltárai* 280-282.

Weitere Dokumente der geistlichen Gerichtsbarkeit in Esztergom findet man in dem VKL. Die mittelalterlichen Gerichtsurkunden bilden hier keinen selbständigen Fonds. Über dieses Archiv siehe:

J. Körmendy, 'Veszprémi Káptalani Levéltár', in Balázs, *Magyarország levéltárai* 328-331.

Ähnliche Urkunden finden sich auch in dem VPL. Über dieses Archiv siehe:

J. Körmendy, 'Veszprémi Püspöki Levéltár', in Balázs, *Magyarország levéltárai* 323-328.

Regesten der Urkunden beider Archive für die Jahre 1301-1387:

Kumorovitz, *Veszprémi regeszták.*

Einige handschriftliche Formelbücher dieses Offizialats sind in Bibliotheken (BBAJ u. FKE) zu finden. Für BBAJ siehe:

R. Szentiványi, *Catalogus concinnus librorum MSS Bibliothecae Batthyanyanae*, 4. Ausg. (Szeged 1958).

Für eine kurze Beschreibung des FKE siehe:

M. Beke, 'Főszékesegyházi Könyvtár', in L. Turányi (ed.), *Schematismus statusque Archidioecesis Strigoniensis anno Domini MCMLXXXII* (Esztergom 1982) 477-479.

3. *1. EPL – Protocolla*:

*Acta Consist. 130 pp, gebunden (Halbleder). 1525, 1532, 1564. Protocollum Annorum 1525, 1532, 1564.

Register der Prozesse aus den Jahren 1525 und 1532: p 2-78; Register der Prozesse aus dem Jahr 1564: p 79-130. Die Akten dieser Prozesse aus den Jahren 1525 und 1532 sind heute im Archiv nicht zu finden.

*Acta Consist. c350 fols, Lederband, Papier. 1553-1786. Regestrum processualium ab a. 1553 usque a. 1786.

Handschriftlich. Geschrieben 1828. Register von 3487 Prozessen. Nach den Kategorien der Prozesse gegliedert. Jede Kategorie ist chronologisch geordnet.

2. EPL – Einzelne Dokumente u. Urkunden:

*AEV 21/1-2. 2 Dok. 16.3.1325. Sentenzen: der Archidiakon von Zvolen entscheidet als Delegierter des Erzbischofs von Esztergom *(amotio a beneficio)*.

*F-2-24. 8.10.1343. Eine Entscheidung des "vicarius in spiritualibus" von Esztergom.

*AEV 18. 30.11.1393. Gerichtliche Privilegien des "Kirchenvolks" von Esztergom.

*O-2-54. 8.4.1439. Der "vicarius in spiritualibus" zu Esztergom droht einer der Parteien mit Interdikt.

*D-26-617. 8.4.1439. Eine Gerichtsurkunde des "vicarius in spiritualibus" zu Esztergom.

*AEV 56. 12.6.1464. Eine Liste der Kirchen, die unter der Jurisdiktion des Erzbischofs von Esztergom stehen.

*AEV 77. 26.11.1471. Eine Gerichtsurkunde des "vicarius in spiritualibus" zu Esztergom.

Hrsg.: Erdélyi, *Szent Benedek Rend története* 7:466-68.

*AEV 75. 16.9.1515. Der Erzbischof beauftragt den "vicarius in spiritualibus" zu Esztergom mit der Erledigung einer Gerichtssache.

*Y 62. 1517. Eine Gerichtsurkunde des "vicarius in spiritualibus" zu Esztergom.

*Acta Consist. 1/1. 1558. Akten eines Prozesses. "Solutio vinculi matrimonialis."

*Acta Consist. 1/2. 1563. Akten eines Prozesses. "Solutio vinculi matrimonialis."

*Acta Consist. 5/1-7. 1560-1563. Akten von 6 Prozessen (die Nr. 3 fehlt). "Processus sponsalistici."

*Acta Consist. 6/1. 1557. "Processus sponsalist. appellatus." Akten eines Prozesses.

*Acta Consist. 9/1-8. 1553-1563. Akten von 8 Prozessen. "Fiscales" (Benefizien, Kirchenvermögen, Geldstrafe).

*AEV 105. 1557. "Processus appellatus a vicario gen. ad Archiepiscopum." Eine Appellationsurkunde gegen Exkommunikationsurteil.

*AEV 105. 1560. 3+98+13 pp. "Processus de Paroechia." Sämtliche Akten.

*AEV 112. 1559, 1561. 2 Urkunden eines Prozesses: Zitation, Exkommunikation.

*AEV 113. 1560. Akten eines Prozesses vor dem "vicarius in spiritualibus."

*AEV 114. 19pp. 1554-55. Zwei Gruppen von Dokumenten; p 1-5: Protokolle einer Vernehmung in einem Prozeß über Häresie vor dem "vicarius in spiritualibus"; p 6-19: Sammlung von Formeln.

*AEV 120. 1350. Eine Appellation gegen das Urteil des Archidiakons von Trenčín zum Apostolischen Stuhl in einer Benefizialsache.

*AEV 121. 1557. "Libellus" in einer Besitzstörungssache. Der "actor" ist der Konvent der Dominikaner in Trnava.

3. *Formelbücher*:

*FKE, MSS II. 507. 428 fols, Papier, 220 X 160 mm. s16/in. "Formularium secundum modum et stilum ecclesie Strigoniensis" etc.

Handgeschriebenes Formelbuch aus der Kanzlei des Generalvikars und Weihbischofs Demetrius von Nyás. Formeln aus den Jahren 1500-1521. Das wichtigste kirchliche Formelbuch des mittelalterlichen Ungarns.

BBAJ, MSS I. 152. 1500-1512. Handgeschriebenes Formelbuch des Matthäus Beneéthy aus der Kanzlei des Generalvikars von Esztergom.

Das obengenannte Formelbuch des Demetrius von Nyás ist eine erweiterte zweite Redaktion dieser Sammlung. Siehe:

Bónis, *Középkori jogunk elemei* 44-5

G. Bónis, 'Un formulaire de l'officialité primatiale hongroise de 1512', *Recueil de Mémoires et Travaux de la Société d'Histoire du Droit Écrit* (= Mélanges Pierre Tisset) 7 (1970) 31-40.

4. *MOL— Einzelne Urkunden*:

Alle diese Aktenstücke sind einzelne Urkunden (meistens Gerichtsurkunden), die vom Generalvikar von Esztergom ausgestellt sind. Diese Liste wurde aufgrund des Registers "O.m., 42" (siehe: 00/1/3) zusammengestellt.

D1.040886.	1.7.1342.	D1.057364.	12. 8.1352.
D1.041129.	1349.	D1.057748.	24.11.1468.
D1.042827.	7.10.1404.	D1.058470.	23. 6.1332.
D1.043145.	29. 4.1412.	D1.058822.	2. 7.1408.
D1.043265.	18.11.1414.	D1.058911.	13. 3.1415.
D1.043382.	19. 1.1418.	D1.058984.	6. 4.1424.
D1.043471.	30. 5.1420.	D1.058993.	30. 8.1424.
D1.044689.	18. 7.1453.	D1.058995.	13. 9.1424.
D1.045064.	12. 9.1463.	D1.059593.	4. 2.1471.
D1.045419.	16. 8.1470.	D1.061418.	13.11.1427.
D1.045711.	14. 3.1478.	D1.061650.	20. 8.1453.
D1.046160.	9. 5.1491.	D1.062559.	14. 3.1409.
D1.046170.	26. 9.1491.	D1.062570.	14. 2.1421.
D1.046296.	8. 9.1495.	D1.062578.	1428.
D1.046848.	21. 2.1508.	D1.062948.	11. 5.1497.
D1.046931.	11. 3.1510.	D1.063070.	12.12.1356.
D1.047493.	28. 2.1523.	D1.063538.	28. 7.1511.
D1.048279.	16. 5.14??.	D1.064717.	18. 6.1303.
D1.050341.	12.11.1438.	D1.064717.	6.10.1357.
D1.050501.	9. 2.1516.	D1.064862.	15. 7.1407.
D1.051046.	24. 2.1337.	D1.064865.	2. 7.1411.
D1.051049.	18. 3.1337.	D1.064870.	5. 5.1419.
D1.053854.	10.10.1415.	D1.064910.	?1366.
D1.056186.	18. 4.1485.	D1.065277.	9.10.1349.
D1.056825.	1332.	D1.065335.	8. 5.1471.
D1.056866.	1351.	D1.065349.	30.11.1481.
D1.056915.	7. 5.1382.	D1.065815.	1. 9.1390.
D1.056952.	13. 1.1414.	D1.065841.	2. 5.1407.
D1.056963.	16. 5.(1.)1425.	D1.065844.	24. 2.1410.
D1.056999.	17. 7.1470.	D1.065876.	7. 6.1435.

D1.065931.	22. 7.1465.
D1.065958.	26. 3.1477.
D1.067100.	12. 5.1485.
D1.067475.	15. 6.1505.
D1.068974.	10. 5.1424.
D1.069224.	8. 8.1343.
D1.069369.	25. 4.1413.
D1.069388.	4.10.1340.
D1.069475.	23. 8.1449.
D1.069596.	29. 7.1525.
D1.070192.	22. 9.1394.
D1.070282.	4. 6.1465.
D1.070295.	7. 9.1470.
D1.072193.	20.11.1520.
D1.072447.	9. 3.1525.
D1.072595.	8. 5.1418.
D1.072596.	8. 7.1418.
D1.072805.	um 1436.
D1.072946.	14. 5.1507.
D1.072991.	16. 3.1401.
D1.073092.	12. 7.1414.
D1.073093.	30. 8.1414.
D1.073332.	9.12.1496.
D1.074679.	16. 1.1485.
D1.074927.	23. 9.1467.
D1.075082.	7. 6.1431.
D1.075570.	31.10.1388.
D1.076057.	10. 7.1454.
D1.077882.	7. 7.1383.
D1.077884.	23. 5.1383.
D1.077891.	16.11.1383.
D1.078514.	23. 8.1402.
D1.079377.	9.11.1416.
D1.079391.	21. 2.1417.
D1.079399.	1. 5.1417.
D1.079478.	20. 6.1408.
D1.079478.	1.10.1408.
D1.079961.	22. 3.1425.
D1.079964.	23. 3.1425.
D1.081029.	23. 8.1451.
D1.082088.	1495.
D1.082586.	11. 9.1522.
D1.083054.	25. 4.1380.
D1.083061.	1.10.1343.
D1.083099.	2. 7.1497.
D1.083227.	14. 2.1341.
D1.083234.	3.10.1341.
D1.083527.	10. 2.1410.
D1.084247.	s14.
D1.084584.	15.11.1503.
D1.084712.	25. 7.1434.
D1.085975.	19. 2.1478.
D1.086012.	10.12.1492.
D1.086497.	14. 3.1478.
D1.087520.	6. 6.1379.
D1.087783.	1402.
D1.088502.	9. 5.1470.
D1.088505.	9. 5.1470.
D1.089164.	4. 7.1522.
D1.089812.	27. 7.1420.
D1.090109.	26. 8.1467.
D1.090115.	27. 4.1468.
D1.090554.	23.12.1418.
D1.090639.	5. 2.1333.
D1.090691.	2. 5.1417.
D1.090728.	16.12.1521.
D1.090807.	24. 4.1474.
D1.090877.	18.10.1431.
D1.093478.	14.12.1474.
D1.093482.	17. 3.1475.
D1.093609.	13. 5.1490.
D1.093749.	1.11.1509.
D1.094366.	27. 1.1335.
D1.095380.	18. 9.1465.
D1.095434.	3. 2.1499.
D1.095497.	s14.
D1.095617.	25. 4.1355.
D1.095791.	s14.
D1.096581.	19. 1.1383.
D1.097226.	1. 7.1451.
D1.097447.	27.10.1484.
D1.097529.	9. 2.1496.
D1.097647.	10. 5.1516.
D1.097865.	12.10.1355.
D1.098025.	10. 9.1447.
D1.098038.	um 1462.
D1.098241.	12. 8.1352.
D1.098384.	2.11.1501.
D1.098413.	26.10.1324.
D1.098415.	25. 5.1325.
D1.098416.	13. 6.1325.
D1.098417.	18.10.1325.
D1.099473.	24. 8.1411.
D1.099521.	26. 7.1485.
D1.102651.	25. 2.1492.
D1.102699.	6. 6.1513.
D1.103094.	18. 8.1511.
D1.104972.	9.10.1420.
D1.105812.	1. 5.1509.
D1.105812.	4. 3.1510.
D1.105812.	2. 5.1510.
D1.106002.	9. 1.1413.
D1.106023.	19. 3.1496.
D1.106894.	9.10.1420.

D1.107031.	17. 1.1478.	D1.107500.	17. 8.1397.
D1.107216.	14. 8.1486.	D1.107619.	12.12.1497.
D1.107217.	16.11.1486.	D1.107636.	26. 9.1504.
D1.107228.	11. 6.1520.		

5. *FKL*:

*Lad. 1 fasc. 1 Nr. 5a. 1297. Königliche Bestätigung des Urteils des Erzbischofs von Esztergom (Zoll, Kirchenvermögen). Kopie aus dem Jahr 1689.

*Lad. 1 fasc. 1 Nr. 5aa. 14.6.1285. Urteil des Erzbischofs von Esztergom (Kirchenvermögen). Kopie aus dem Jahr 1689.

*Lad. 1 fasc. 1 Nr. 11. 6.5.1292. "Protestatio in synodo provinciali" *(iniuria)*.

*Lad. 1 fasc. 1 Nr. 12. 20.10.1295. Urteil des Erzbischofs (Kirchenvermögen, Zoll). Kopie aus dem Jahr 1689.

*Lad. 1 fasc. 1 Nr. 13-16. 4 Dok. 7.7.1285, 21.5.1302, 1.6.1326, 22.7.1326. Weitere Urkunden desselben Prozesses. Kopien aus dem Jahr 1689.

*Lad. 2 fasc. 3 Nr. 13. 8.12.1403. Fristverlängerung *(decimae)*.

*Lad. 24 fasc. 3 Nr. 27. 4.1.1497. Eine Gerichtsurkunde des Generalvikars von Esztergom.

*Lad. 38 fasc. 9 Nr. 24. 1.9.1467. Urteil des Generalvikars ("super censu molendini").

*Lad. 45 fasc. 1 Nr. 6. 15.9.1365. Eine Gerichtsurkunde des Generalvikars *(decimae)*.

*Lad. 45 fasc. 1 Nr. 11. 28.2.1396. Eine Gerichtsurkunde des Generalvikars *(decimae)*.

*Lad. 45 fasc. 1 Nr. 12. 18.9.1396. Urteil.

*Lad. 45 fasc. 2 Nr. 2-3. 2 Dok. 9.10.1433, 14.10.1433. 2 Urkunden: "Appellatio contra sent. interlocutoriam ad Concilium Basiliense in causa decimali."

*Lad. 45 fasc. 2 Nr. 11-12. 2 Dok. 29.7.1435. 2 Urkunden: "Sententia Concilii Basilien. in eadem causa" *(decimae)*.

*Lad. 45 fasc. 2 Nr. 13. 13.8.1435. Urteil des Konzils von Basel in demselben Prozeß über "spoliatio, usurpatio etc.".

*Lad. 45 fasc. 3 Nr. 1. 23.8.1435. Urteil des Konzils von Basel in demselben Prozeß *(decimae)*.

*Lad. 45 fasc. 3 Nr. 3. 24.8.1435. "Bulla executionalis" des Konzils von Basel in demselben Prozeß.

*Lad. 45 fasc. 4 Nr. 18. 30.7.1453. "Compulsoria" in demselben Prozeß.

*Lad. 45 fasc. 4 Nr. 19. 2.9.1453. "Executio citationis" in demselben Prozeß. "Causa ... per Capitulum Strigonien. Romam appellata" *(decimae)*.

*Lad. 45 fasc. 4 Nr. 21. 8.9.1453. Ladung nach Rom in demselben Prozeß.

*Lad. 45 fasc. 4 Nr. 24. 1453. "Inhibitio" in demselben Prozeß.

*Lad. 45 fasc. 6 Nr. 1. 24.7.1458. "Relatio ... commissariorum ad auditorem in Curia" in demselben Prozeß.

*Lad. 45 fasc. 6 Nr. 24. 2.5.1459. Eine Urkunde in demselben Prozeß. "Inhibitio ad Archiep. Card. Strigonien. eiusque vicarium ne in causa ... aliquid innovare praesumant."

*Lad. 45 fasc. 8 Nr. 6. 21.9.1470. Eine Urkunde desselben Prozesses. Teil eines Protokolls?

*Lad. 45 fasc. 12 Nr. 4-5. 2 Dok. 21.7.1436, 13.8.1435. Entscheidungen des Konzils von Basel in demselben Prozeß.

*Lad. 45 fasc. 12 Nr. 20. 1458. Brief des Prokurators in demselben Prozeß.

*Lad. 45 fasc. 12 Nr. 21. 6 pp, Papier. 1458. "Litterae procuratoris Capituli Strigonien. ex Urbe Roma" in demselben Prozeß.

*Lad. 45 fasc. 13 Nr. 7. 7 pp, Papier. 1461. "Diversae observationes in facto decimarum de Sasad" (derselbe Prozeß).

*Lad. 45 fasc. 13 Nr. 14. 26.8.1469. "Prohibitio" in demselben Prozeß.

*Lad. 45 fasc. 14 Nr. 1. 22 pp, Papier. 1484. Akten eines vor dem "generalis auditor" des Erzbischofs von Esztergom geführten Prozesses *(decimae)*.

*Lad. 45 fasc. 14 Nr. 22. c1450. "Primus conceptus maculatus Bullae Pii Papae 2di ad Dionysium Cardinalem Strigonien. in causa decimarum Sasadiensium, in qua is iudex constituitur."

*Lad. 45 fasc. 14 Nr. 24. 7 fols, Papier. c1470. "Informatio brevis et summaria in causa decimarum Wijmal et Gombamal."

*Lad. 46 fasc. 4 Nr. 8. 25 pp, Papier. 1512-1518. "Processus de Capella B.M.V. in causa Philippi contra Capit. Strigonien." Akten.

*Lad. 46 fasc. 5 Nr. 5. 4 pp, Papier. 28.9.1522. "Concordia de proventibus Capellae B.M.V." in demselben Prozeß.

*Lad. 46 fasc. 4 Nr. 22-23. 2 Dok. 4 +4 pp, Papier. s/16/in. Dokumente desselben Prozesses.

*Lad. 48 fasc. 1 Nr. 2. 6.7.1362. Eine Gerichtsurkunde des Generalvikars von Esztergom *(decimae)*.

*Lad. 48 fasc. 1 Nr. 9. 17.11.1439. Eine Gerichtsurkunde *(decimae)*.

*Lad. 48 fasc. 1 Nr. 11. 21.7.1469. Eine Gerichtsurkunde des Generalvikars von Esztergom in demselben Prozeß "causa decimarum de Sagh."

*Lad. 48 fasc. 1 Nr. 16. 30.7.1478. Eine Gerichtsurkunde des Generalvikars von Esztergom in demselben Prozeß.

*Lad. 48 fasc. 1 Nr. 20. 7 pp, Papier. 2.8.1479. "Appellatio a Vicario Strigonien." in demselben Prozeß.

*Lad. 48 fasc. 2 Nr. 2. 21.7.1469. Eine Gerichtsurkunde des Generalvikars von Esztergom in demselben Prozeß.

*Lad. 48 fasc. 2 Nr. 3-4. 2 Dok. 8+4 pp, Papier. 1479. Akten desselben Prozesses.

*Lad. 48 fasc. 2 Nr. 8. 8 pp, Papier. 1484. Akten desselben Prozesses.

*Lad. 48 fasc. 2 Nr. 11. 1.4.1484. Eine Urkunde des Generalvikars von Esztergom in demselben Prozeß.

*Lad. 48 fasc. 2 Nr. 12. 4 pp, Papier. 1484. Dokumente desselben Prozesses.

*Lad. 48 fasc. 2 Nr. 18. 7.8.1485. Eine Gerichtsurkunde des Generalvikars von Esztergom. "Decimae in Barsiensi comitatu."

*Lad. 51 fasc. 1 Nr. 30. 1390. Eine Gerichtsurkunde des Generalvikars von Esztergom. Kompromiß (Jurisdiktionsstreit).

*Lad. 51 fasc. 2 Nr. 1. 13.10.1399. Eine Gerichtsurkunde des Generalvikars von Esztergom *(testamentum)*.

*Lad. 51 fasc. 2 Nr. 4. 3.4.1403. Eine Gerichtsurkunde des Generalvikars von Esztergom ("de quartis in possessione Damas proventibus").

*Lad. 51 fasc. 2 Nr. 7. 26.8.1446. Eine Gerichtsurkunde des Generalvikars von Esztergom ("super censu").

*Lad. 51 fasc. 2 Nr. 8. 20.9.1454. Protestbrief *(beneficium)*.

*Lad. 53 fasc. 3 Nr. 4. 13.5.1419. Entscheidung des Generalvikars von Esztergom ("de censu annuo").

*Lad. 53 fasc. 3 Nr. 21 a-b, 22. 3 Dok. 22.2.1501 2, 30.10.1510 1. Akten eines vor dem Generalvikar von Esztergom geführten Prozesses *(testamentum)*.

*Lad. 53 fasc. 3 Nr. 34. 2.5.1519. Exkommunikation in einem vor dem Generalvikar von Esztergom geführten Prozeß ("ob non solutum censum").

*Lad. 53 fasc. 3 Nr. 45. 30.10.1510. Eine Gerichtsurkunde des Generalvikars von Esztergom *(testamentum)*.

*Lad. 53 fasc. 4 Nr. 9. 8.10.1500. Eine Gerichtsurkunde des Generalvikars von Esztergom (Kirchenvermögen).

*Lad. 66 fasc. 2 Nr. 5. 15.6.1465. Vernehmungen in einem vor dem Generalvikar von Esztergom geführten Prozeß (Kirchenvermögen).

*Lad. 72 fasc. 1 Nr. 2. 12.8.1429. Eine Gerichtsurkunde des Generalvikars von Esztergom (Kirchenvermögen).

*Lad. 72 fasc. 1 Nr. 3. 26.6.1434. Urteil des Delegierten des Erzbischofs von Esztergom ("pro censu annuo").

*Lad. 72 fasc. 2 Nr. 4. 9.1.1480. Eine Urkunde des Generalvikars von Esztergom *(beneficium)*.

*Lad. 73 capsa cerul. Nr. 22. 20.12.1358. Gerichtsurkunde des Vikars von Esztergom (Dienstleistungen für das Kloster der Augustiner zu Esztergom).

*Lad. 76 sine fasc. ohne Nr. 1330. Gerichtsurkunde des Generalvikars (?*beneficium*).

*Capsa Ecclesiasticorum, 1-1-ohne Nr. 2 fols, Papier. 1514. Atken eines Prozesses *(decimae)*.

6. *VPL*:

Csolnok 11. 4.9.1322. Eine Gerichtsurkunde des Vikars von Esztergom *(iniuria)*.

Regest.: Kumorovitz, *Veszprémi regeszták* 59, Nr. 123.

Decimae episcopales 14. 9.4.1359. Eine Gerichtsurkunde *(testamentum)*.

Regest.: Kumorovitz, *Veszprémi regeszták* 201-2, Nr. 507.

Kálóz 1. 14.5.1326. Ladung in einem vor dem Erzbischof von Esztergom geführten Prozeß *(iniuria)*.

Regest.: Kumorovitz, *Veszprémi regeszták* 73, Nr. 163.

Litterae mancae 18. 31.7 X 27.8.1349. Eine Gerichtsurkunde des Vikars von Esztergom.

Regest.: Kumorovitz, *Veszprémi regeszták* 169, Nr. 420.

Miscell. 11. 13.11.1320. Berufung zum Papst gegen das Urteil des Erzbischofs von Esztergom (Gehorsam einiger Pfarrer gegen den Bischof).

Regest.: Kumorovitz, *Veszprémi regeszták* 55, Nr. 110.

Miscell. 24. 6.5.1349. Eine Gerichtsurkunde des Vikars von Esztergom. Fristverlängerung *(decimae)*.

Regest.: Kumorovitz, *Veszprémi regeszták* 167, Nr. 414. Hrsg.: Knauz, *Monumenta* 3:680.

Miscell. 25. 3.6.1349. Protestbrief in einem vor dem Vikar von Esztergom geführten Prozeß.

Regest.: Kumorovitz, *Veszprémi regeszták* 168, Nr. 416. Hrsg.: Knauz, *Monumenta* 3:684.

Miscell. 26. 31.7.1349. Ladung.

Regest.: Kumorovitz, *Veszprémi regeszták* 169, Nr. 419. Hrsg.: Knauz, *Monumenta* 3:690.

Miscell. 124. 1.12.1347. Fristverlängerung (*decimae*).

Regest.: Kumorovitz, *Veszprémi regeszták* 165, Nr. 407. Hrsg.: Knauz, *Monumenta* 3:651.

Miscell. 125. 6.5.1350. Fristverlängerung.

Regest.: Kumorovitz, *Veszprémi regeszták* 169, Nr. 422.

Miscell. 145. 2.6.1349. Fristverlängerung.

Regest.: Kumorovitz, *Veszprémi regeszták* 167, Nr. 415. Hrsg.: Knauz, *Monumenta* 3:684.

7. *VKL*:

Kolon 6. 1327. Vernehmungen in einem vor dem Erzbischof von Esztergom geführten Prozeß (*decimae*).

Regest.: Kumorovitz, *Veszprémi regeszták* 77, Nr. 178.

Kolon 7. 28.11.1327. Urteil des Vikars von Esztergom (*decimae*).

Regest.: Kumorovitz, *Veszprémi regeszták* 78-9, Nr. 181.

Veszpr. eccl. et capit. 16. 6.12.1319. Berufung gegen das Urteil des Erzbischofs von Esztergom (Gehorsam gegen den Bischof).

Regest.: Kumorovitz, *Veszprémi regeszták* 53, Nr. 104.

4. Die Kompetenz der kirchlichen Gerichte war in Ungarn einheitlich. Im s14 wurde diese Kompetenz nur gewohnheitsrechtlich geregelt. Im s15 zählte eine Reihe staatlicher Gesetze die Kompetenzen der geistlichen Gerichte auf. Zur Zuständigkeit der kirchlichen Gerichte gehörten: "(1) die Angelegenheiten der Sakramente; (2) die Fragen des Glaubens und der Ketzerei; (3) Testamente; (4) Ehesachen und ihre Akzessorien, besonders Dotal-, Paraphrenal- und Tochterviertelansprüche, und "donationes propter nuptias"; (5) die Streitigkeiten über dingliche und persönliche Zehnten mit ihren Akzessorien; (6) Wucher; (7) Angelegenheiten der Witwen und Armen mit Ausnahme von Eigentumsfragen; (8) Eidbruch und Meineid (d. h. die Klagen aus unter Eid eingegangenen Verträgen), mit den auf Bestrafung der Sünden abzielenden Rechtsstreitigkeiten; (9) jede Sache, in welcher der Kirchenbann erfolgte." Über die Kompetenzstreitigkeiten zwischen den geistlichen und weltlichen Richtern sollte — nach Art. 14 des königlichen

Gesetzes vom 15.4.1405 — die "specialis presentia" des Königs entscheiden. Siehe:

Bónis, 'Entwicklung', 224-5

G. Bónis, 'Az egyházi és világi jog határai a középkorban', in G. Székely (ed.), *Eszmetörténeti tanulmányok a magyar középkorról* Memoria Saeculorum Hungariae 4 (Budapest 1984) 235-41.

Aufgrund der überlieferten Urkunden kann man vermuten, daß die eigentlichen Eheprozesse (Klagen auf Zuerkennung des Partners als Ehegatten, Feststellung der Rechtmäßigkeit der Ehe, Verlöbnisverfahren, Nichtigerklärung der Ehe, Ehetrennung) relativ selten waren (3-5% sämtlicher Gerichtssachen), während die mit der Ehe zusammenhängenden vermögensrechtlichen Sachen (Dotal-, Paraphrenal- und Tochterviertelansprüche, "donationes propter nuptias") die Mehrheit sämtlicher Prozesse ausmachten. Alle diese Feststellungen gelten für das ganze Land. Siehe:

P. Erdő, 'Eheprozesse in mittelalterlichen Ungarn', ZRG KA 72 (1986) 250-76.

Eine Spezialität des kirchlichen Gerichts von Esztergom war, daß der Erzbischof als Primas Hungariae befugt war, in allen kirchlichen Sachen des Landes erstinstanzlich zu verfahren und gegen Urteile jedes kirchlichen Richters des Landes Appellationen anzunehmen. Obwohl diese Befugnisse schon im Spätmittelalter dokumentiert sind (1451; 1513), gibt es keinen Fonds, in dem die Urkunden des Primatialgerichts aus der Zeit vor 1563 gesondert zu finden wären. Siehe:

P. Erdő, 'Il potere giudiziario del Primate d'Ungheria', *Apollinaris* 53 (1980) 272-92; 54 (1981) 213-31

A. Szentirmai, 'The Primate of Hungary', *The Jurist* 20 (1961) 36-7.

[02.]

1. Esztergom, Offizialat des Dekans von Braşov.

2. In der Volksrepublik Ungarn sind meistens nur die gedruckten Dokumente dieses Offizialats zugänglich.

3. *1. Ausgaben von einzelnen Dokumenten*:

Zimmermann, *Urkundenbuch* 2:506, 533, 534, 595; 3:96, 138, 208, 220, 522; 4:125, 344, 596; 5:111, 118, 151, 186, 218, 297, 314, 341, 495.

Bunyitay, *Egyháztörténelmi* 1:140, 201.

4. Für die Jurisdiktion dieses Offizialats siehe: 01/4. Siehe auch:

Teutsch, *Geschichte* 42, 87, 252-3.

Anmerkung: "...schon 1295 erscheint das Dekanat von Kronstadt [Braşov] unmittelbar unter dem Erzbischof von Gran [Esztergom] stehend, der 1336 für die Gesamtheiten der Pfarrer von Hermannstadt [Sibiu] und Kronstadt Verfügungen erläßt, bestimmt u.a. ... die Gerichtsbarkeit in geistlichen Angelegenheiten" (Teutsch, *Geschichte* 87).

[03.]

1. Esztergom, Offizialat des Propstes von Bratislava.

2. *MOL (siehe 01/2).

In diesem Archiv findet man nur einzelne Urkunden des geistlichen Gerichts von Bratislava. Die Liste der Urkunden wurde aufgrund des Registers "O.m., 42" (siehe: 00/1/3) zusammengestellt.

Für die weitere Forschung: Archív Mesta Bratislavy, Bratislava, Tschechoslowakei. In diesem Archiv besonders: "Cirkevné fondy 7, Capitulum Posoniense". Siehe:

D. Lehotská u.a. (ed.), *Archív Mesta Bratislavy. Sprievodca po fondoch a zbierkach* (Praha 1955) 80, 85-6.

Regesten der mittelalterlichen Urkunden dieses Archivs:

D. Lehotská u.a. (ed.), *Archív Mesta Bratislavy. Inventár stredovekých listín, listov a iných príbuzných písomnosti*, 1 (Praha 1956)

V. Horváth (ed.), *Archív Mesta Bratislavy. Inventár listín a listov*, 2: *(1501-1563)* (Bratislava 1966).

Sämtliche Akten einiger Prozesse (in Buchformat) gehörten zur Handschriftensammlung des Kapitels von Bratislava und wurden besprochen bzw. herausgegeben in Knauz, *Codices manuscripti*.

3. *1. Sämtliche Akten einiger Prozesse in Buchformat*:

Knauz, *Codices manuscripti* 27, Nr. 28. 7 fols, Papier. 1526. Prozeß zwischen dem Kapitel zu Bratislava und seinem Propst (erwähnt wird auch die Jurisdiktion des Propstes).

Ebd. 27, Nr. 29. 10 fols, Papier. 1531. Eheprozeß vor dem geistlichen Gericht von Bratislava.

Ebd. 27-94, Nr. 31. 83 fols, Papier. 1506-8. Prozeß zwischen dem Kapitel und seinem Propst (mit mehreren Dokumenten der richterlichen Tätigkeit der Propstei von Bratislava) (teilweise herausgegeben).

2. MOL – Einzelne Urkunden:

Alle Aktenstücke sind Gerichtsurkunden, die vom Vikar des Propstes oder von anderen Behörden ausgestellt sind.

D1.18015.	16. 1.1478.	D1.84265.	5. 3.1346.
D1 62051.	3.12.1519.	D1.88494.	26. 3.1470.
D1.62056.	15.12.1519.	D1.88496.	30. 3.1470.
D1.62057.	17.12.1519.	D1.94990.	14.11.1501.
D1.62060.	20. 1.1520.		

4. Für die Jurisdiktion dieses Offizialats ist anzumerken, daß der Propst als "in spiritualibus et temporalibus vicarius generalis" eine gewisse richterliche Tätigkeit schon im s15 ausgeübt hat. Siehe:

Knauz, *Monumenta* 2:505-6; 3:668-9, 715.

Im Jahre 1469 ernannte der Erzbischof von Esztergom den Propst von Bratislava und seine Nachfolger zum Offizial und Generalvikar "tam in foro contentioso, quam conscientiae" für das Gebiet der Propstei bzw. des Archidiakonats von Bratislava. Der Propst ernannte selbst seinen Vikar, der das Gericht leitete. Siehe:

C. Rimely, *Capitulum insignis Ecclesiae Collegiatae Posoniensis* (Posonii 1880) 32-3, 231, 324-7.

Für die geographischen Grenzen der Jurisdiktion des Propstes siehe:

Ortvay, *Geographia* 1:7-16.

Für die Geschichte dieser Propstei siehe:

N. Knauz, *A pozsonyi prépostság* (Esztergom 1881).

[04.]

1. Esztergom, Offizialat des exemten Abtes von Pannonhalma.

Pannonhalma lag außerhalb der Diözese Esztergom, und war von der Jurisdiktion des Erzbischofs von Esztergom unabhängig.

2. Bencés Főapátsági Levéltár, Főmonostor, H-9090 Pannonhalma, Ungarn [BFL].

Über dieses Archiv siehe:

Nagy, *Magyarországi katolikus egyház levéltári* 119-123

P. Balázs, 'Bencés Főapátsági Levéltár', in Balázs, *Magyarország levéltárai* 335-339.

Die Urkunden des geistlichen Gerichts bilden hier keinen selbständigen Fonds.

3. *1. BFL—Einzelne Urkunden*:

Capsa 47. O. 24.9.1501. Eine Gerichtsurkunde (Jurisdiktionsstreit zwischen der Abtei von Pannonhalma und dem Bischof von Győr). Hrsg.: Erdélyi, *Szent Benedek Rend története* 3:574.

Capsa 50. A4. 1501. Libellus in demselben Prozeß. Hrsg.: Erdélyi, *Szent*

Benedek Rend története 3:572.

Capsa 51. C3. 1505. Eine Urkunde eines vor dem geistlichen Gericht des Abtes von Pannonhalma geführten Prozesses. Hrsg.: Erdélyi, *Szent Benedek Rend története* 8:545.

Capsa 63. Nn. ?1503. Eine Urkunde des Abtes. Urteil (Entzug des Benefiziums eines Pfarrers wegen Unzucht, Nachlässigkeit und unerlaubter ärztlicher Praxis). Hrsg. (teilweise): Erdélyi, *Szent Benedek Rend története* 3:175.

4. Für die Jurisdiktion dieses Offizialats siehe:

   Erdélyi, *Szent Benedek Rend története* 4:168-175.

[05.]

1. Esztergom, Offizialat des Dekans von Sibiu.

2. In der Volksrepublik Ungarn sind meistens nur die gedruckten Dokumente dieses Offizialats zugänglich.

3. *1. Ausgaben von einzelnen Dokumenten*:

   Zimmermann, *Urkundenbuch* 1:91-2, 200, 259, 414, 481-4; 2:58, 81-3, 172-3, 215; 3:19-22, 85-95, 243, 270, 482-6, 604-6; 4:124, 167, 415; 5:121, 122, 125, 130, 175, 218, 314.

   Bunyitay, *Egyháztörténelmi* 1:18, 108, 114, 115, 120, 140, 153, 179, 217, 218, 223.

4. Für die Jurisdiktion dieses Offizialats siehe:

   Teutsch, *Geschichte* 42, 244-5, 250, 267, 293, 320

   G.E. Müller, *Die deutschen Landkapitel in Siebenbürgen und ihre Dechanten 1192-1848*, 3 Bde. (fortlaufende Seitenzahlen) (Hermannstadt 1934-1936) 444-96

   F. Schuler Libloy, *Siebenbürgische Rechtsgeschichte*, 2. Ausg. (Hermannstadt 1868) 2:345

   Ortvay, *Geographia* 1:57-63.

Anmerkung: "...nach dem Andreanischen Freibrief (1224) wählten sich die Ansiedler auch die Pfarrer selbst, gaben ihnen, nicht dem Bischof, den Zehnten und die übrigen kirchlichen Abgaben und waren in allen kirchlichen Angelegenheiten unmittelbar ihrem Gericht unterstellt.... Auf dem Gebiete des kirchlichen Lebens bildeten die einzelnen Gemeinden, gewiß nach den ursprünglichen Einwanderergruppen, je ein Kapitel, in dem die freie Wahl der Pfarrer den Dechanten an die Spitze stellte, der in vielen Fällen, wie sonst der Bischof und unabhängig von ihm, die kirchliche Verwaltung führte" (Teutsch, *Geschichte* 42).

[06.]

1. Esztergom, Offizialat des Propstes von Spiška Kapitula.

2. *MOL (siehe 01/2).

In diesem Archiv findet man nur einzelne Urkunden des Offizialats von Spiš. Die Liste der Urkunden wurde aufgrund des Registers "O.m., 42." (siehe: 00/1/3) zusammengestellt.

Für weitere Forschungen: Štátny Oblastný Archív, Mierové Námestie 60, Levoča, Tschechoslowakei. Ein Teil des Materials dieses Archivs ist, in Form von Mikrofilm, auch in Ungarn (MOL) zugänglich. Siehe:

Borsa, *Csehszlovákiai levéltári*

Bándi, *Csehszlovákiai levéltári.*

3. *1. MOL—Einzelne Urkunden*:

D1.045419.	16. 8.1470.	D1.068942.	10.10.1387.
D1.045543.	27.10.1473.	D1.070488.	2. 3.1393.
D1.045599.	2. 3.1475.	D1.071611.	21. 2.1371.
D1.060278.	10. 5.1359.	D1.071611.	10. 5.1384.
D1.060435.	13. 3.1388.	D1.071647.	10. 5.1384.
D1.060521.	7.12.1406.	D1.071653.	5. 5.1396.
D1.060583.	11. 6.1414.	D1.071653.	26. 4.1414.
D1.060584.	9. 7.1414.	D1.071654.	1.10.1423.
D1.060614.	6. 2.1419.	D1.071664.	25.11.1428.
D1.060718.	4.10.1434.	D1.074869.	20. 1.1415.
D1.060727.	25. 2.1435.	D1.074881.	19.11.1418.
D1.060954.	vor 1410.	D1.075020.	4. 8.1398.
D1.060981.	7.12.1361.	D1.083247.	18. 5.1347.
D1.060985.	8.10.1375.	D1.083449.	27. 1.1395.
D1.060988.	8.10.1379.	D1.083527.	13.12.1409.
D1.060993.	29. 4.1393.	D1.083663.	30. 6.1432.
D1.063695.	8. 5.1374.	D1.083677.	24. 5.1434.
D1.063697.	18.11.1378.	D1.083681.	28. 5.1434.
D1.063702.	8.10.1386.	D1.096020.	7. 5.1408.
D1.063737.	22. 9.1413.	D1.101742.	3. 6.1420.
D1.065308.	9. 3.1436.	D1.101742.	18. 2.1421.
D1.065340.	22. 1.1479.	D1.103176.	15. 5.1416.
D1.065341.	24. 3.1479.		

4. Über das Richteramt und die beinahe bischöfliche Stellung des Propstes von Spiš siehe:

Wagner, *Analecta* 1:319-321, 344-347, 366-372

Conc. Scepusien. a. 1460, c. 22-23, in Péterffy, *Sacra concilia* 193; vgl. ebd. 185-186.

Der Propst von Spiš war "tamquam vicarius in ipsa Ecclesia Scepusiensi in spiritualibus" des Erzbischofs von Esztergom, siehe: Brief vom 1.6.1560 des Erzbischofs Nikolaus Oláh: Wagner, *Analecta* 1:380-382. Der Propst ernannte selbst seinen Vikar, der das Gericht von Spiš leitete, siehe: Wagner,

Analecta 1:374-375. Die "canonica visitatio" hat im Jahre 1629 festgestellt: "utraque iurisdictione, tam fori judicialis, seu contentiosa, quam voluntaria Praepositos praedictos usos fuisse" (Wagner, *Analecta* 2:283).

Für die geographischen Grenzen der Jurisdiktion dieses Propstes, siehe:

Wagner, *Analecta* 2:283-284 und

Ortvay, *Geographia* 1:53-57.

Zur Geschichte der Propstei siehe:

M. Pirhala, *A szepesi prépostság vázlatos története kezdetétől a püspökség felállításáig* (Löcse 1899).

[07.]

1. Esztergom, Eger, Offizialat des Bischofs.

2. *MOL (siehe 01/2).

In diesem Archiv findet man nur einzelne Urkunden des Offizialats von Eger. Die Liste der Urkunden wurde aufgrund des Registers "O.m., 42" (siehe: 00/1/3) zusammengestellt.

Klimó Könyvtár, István tér 23, H-7624 Pécs, Ungarn [KKP].

Nationalbibliothek, Josefplatz 1, Wien, Österreich [NBÖ].

Ein Formelbuch dieses Offizialats ist in der KKP zu finden. Ein anderes Formelbuch, das teilweise aufgrund der Praxis dieses Offizialats zusammengestellt wurde, findet sich in der NBÖ. Siehe: *Tabulae codicum.*

Das Diözesanarchiv von Eger (Egri Érseki Levéltár, Széchenyi u. 1, H-3301 Eger, Ungarn) hat sehr viele Protokollbücher: "Protocolla consistorialia et dioecesana ab. a. 1600 usque ad a. 1960," 336 vols. Siehe:

I. Soós, 'Egri Érseki Levéltár', in P. Balázs, *Magyarország levéltárai* 290.

Dieses Archiv hat aber keine mittelalterliche Gerichtsurkunden und keine Protokollbücher für die Jahre vor 1563.

3. *1. Formelbücher*:

KKP, DD III. 18. Formelbuch des Johannes Magyi.

Enthält auch Formeln des Offizialats von Eger aus den Jahren 1468-1476. Hrsg.: Kovachich, *Formulae* 155-458. Siehe:

G. Bónis, 'Magyi János formuláskönyve és a gyakorlati jogtanítás', in A. Csizmadia (ed.), *Jubileumi tanulmányok.* 1: *A pécsi egyetem történetéből* (Pécs 1967) 232-3.

NBÖ, Cod. 3452. 33 fols, Papier, 215 X 145 mm. s15. Ars Notaria des Johannes Uzsai.

NBÖ, Cod. 4276. Fol. 104-139, Papier, 215 X 145 mm. s15-16. Ars Notaria des Johannes Uzsai.

Enthält auch Formeln des Offizialats von Eger aus den Jahren 1346-1350. Siehe: *Tabulae codicum* 2 (Vindobonae 1868) 292; 3 (Vindobonae 1869) 225.

Hrsg.: Kovachich, *Formulae* 1-154. Darüber siehe:

G. Bónis, 'Uzsai János Ars Notariája', *Filológiai Közlöny* 6 (1961) 229-260.

2. *MOL — Einzelne Urkunden*:

Alle Aktenstücke sind vom Generalvikar von Eger ausgestellt (meistens Gerichtsurkunden).

D1.039912.	12. 3.1435.	D1.050951.	5. 5.1333.
D1.040616.	?1332.	D1.050954.	7.10.1333.
D1.040963.	29.11.1344.	D1.050961.	7. 4.1334.
D1.041110.	6. 7.1349.	D1.051244.	12. 8.1343.
D1.041136.	15. 3.1350.	D1.051268.	13. 1.1344.
D1.041146.	11.12.1349.	D1.051269.	13. 1.1344.
D1.041309.	5. 5.1357.	D1.051482.	22. 6.1348.
D1.041535.	8. 1.1343.	D1.051493.	18.10.1348.
D1.041535.	5. 7.1361.	D1.051494.	19.10.1348.
D1.041854.	11.10.1371.	D1.051500.	18.11.1348.
D1.042034.	8. 7.1376.	D1.051504.	11.12.1348.
D1.042045.	13. 1.1349.	D1.051506.	nach 8. 1.1348.
D1.042054.	nach 4. 7.1377.	D1.051507.	18. 1.1349.
D1.042054.	18. 9.1377.	D1.051513.	29. 3.1349.
D1.042155.	8. 5.1380.	D1.051521.	24. 7.1349.
D1.042727.	6. 1.1400.	D1.051532.	26. 8.1349.
D1.042854.	20. 9.1405.	D1.051551.	17. 1.1350.
D1.042854.	6.10.1401 und 1383.	D1.051593.	16. 6.1351.
D1.043004.	19. 5.1405.	D1.051638.	9.11.1353.
D1.043263.	8.11.1414.	D1.051858.	5. 8.1359.
D1.043768.	8.11.1428.	D1.051871.	11.12.1359.
D1.043851.	15. 9.1430.	D1.051943.	19.11.1361.
D1.043937.	1. 2.1433.	D1.051944.	19.11.1361.
D1.044184.	24.12.1437.	D1.051948a.	12. 1.1362.
D1.044935.	1459.	D1.052019.	5. 5.1364.
D1.047966.	s14.	D1.052020.	5. 5.1364.
D1.050292.	1376.	D1.052021.	5. 5.1364.
D1.050334.	22. 6.1329.	D1.052300.	25. 8.1379.
D1.050360.	1. 8.1414.	D1.052314.	20.12.1379.
D1.050769.	31. 5.1325.	D1.052332.	25. 5.1380.
D1.050772.	6. 6.1325.	D1.052360.	30. 3.1381.
D1.050843.	8. 5.1327.	D1.052391.	9. 6.1379.
D1.050854.	24. 2.1328.	D1.052503.	1. 6.1385.
D1.050855.	24. 2.1328.	D1.052504.	17. 1.1385.
D1.050861.	8. 7.1328.	D1.052506.	11. 10.1385.
D1.050862.	8. 7.1328.	D1.052684.	18. 5.1390.
D1.050863.	8. 7.1328.	D1.052691.	18. 5.1390.
D1.050929.	7. 9.1332.	D1.052779.	4. 5.1393.
D1.050931.	26. 9.1332.	D1.052796.	1385.
D1.050935.	7.12.1332.	D1.052796.	25. 8.1391.

D1.052828.	14. 3.1393.	D1.057073.	17. 7.1328.
D1.053037.	26. 7.1399.	D1.057141.	17. 9.1495.
D1.053075.	25. 8.1400.	D1.057290.	1. 4.1329.
D1.053078.	18. 9.1400.	D1.057311.	5. 5.1341.
D1.053400.	11.12.1387.	D1.057315.	1342.
D1.053457.	16. 1.1409.	D1.057377.	19. 8.1383.
D1.053581.	26. 3.1411.	D1.057421.	18.11.1411.
D1.053593.	1. 7.1411.	D1.057631.	6.10.1434.
D1.053641.	11.11.1412.	D1.057693.	14.12.1439.
D1.053644.	7.12.1412.	D1.058527.	12.12.1349.
D1.053646.	13. 1.1413.	D1.060167.	21. 1.1317.
D1.053661.	18. 4.1413.	D1.060168.	12. 6.1317.
D1.053670.	26. 5.1413.	D1.060169.	5. 3.1317.
D1.053690.	25. 8.1413.	D1.060170.	1317.
D1.053691.	26. 8.1413.	D1.060224.	20. 7.1337.
D1.053692.	31. 8.1413.	D1.060225.	31. 7.1337.
D1.053693.	3. 9.1416.	D1.060231.	8. 8.1338.
D1.053699.	9. 9.1413.	D1.060268.	11.12.1352.
D1.053700.	13. 9.1413.	D1.060269.	18. 1.1353.
D1.053704.	24.10.1413.	D1.060270.	18. 1.1353.
D1.053708.	8.11.1413.	D1.060399.	13. 1.1382.
D1.053718.	7.12.1413.	D1.060407.	1. 5.1383.
D1.053754.	1. 5.1414.	D1.060413.	13. 1.1384.
D1.053755.	1. 5.1414.	D1.060446.	10. 5.1389.
D1.053782.	1. 8.1414.	D1.060450.	6. 6.1389.
D1.053793.	6.10.1414.	D1.060451.	6. 6.1389.
D1.053806.	7.12.1414.	D1.060453.	11. 1.1390.
D1.053815.	vor 20. 2.1415.	D1.060454.	22.11.1390.
D1.053816.	20. 2.1415.	D1.060455.	19. 3.1390.
D1.053830.	1. 5.1415.	D1.060456.	13. 4.1390.
D1.053866.	11.12.1415.	D1.060461.	21. 2.1391.
D1.053873.	16. 1.1416.	D1.060567.	13. 1.1413.
D1.053905.	1. 8.1416.	D1.060571.	20. 9.1413.
D1.054595.	1. 8.1411.	D1.060572.	6.10.1413.
D1.054669.	1. 5.1429.	D1.060573.	10.10.1413.
D1.055471.	12.11.1450.	D1.060576.	7.12.1413.
D1.055473.	11.12.1450.	D1.060578.	8. 1.1414.
D1.055475.	12. 1.1451.	D1.060594.	1. 7.1415.
D1.055542.	5. 7.1453.	D1.060595.	26.10.1415.
D1.055545.	4. 8.1453.	D1.060606.	6. 6.1417.
D1.055552.	19.12.1453.	D1.060609.	12.10.1417.
D1.055636.	10. 3.1459.	D1.060707.	1. 8.1433.
D1.055637.	10. 3.1459.	D1.060712.	29. 5.1434.
D1.055647.	1. 8.1459.	D1.060714.	1. 7.1434.
D1.055651.	7. 9.1459.	D1.060719.	6.10.1434.
D1.055666.	8. 5.1460.	D1.060721.	11.10.1434.
D1.055667.	18. 6.1460.	D1.060850.	7. 7.1480.
D1.055853.	18. 6.1467.	D1.060909.	10. 9.1506.
D1.055897.	5.12.1469.	D1.060929.	20.12.1516.
D1.055960.	20. 5.1472.	D1.062276.	s15.
D1.056395.	28. 1.1512.	D1.063840.	8. 4.1448.
D1.057073.	12. 7.1328.	D1.064055.	5. 5.1359.

D1.064099.	9.10.1380.	D1.077219.	11. 3.1358.
D1.064155.	9. 7.1411.	D1.077223.	6. 5.1358.
D1.066661.	29. 4.1333.	D1.077243.	22.11.1358.
D1.066670.	1381.	D1.077252.	5. 5.1359.
D1.066800.	8. 6.1341.	D1.077255.	20. 6.1359.
D1.066831.	12.12.1378.	D1.077257.	5. 7.1359.
D1.066838.	12. 1.1385.	D1.077281.	5. 7.1360.
D1.067115.	25. 8.1492.	D1.077289.	18. 1.1361.
D1.067465.	3. 9.1493.	D1.077294.	5. 5.1361.
D1.068629.	28.11.1344.	D1.077301.	3. 4.1362.
D1.068866.	25. 2.1347.	D1.077534.	13.12.1372.
D1.068869.	25. 2.1347.	D1.077599.	10.10.1374.
D1.068871.	8. 4.1347.	D1.077618.	8. 4.1375.
D1.068908.	12. 1.1357.	D1.077797.	10.10.1380.
D1.068934.	1. 7.1374.	D1.077887.	6.10.1383.
D1.068970.	29. 2.1372.	D1.077919.	4. 8.1385.
D1.069287.	14. 7.1395.	D1.077928.	5. 5.1386.
D1.069705.	5. 5.1379.	D1.077934.	1. 7.1386.
D1.069706.	5. 5.1379.	D1.077935.	2. 7.1386.
D1.069817.	22.11.1438.	D1.078238.	23. 3.1398.
D1.069943.	s14.	D1.078246.	5. 6.1398.
D1.070168.	22.12.1347.	D1.078261.	20. 9.1398.
D1.070184.	16.12.1371.	D1.078265.	30.10.1398.
D1.070184.	13. 2.1372.	D1.078465.	10.10.1401.
D1.070184.	26. 5.1372.	D1.078498.	24. 5.1402.
D1.070184.	6.10.1372.	D1.078517.	20. 9.1402.
D1.070184.	13. 3.1380.	D1.078926.	6. 8.1336.
D1.070189.	16. 1.1384.	D1.078952.	1. 8.1410.
D1.070190.	12.12.1386.	D1.079125.	23. 3.1413.
D1.070269.	20.11.1462.	D1.079216.	6.10.1414.
D1.070297.	14. 1.1471.	D1.079229.	7.12.1414.
D1.070375.	s14.	D1.079250.	13. 3.1415.
D1.070376.	s14.	D1.079259.	5. 5.1415.
D1.070796.	7.12.1411.	D1.079284.	15. 9.1415.
D1.072421.	1456.	D1.079446.	13. 1.1418.
D1.072996.	1. 5.1471.	D1.079535.	29. 3.1419.
D1.074549.	22. 5.1508.	D1.079738.	7. 6.1422.
D1.074833.	28.11.1473.	D1.079901.	21. 6.1424.
D1.074943.	18. 9.1472.	D1.080490.	12. 1.1435.
D1.074947.	28. 9.1473.	D1.080870.	1. 8.1333.
D1.075085.	6.10.1434.	D1.080870.	6.10.1418.
D1.075261.	31. 5.1365.	D1.080890.	1. 8.1450.
D1.075720.	8. 5.1503.	D1.081058.	28. 4.1452.
D1.075846.	8. 6.1389.	D1.081152.	22. 3.1454.
D1.075870.	30. 8.1397.	D1.081153.	8. 4.1454.
D1.076360.	5. 5.1326.	D1.081199.	7. 3.1455.
D1.076393.	25. 6.1328.	D1.081245.	6. 1.1457.
D1.076461.	26. 9.1332.	D1.081252.	22. 2.1457.
D1.077117.	7. 2.1355.	D1.081263.	14. 6.1457.
D1.077155.	23.11.1355.	D1.081781.	21. 6.1476.
D1.077167.	26. 6.1356.	D1.081875.	29.11.1482.
D1.077194.	8. 5.1357.	D1.082008.	8. 8.1489.

D1.082051.	13. 2.1493.
D1.082345.	21. 5.1512.
D1.082943.	1435.
D1.082951.	s14.
D1.082953.	12. 1.1384.
D1.082953.	9. 2.1384.
D1.082953.	5. 5.1391 um 1397.
D1.083278.	5. 5.1356.
D1.083367.	13. 1.1380.
D1.083373.	29. 7.1380.
D1.083403.	5. 7.1383.
D1.083419.	5. 8.1389.
D1.083420.	4. 8.1389.
D1.083422.	9.10.1389.
D1.083424.	16. 1.1390.
D1.083425.	19. 3.1390.
D1.083426.	1. 6.1390.
D1.083428.	9.10.1390.
D1.083429.	10.10.1390.
D1.083560.	22.11.1413.
D1.083561.	23.11.1413.
D1.083563.	11.12.1413.
D1.083564.	18.12.1413.
D1.083588.	3. 3.1417.
D1.083591.	18. 4.1417.
D1.083675.	9. 3.1434.
D1.083679.	6.10.1434.
D1.083680.	11.10.1434.
D1.083713.	30. 4.1440.
D1.083728.	18.12.1448.
D1.083906.	19. 6.1484.
D1.083929.	11. 8.1479.
D1.083961.	29. 5.1493.
D1.084049.	26. 5.1507.
D1.084297.	15. 2.1380.
D1.084374.	6.10.1424.
D1.084594.	1507.
D1.084894.	29. 1.1448.
D1.084902.	12.11.1448.
D1.084963.	12. 5.1462.
D1.085133.	30. 6.1489.
D1.085224.	1331.
D1.085258.	2. 1.1345.
D1.085328.	17.10.1358.
D1.085356.	4. 5.1349.
D1.085488.	4. 7.1389.
D1.085498.	19. 1.1391.
D1.085561.	18. 5.1407.
D1.085887.	nach 22. 3.1452.
D1.085890.	26. 8.1452.
D1.086007.	9. 4.1491.
D1.087355.	um 18.13.1360.
D1.087772.	21. 7.1406.
D1.088534.	29.11.1472.
D1.088582.	1. 7.1476.
D1.088617.	20.12.1487.
D1.089274.	13. 1.1336.
D1.089473.	4. 7.1402.
D1.089485.	21. 1.1380.
D1.089545.	11. 3.1388.
D1.089570.	1391.
D1.089704.	22. 8.1412.
D1.089713.	6. 7.1402.
D1.089721.	5. 9.1413.
D1.089724.	10.12.1413.
D1.089734.	1. 8.1414.
D1.089743.	22.11.1414.
D1.089745.	9. 2.1415.
D1.089918.	1. 7.1376.
D1.089919.	1. 7.1431.
D1.089960.	14.11.1446.
D1.090104.	14. 5.1476.
D1.090332.	s15.
D1.090765.	15. 5.1340.
D1.090816.	19. 9.1340.
D1.094900.	17. 1.1342.
D1.096278.	12. 4.1347.
D1.096282.	5. 7.1347.
D1.096306.	11.10.1349.
D1.096309.	17. 1.1350.
D1.096313.	27. 5.1350.
D1.096317.	10.10.1350.
D1.096319.	Anfang 1351.
D1.096320.	12. 5.1351.
D1.096326.	27. 8.1351.
D1.096329.	11.12.1351.
D1.096334.	31. 3.1353.
D1.096354.	22.11.1356.
D1.096361.	23.12.1357.
D1.096363.	8. 4.1358.
D1.096533.	5. 8.1379.
D1.096558.	23. 1.1381.
D1.096565.	1. 7.1381.
D1.096576.	15. 5.1382.
D1.096695.	26. 8.1397.
D1.096829.	25. 8.1412.
D1.096831.	21.10.1412.
D1.096873.	13. 2.1415.
D1.096881.	5. 8.1415.
D1.097218.	16. 6.1449.
D1.097332.	23.10.1470.
D1.097439.	23. 1.1484.
D1.097464.	28. 7.1487.
D1.097722.	30. 4.1526.

D1.097827.	5. 5.1395.	D1.099500.	6. 3.1435.
D1.097852.	26. 6.1356.	D1.099506.	13. 1.1439.
D1.098243.	22. 7.1379.	D1.099518.	28.11.1475.
D1.099403.	13.12.1324.	D1.099565.	6. 8.1341.
D1.099416.	19. 1.1341.	D1.099566.	6. 8.1341.
D1.099419.	12. 1.1348.	D1.099566.	13. 9.1341.
D1.099420.	20. 9.1348.	D1.102907.	14. 2.1383.
D1.099455.	25. 8.1374.	D1.103273.	1348.
D1.099470.	1. 7.1410.	D1.104440.	10. 6.1525.
D1.099472.	16. 1.1411.	D1.104781.	8.11.1338.
D1.099485.	6. 7.1421.	D1.105778.	26. 6.1356.
D1.099499.	1. 3.1435.	D1.105828.	17. 1.1385.

4. Für die Jurisdiktion dieses Offizialats siehe: 01/4.

[08.]

1. Esztergom, Győr, Offizialat des Bischofs.

2. *MOL (siehe 01/2).

In diesem Archiv findet man nur einzelne Urkunden des Offizialats von Győr. Die Liste der Urkunden wurde aufgrund des Registers "O.m., 42" (siehe: 00/1/3) zusammengestellt.

*Győri Káptalani Levéltár, Káptalandomb 1, Tel. 12-087, H-9002 Győr, Ungarn [GKL].

Über dieses Archiv siehe:

Nagy, *Magyarországi katolikus egyház levéltári* 89-92

P. Balázs, 'Győri Káptalani Levéltár', in Balázs, *Magyarország levéltárai* 300-301.

In diesem Archiv des Kapitels von Győr findet man einige Urkunden aus dem mittelalterlichen Diözesanarchiv. Die Gerichtsurkunden bilden keinen selbständigen Fonds. Außer den von uns gefundenen kann man bei weiterer Suche vielleicht noch andere Gerichtsurkunden finden.

3. *1. MOL — Einzelne Urkunden*:

Alle Aktenstücke sind einzelne Urkunden (meistens Gerichtsurkunden), die vom Generalvikar von Győr ausgestellt sind.

D1.042116.	nach 27. 2.1379.	D1.043586.	24. 3.1424.
D1.042378.	13.12.1387.	D1.043863.	14.11.1430.
D1.042988.	8. 6.1409.	D1.043865.	1.12.1430.
D1.043477.	1. 9.1420.	D1.043866.	1.12.1430.
D1.043485.	12.10.1420.	D1.043867.	2.12.1430.
D1.043537.	13.12.1422.	D1.043870.	16.12.1430.

D1.043871.	16.12.1430.	D1.061246.	29. 3.1384.
D1.043883.	26. 2.1431.	D1.061282.	7. 6.1404.
D1.044057.	21. 9.1435.	D1.061283.	7. 6.1404.
D1.044064.	31.10.1435.	D1.061335.	7. 9.1415.
D1.044160.	17. 8.1437.	D1.061388.	16. 5.1423.
D1.044190.	19. 1.1438.	D1.061411.	14. 9.1426.
D1.044220.	18.11.1438.	D1.061415.	21. 3.1427.
D1.044507.	1. 4.1448.	D1.061545.	7. 8.1438.
D1.044746.	25.10.1454.	D1.061711.	19. 4.1464.
D1.045285.	5. 3.1468.	D1.061722.	1465.
D1.045612.	29. 5.1475.	D1.061852.	1484.
D1.045625.	14.11.1475.	D1.062099.	20. 4.1525.
D1.045628.	13.12.1475.	D1.065529.	8. 4.1434.
D1.045668.	20.11.1476.	D1.065530.	24. 5.1434.
D1.045781.	29. 4.1479.	D1.065554.	21. 8.1466.
D1.045786.	10. 6.1479.	D1.065565.	19.10.1473.
D1.045830.	22. 6.1480.	D1.065567.	19. 6.1480.
D1.046228.	4. 6.1493.	D1.065622.	7. 1.1469.
D1.047048.	1513.	D1.067959.	19. 6.1481.
D1.047618.	27. 7.1525.	D1.068354.	19. 3.1431.
D1.048480.	31.12.1485.	D1.068383.	vor 19. 6.1458.
D1.048683.	16. 6.1430.	D1.068448.	8. 6.1492.
D1.048803.	19. 6.1325.	D1.068490.	28.11.1508.
D1.048903.	8. 1.1456.	D1.071234.	8. 7.1462.
D1.049618.	7. 5.1379.	D1.086240.	21. 9.1408.
D1.049656.	24. 6.1462.	D1.088611.	9. 9.1478.
D1.049666.	30. 8.1450.	D1.088612.	6.11.1478.
D1.049791.	15.11.1449.	D1.092589.	10. 3.1422.
D1.049941.	6. 5.1400.	D1.092861.	7. 7.1436.
D1.049945.	10. 6.1401.	D1.093485.	27. 6.1475.
D1.049946.	7. 5.1401.	D1.093745.	25. 5.1509.
D1.049998.	1450.	D1.095798.	25. 8.1499.
D1.050408.	8.11.1405.	D1.102408.	13.12.1387.
D1.050489.	26. 6.1465.	D1.102458.	2.12.1435.
D1.058018.	25. 9.1350.	D1.103515.	22.11.1427.
D1.058079.	20. 9.1433.	D1.103541.	26. 6.1430.
D1.058087.	17. 8.1437.	D1.105053.	19.10.1433.
D1.058089.	14. 2.1438.	D1.107278.	27. 6.1488.
D1.058376.	s15.		

2. GKL:

*PP. Cath. III. f. 24 Nr. 109. 1426. Bischöfliche Urkunde (Frage der Jurisdiktion über die Augustiner Eremiten).

*PP. Cath. III. f. 24 Nr. 110. 1482. Eine Gerichtsurkunde des "vicarius" von Győr *(testamentum)*.

*PP. Cath. III. f. 24 Nr. 108. 1363. Eine Gerichtsurkunde des Bischofs von Győr *(beneficium)*.

4. Für die Jurisdiktion dieses Offizialats siehe: 01/4.

[09.]

1. Esztergom, Nitra, Offizialat des Bischofs.

2. *MOL (siehe 01/2).

In diesem Archiv findet man nur einzelne Urkunden des Offizialats von Nitra. Die Liste der Urkunden wurde aufgrund des Registers "O.m., 42" (siehe: 00/1/3) zusammengestellt.

Für die weitere Forschung: Archív R. Kat. Biskupstva, Nitra, Tschechoslowakei und Kapitulský Archív Nitre, Nitra, Tschechoslowakei. Ein Teil des Bestandes dieser Archive ist, in Form von Mikrofilm, auch in Ungarn (MOL) zugänglich. Siehe:

Borsa, *Csehszlovákiai levéltári* 51-52, 89

Bándi, *Csehszlovákiai levéltári* 81-82.

3. *1. MOL—Einzelne Urkunden*:

Alle Aktenstücke sind Gerichtsurkunden, die vom Generalvikar oder von anderen Behörden ausgestellt sind.

D1.010511.	7.12.1416.	D1.072807.	um 1510.
D1.043480.	6. 9.1420.	D1.095498.	s15.
D1.050312.	29.12.1484.	D1.105892.	28. 6.1409.
D1.062095.	1524.		

4. Für die Jurisdiktion dieses Offizialats siehe: 01/4.

Zur Geschichte des Bistums siehe:

J. Vurum, *Episcopatus Nitriensis* ... (Posonii 1835)

A. Stransky, *Dejiny biskupstva nitrianskeho od najstarších dôb až* do konca *stredoveku* (Trnava 1933)

Gyetvai, *Egyházi szervezés* 22-23, 26-30.

[10.]

1. Esztergom, Pécs, Offizialat des Bischofs.

2. *MOL (siehe 01/2).

In diesem Archiv findet man nur einzelne Urkunden des Offizialats von Pécs. Die Liste der Urkunden wurde aufgrund des Registers "O.m., 42" (siehe: 00/1/3) zusammengestellt.

*Főkáptalani Levéltár [FKL] (siehe 01/2).

Ein Formelbuch des Offizialats von Pécs ist in dem Archiv des Kapitels von Esztergom [FKL] zu finden.

Stiftsbibliothek, Klosterneuburg, Österreich [SKÖ].

Ein anderes Formelbuch findet man in der SKÖ. Über diese Bibliothek siehe:

L. Petzhold, *Adressenbuch der Bibliotheken Deutschlands, Österreich-Ungarns und der Schweiz* (Dresden 1875) 221.

3. *1. Formelbücher*:

*FKL, Ladula 50, liber primus. 189 pp, Lederband., Papier. s16/in. Handgeschriebenes Formelbuch des Doktors Michael (Vikar von Pécs).

P 1-70 und 132-185: gerichtliche Formeln des Offizialats von Pécs (einige auch datiert, z.B. 1515, 1516); p 74-131: Aufzeichnungen des Kapitels von Esztergom aus den Jahren 1526-1616 *(colligatum)*. Über dieses Formelbuch (mit einigen gedruckten Formeln) siehe:

Szentirmai, 'Ungarische Diözesankurie', 209, 210-211, 215, 217.

SKÖ, MS 941. 370 pp, Papier. s15. Formelbuch des Vitus Huendler (Vikar von Pécs).

Ein Teil dieses Formelbuchs ist gedruckt worden:

Koller, *Historia Quinqueecclesiarum* 4:246-359.

Siehe:

J.Csontosi, 'Könyvtárbúvárlatok Ausztriában', in *Magyar Könyvszemle* 15 (1890) 38-39

Bónis, *Középkori jogunk elemei* 43.

Einige Formeln des Offizialats von Pécs finden sich auch im Formelbuch des Johannes Magyi, siehe: 06/3/1.

2. MOL – Einzelne Urkunden:

Alle Aktenstücke sind einzelne Urkunden (meistens Gerichtsurkunden), die vom Vikar von Pécs ausgestellt sind.

D1.042622.	24.11.1395.	D1.067911.	s14.
*D1.044391.	19. 3.1445.	*D1.081030.	25. 8.1451.
*D1.067713.	19. 8.1343.	D1.081767.	7. 9.1474.
*D1.067714.	18. 9.1343.	D1.107388.	4.10.1393.
*D1.067719.	14. 6.1352.		

4. Werke mit mehreren Dokumenten für die Jurisdiktion dieses Offizialats:

I. Nagy u. G. Nagy (ed.), *Anjoukori okmánytár*, 7 Bde. (Budapest 1879-1920) 1:324, 327, 336, 377; 6:251

E. Mályusz (ed.), *Zsigmondkori Oklevéltár* (Budapest 1951-1958) 1: Nr. 6185; 2: Nr. 6855, 7049, 7310, 7397

Koller, *Historia Quinqueecclesiarum* 3:299; 4:206-219, 246-359.

[11.]

1. Esztergom, Vác, Offizialat des Bischofs.

2. *MOL (siehe 01/2).

In diesem Archiv findet man nur einzelne Urkunden des Offizialats von Vác. Die Liste der Urkunden wurde aufgrund des Registers "O.m., 42" (siehe: 00/1/3) zusammengestellt.

Das mittelalterliche Archiv der Diözese Vác wurde während der Türkenzeit vernichtet. Vgl.:

P. Balázs, 'Váci Püspöki Levéltár', in Balázs, *Magyarország levéltárai* 320.

3. *1. MOL – Einzelne Urkunden*:

Alle Aktenstücke sind einzelne Urkunden (meistens Gerichtsurkunden), die von dem Vikar von Vác ausgestellt sind.

D1.042007.	30. 9.1331.	D1.069757.	15.10.1415.
D1.042007.	18. 1.1332.	D1.069765.	7. 6.1417.
D1.042706.	31. 3.1399.	D1.069767.	23. 6.1417.
D1.042956.	26. 7.1408.	D1.080555.	12. 3.1436.
D1.043358.	13. 5.1417.	D1.093586.	17. 5.1488.
D1.043426.	7.12.1418.	D1.098140.	13.12.1450.
D1.044473.	13. 7.1447.	D1.098158.	4.11.1474.
D1.046953.	20. 9.1510.	D1.098256.	11. 4.1469.
D1.057722.	13. 2.1456.	D1.105841.	20. 5.1468.
D1.064845.	17. 1.1470.	D1.105842.	28. 4.1468.
D1.065293.	5. 4.1418.	D1.105843.	13. 4.1469.
D1.067994.	17. 8.1513.	D1.105844.	7. 7.1469.
D1.069739.	12.10.1399.	D1.105846.	13. 4.1469.

4. Für die Jurisdiktion dieses Offizialats siehe: 01/4.

Werke mit mehreren Dokumenten für die Jurisdiktion dieses Offizialats:

E. Mályusz (ed.), *Zsigmondkori Oklevéltár* (Budapest 1951-1958).

L.B. Szabó, *Pest megye történetének okleveles emlékei 1002-1599* (Budapest 1938).

[12.]

1. Esztergom, Veszprém, Offizialat des Bischofs.

2. *MOL (siehe 01/2).

In diesem Archiv findet man nur einzelne Urkunden des Offizialats von Veszprém. Die Liste der Urkunden wurde aufgrund des Registers "O.m., 42" (siehe: 00/1/3) zusammengestellt.

3. *1. MOL – Einzelne Urkunden*:

Alle Aktenstücke sind einzelne Urkunden (meistens Gerichtsurkunden), die vom Vikar von Veszprém ausgestellt sind.

D1.040074.	18. 9.1263.	D1.066142.	15. 6.1353.
D1.042788.	19. 1.1403.	D1.066147.	25. 7.1360.
D1.043212.	14. 7.1413.	D1.066260.	20. 7.1438.
D1.049764.	19. 9.1444.	D1.066261.	8. 8.1438.
D1.049873.	1486.	D1.068485.	4. 6.1507.
* D1.050169.	25. 5.1401.	D1.073284.	23. 3.1401.
* D1.050182.	6.10.1401.	D1.073301.	14. 5.1449.
D1.065531.	26. 4.1460.	D1.088380.	18. 8.1462.
D1.066135.	19.10.1348.	D1.088525.	7. 4.1471.

D1.092507.	23. 8.1417.	D1.093583.	21.12.1487.
D1.092512.	31.10.1417.	D1.093718.	14. 5.1505.
D1.092517.	19.11.1417.	D1.093738.	17. 7.1508.
D1.092556.	21. 3.1420.	D1.100538.	2.11.1437.
D1.092744.	15. 5.1428.	D1.104444.	21. 6.1525.
D1.093184.	29. 8.1450.	D1.106714.	21. 3.1502.
D1.093455.	10. 4.1472.	D1.107484.	16.12.1508.

4. Für einige Dokumente über die Jurisdiktion des Offizialats von Veszprém siehe:

Monumenta Romana Episcopatus Vesprimiensis, 4 Bde. (Budapest 1896-1908).

[13.]

1. Kalocsa, Offizialat des Erzbischofs.

2. *MOL (siehe 01/2).

In diesem Archiv findet man nur einzelne Urkunden des Offizialats. Die Liste der Urkunden wurde aufgrund des Registers "O.m., 42" (siehe: 00/1/3) zusammengestellt.

Das mittelalterliche Archiv der Erzdiözese Kalocsa wurde während der Türkenzeit völlig vernichtet. Siehe:

J. Hamvas, 'Kalocsai Érseki Levéltár', in Balázs, *Magyarország levéltárai* 282.

3. *1. MOL – Einzelne Urkunden*:

Alle diese Aktenstücke sind einzelne Urkunden (meistens Gerichtsurkunden), die vom "vicarius bachiensis" ausgestellt sind.

D1.055913.	23. 7.1470.	D1.081109.	16.10.1453.
D1.081099.	6. 8.1453.	D1.082516.	26. 3.1519.
D1.081101.	22. 8.1453.	D1.091986.	10. 2.1392.
D1.081105.	24. 9.1453.		

Alle diese Aktenstücke sind einzelne Urkunden (meistens Gerichtsurkunden), die vom "vicarius colocensis" ausgestellt sind.

D1.041900.	16. 4.1373.	D1.069853.	6. 5.1474.
D1.046101.	14.14.1489.	D1.081419.	1. 1.1461.
D1.054883.	nach 8. 8.1434.	D1.081885.	5. 5.1483.
D1.054892.	22.10.1434.	D1.091988.	29. 3.1392.

4. Die Erzdiözese Kalocsa-Bács kam in s12 durch die Vereinigung von zwei früheren Diözesen (Kalocsa und Bács) zustande. Siehe z.B.:

G. Székely (ed.), *Magyarország története. Előzmények és magyar történet 1242-ig*, Magyarország története 1/2 (Budapest 1984) 2:917, 1117.

Darum hatte das Erzbistum bis zum Ende des Mittelalters 2 Sitze und 2 Kapitel (mit 2 Vikariaten), die gemeinsam den Erzbischof wählten. Siehe:

T. Bogyay, 'Kalocsa', in *Lexikon für Theologie und Kirche*, 5 (Freiburg 1960) 1264.

In den Gerichtsakten nennen sich die Vikare des Erzbischofs bald "vicarius colocensis" bald "vicarius bachiensis". Beide Bezeichnungen kommen auch in den Akten der zweitinstanzlichen Prozesse vor.

Für die Jurisdiktion dieses Offizialats siehe:

M. Érdújhelyi, *A kalocsai érsekség a renaissance-korban* (Zenta 1899) 166-194.

Werke mit mehreren Dokumenten für die Jurisdiktion dieses Offizialats:

S. Katona, *Historia metropolitanae Colocensis ecclesiae*, 2 Bde. (Colocae 1800) 1:363, 477, 494

I. Nagy, u. a. (ed.), *A Zichy család idősebb ágának okmánytára*, 12 Bde. (Budapest 1872-1931)

Zimmermann, *Urkundenbuch* 5:344, 366, 427.

Weitere Literatur zu den 2 Kapiteln und 2 Vikariaten:

J. Városy, 'Disquisitio historica de unione ecclesiarum Colochensis et Bachienisis', in *Schematismus* (Kalocsa 1885) vii-xxxvii

Ortvay, *Geographia* 1:336-7

P. Winkler, *A kalocsai és bácsi érsekség* (Kalocsa 1926)

P. Winkler, *A kalocsai és bácsi főkápalan története alapításától 1935-ig* (Kalocsa 1935)

L. Ipolyi, 'Kalocsai Főegyházmegye', in *Schematismus Dioecesium Hungariae* (Budapest 1984) 745-50

Gyetvai, *Egyházi szervezés* 31-49.

[14.]

1. Kalocsa, Alba Julia (Siebenbürgen), Offizialat des Bischofs.

2. *MOL (siehe 01/2).

Die Liste der einzelnen Urkunden wurde vor allem aufgrund des Registers "O.m., 42." (siehe: 00/1/3) zusammengestellt. Ein bedeutender Teil des Bestandes des Kapitelarchives von Alba Julia und des Konventarchives von Cluj-Mănăştur (Kolozsmonostor) wurde im Jahre 1882 in dieses Archiv überführt. Über die im Jahre 1882 von Alba Julia nach Budapest verschafften Archivalien siehe:

A. Beke, *A Gyulafehérvári Káptalani Levéltárnak czimjegyzéke* (Budapest 1884).

Unter diesen Archivalien kann die weitere Forschung noch Dokumente der geistlichen Gerichtsbarkeit entdecken, vor allem in den Fonds F 2 (Protocolla 1540-1836), F 8 (Metales s16-s18), F 14 (Hilfsbücher s13-s19), und aus dem Konventarchiv von Cluj-Mănăştur (Kolozsmonostor): F 15-16 (Protocolla 1529-1827), F 22 (Protestatoria 1438-1667), F 23 (Testamentaria s16-s19), F 34 (Hilfsbücher s16-s19); Siehe:

Magyar Országos Levéltár 1:77-78.

Capitul rom. cat. din Alba Iulia, Alba Iulia, Rumänien.

Ein Teil des Materials dieses Archivs ist, in Form von Mikrofilm, auch in Ungarn (MOL) zugänglich. Siehe:

I. Borsa, *Romániai levéltári anyagról készült mikrofilmek az Országos Levéltár Filmtárában (1964. január 1-én)* Levéltári leltárak 28 (Budapest: Levéltárak Országos Központja, 1964) 35.

3. *1. MOL – Einzelne Urkunden*:

D1.041523.	15. 7.1363.	D1.073084.	5. 7.1371.
D1.042694.	6. 5.1356.	D1.073661.	16. 1.1349.
D1.042803.	13. 1.1404.	D1.073747.	5. 5.1376.
D1.047434.	28.11.1521.	D1.073771.	4. 7.1382.
D1.047548.	24.11.1524.	D1.073805.	22. 8.1394.
D1.062217.	13.10.1348.	D1.073805.	13.12.1394.
D1.062218.	13.10.1348.	D1.073877.	1. 8.1407.
D1.062272.	8. 5.1348.	D1.073894.	10. 6.1408.
D1.062739.	8.11.1382.	D1.074003.	5. 4.1424.
D1.062748.	29. 5.1390.	D1.074077.	30. 8.1442.
D1.062761.	1. 5.1399.	D1.074080.	10.12.1443.
D1.062844.	11. 5.1448.	D1.074113.	10. 9.1449.
D1.064976.	7. 4.1395.	D1.074114.	13. 5.1451.
D1.064977.	1395.	D1.076994.	4. 5.1351.
D1.065390.	23. 8.1377.	D1.079350.	1401.
D1.067240.	15. 9.1398.	D1.082565.	14.12.1520.
D1.067241.	9. 2.1403.	D1.082569.	26. 3.1521.
D1.067242.	21. 1.1407.	D1.099242.	5.10.1509.
D1.067253.	15. 3.1510.	D1.099253.	31. 1.1511.

4. Für weitere Dokumente und Hinweise auf die Jurisdiktion des geistlichen Gerichts von Alba Julia siehe:

Zimmermann, *Urkundenbuch* 1:226, 2:623, 3:180, 292, 599-602.

F. Zimmermann, *Die Zeugenreihe in den mittelalterlichen Urkunden des Weißenburger Kapitels* (Hermannstadt 1887) 6-11 (= *Archiv des Vereins für siebenbürgische Landeskunde* Neue Folge 21 [1887] 126-131).

Szentirmai, 'Ungarische Diözesankurie', 208.

[15.]

1. Kalocsa, Alba Julia, Offizialat des Vikars "extra Meszes."

2. *MOL (siehe 01/2).

In diesem Archiv findet man nur einzelne Urkunden des Offizialats "extra Meszes". Die Liste der Urkunden wurde aufgrund des Registers "O.m., 42" (siehe: 00/1/3) zusammengestellt.

3. *1. MOL – Einzelne Urkunden*:

Alle diese Aktenstücke sind einzelne Urkunden (meistens Gerichtsurkunden), die von dem Vikar "extra Meszes" des Bischofs von Alba Julia (Siebenbürgen) ausgestellt sind.

D1.070671.	23.12.1337.	D1.072380.	9.11.1350.

D1.076384.	16. 6.1327.	D1.096222.	13. 1.1342.
D1.076892.	18. 7.1348.	D1.096245.	15. 5.1344.
D1.076893.	29. 8.1348.	D1.096246.	14. 6.1344.
D1.090747.	25.10.1349.	D1.096266.	17. 2.1346.
D1.095149.	135?.	D1.096274.	8.11.1346.
D1.095525.	19.11.1399.	D1.096310.	12. 2.1350.
D1.095526.	29.11.1399.	D1.096636.	2. 6.1390.
D1.096061.	18. 4.1315.	D1.096684.	7. 6.1395.
D1.096063.	1316.	D1.098562.	25.10.1349.
D1.096076.	25. 3.1321.	D1.098765.	6. 5.1402.
D1.096218.	7. 5.1341.		

Die folgenden Aktestücke sind meistens Gerichtsurkunden, die vom Pfarrer von Tăşnad (Tasnád) als Vikar für das Gebiet "extra Meszes" ausgestellt sind.

D1.044990.	9.10.1461.	D1.055430.	28. 7.1449.
D1.053142.	14. 1.1402.	D1.055589.	24. 2.1456.
D1.053143.	18. 2.1402.	D1.055593.	5. 5.1456.
D1.053155.	2. 5.1402.	D1.055595.	23. 5.1456.
D1.053156.	19.11.1401.	D1.055596.	1. 7.1456.
D1.053447.	9.11.1408.	D1.055601.	6.10.1456.
D1.053559.	21.11.1410.	D1.055603.	9. 2.1457.
D1.053568.	13. 1.1411.	D1.055605.	30. 3.1457.
D1.053604.	6.10.1411.	D1.055607.	1. 5.1457.
D1.053612.	13. 1.1411.	D1.055608.	1. 7.1457.
D1.053625.	1. 5.1412.	D1.055611.	1. 8.1457.
D1.053983.	13. 1.1418.	D1.055613.	15. 9.1457.
D1.054148.	1420.	D1.055614.	6.10.1457.
D1.054245.	1. 9.1422.	D1.055615.	1457.
D1.054414.	27.12.1424.	D1.055616.	15. 3.1458.
D1.054415.	27.12.1424.	D1.055619.	1. 5.1458.
D1.054417.	16. 1.1425.	D1.055620.	1. 7.1458.
D1.054418.	16. 1.1425.	D1.055738.	17. 9.1462.
D1.054429.	25. 3.1425.	D1.055740.	8.11.1462.
D1.054436.	5. 5.1425.	D1.055741.	17.12.1462.
D1.054437.	5. 5.1425.	D1.055747.	24. 2.1463.
D1.054442.	7. 6.1425.	D1.055751.	17. 3.1463.
D1.054452.	4. 7.1425.	D1.055756.	2. 6.1463.
D1.054520a.	4. 8.1426.	D1.055798.	9. 7.1465.
D1.054801.	11.11.1432.	D1.055804.	9. 1.1466.
D1.054847.	10.12.1433.	D1.056416.	16. 1.1520.
D1.054851.	13. 1.1434.	D1.060761.	8. 4.1440.
D1.054853.	9. 2.1434.	D1.062313.	8.11.1454.
D1.054854.	12. 2.1434.	D1.062315.	7.12.1454.
D1.054855.	11. 2.1434.	D1.062316.	13. 1.1455.
D1.054861.	21. 2.1434.	D1.062317.	13. 1.1455.
D1.054863.	13. 3.1434.	D1.062318.	9. 2.1455.
D1.054866.	5. 5.1434.	D1.062325.	7.12.1463.
D1.055205.	25. 5.1440.	D1.064347.	7. 4.1451.
D1.055214.	4. 7.1440.	D1.065025.	27. 3.1430.
D1.055219.	1. 8.1440.	D1.065068.	1. 7.1452.
D1.055330.	1. 7.1446.	D1.065069.	18. 3.1453.
D1.055336.	1. 8.1446.	D1.065093.	27. 8.1468.
D1.055416.	16. 2.1449.	D1.065094.	9.12.1468.

D1.065081.	4. 6.1460.	D1.086491.	29. 8.1375.
D1.065082.	4. 6.1460.	D1.086491.	?13. 1.1404.
D1.065098.	1469.	D1.096699.	26. 8.1398.
D1.065100.	30. 4.1470.	D1.096740.	2. 8.1402.
D1.065129.	24. 1.1483.	D1.096765.	13. 8.1408.
D1.065160.	25.11.1494.	D1.096981.	4. 5.1420.
D1.065200.	9.10.1512.	D1.096983.	5. 6.1420.
D1.065210.	18. 3.1519.	D1.096990.	13. 1.1421.
D1.065240.	ohne Jahr.	D1.096991.	17. 1.1421.
D1.065473.	30. 5.1520.	D1.096992.	14. 2.1421.
D1.065473.	5. 6.1520.	D1.096993.	10. 3.1421.
D1.065473.	16. 6.1520.	D1.096997.	18. 4.1421.
D1.065473.	3. 9.1520.	D1.096998.	4. 5.1421.
D1.066905.	22. 8.1443.	D1.097001.	5. 7.1420.
D1.066906.	13. 1.1444.	D1.097005.	9.10.1421.
D1.066908.	9.10.1444.	D1.097006.	25.10.1421.
D1.066909.	6.10.1445.	D1.097007.	1421.
D1.066912.	11.11.1445.	D1.097011.	22. 4.1422.
D1.066916.	13. 6.1524.	D1.097014.	12. 2.1423.
D1.070571.	1500.	D1.097019.	4. 6.1423.
D1.070816.	5.10.1419.	D1.097024.	1423.
D1.070971.	17. 1.1474.	D1.097027.	4. 7.1424.
D1.072418.	1. 7.1440.	D1.097031.	28. 2.1425.
D1.072419.	1. 5.1448.	D1.097213.	15. 9.1448.
D1.072420.	10.12.1453.	D1.097264.	13.12.1461.
D1.079350.	um 7.6.1416.	D1.097362.	9. 1.1475.
D1.079622.	25. 7.1420.	D1.098742.	2. 7.1404.
D1.079802.	3. 6.1423.	D1.098804.	23. 8.1414.
D1.079970.	5. 5.1425.	D1.098807.	1414.
D1.079971.	5. 5.1425.	D1.098808.	1414.
D1.079997.	25. 8.1425.	D1.098912.	19. 9.1434.
D1.080423.	1. 5.1433.	D1.098987.	13. 1.1448.
D1.081259.	18. 5.1457.	D1.098994.	11.12.1454.
D1.082009.	22. 8.1489.	D1.099146.	25. 6.1492.
D1.082240.	18. 2.1506.	D1.099185.	26. 9.1498.
D1.082324.	18. 2.1511.	D1.099194.	2. 5.1499.
D1.084330.	1. 5.1408.	D1.105483.	1. 7.1378.
D1.084538.	24.12.1474.	D1.107486.	30. 3.1498.

4. Dem "vicarius de extra Mezes" des siebenbürgischen Bischofs fielen "die Rechtsstreitigkeiten des in der Großen Tiefebene gelegenen Teiles der Diözese zu. Dieses Amt wurde regelmäßig von dem Pfarrer von Szatmárnémeti oder von Tasnád versehen" (G. Bónis, 'Entwicklung', 204). Siehe noch:

J. Karácsonyi, 'Az erdélyi püspökség Erdélyen kivül eső főesperestségei', *Batthyáneum* 1 (1911) 38-46.

[16.]

1. Kalocsa, Csanád, Offizialat des Bischofs.

2. *MOL (siehe 01/2).

In diesem Archiv findet man nur einzelne Urkunden des Offizialats von Csanád. Die Liste der Urkunden wurde aufgrund des Registers "O.m., 42" (siehe: 00/1/3) zusammengestellt.

3. *1. MOL — Einzelne Urkunden*:

Alle Aktenstücke sind einzelne Urkunden (meistens Gerichtsurkunden), die von dem Vikar von Csanád ausgestellt sind.

D1.040469.	6. 6.1325.	D1.054829.	7.11.1433.
D1.042478.	2. 4.1391.	D1.054830.	8.11.1433.
D1.042801.	15.12.1401 und 1403.	D1.054833.	16.11.1433.
D1.042974.	9. 2.1409.	D1.054848.	21.10.1433.
D1.044482.	19. 7.1370.	D1.054852.	17. 1.1434.
D1.051667.	5. 5.1355.	D1.054867.	7. 5.1434.
D1.053237.	4. 5.1405.	D1.054877.	7. 7.1434.
D1.053544.	4. 8.1410.	D1.054909.	22. 2.1435.
D1.053601.	19. 9.1411.	D1.054915.	12. 3.1435.
D1.054821.	19. 8.1433.	D1.085553.	8. 3.1403.
D1.054824.	31. 8.1433.	D1.085554.	10. 3.1403.
D1.054825.	31. 8.1433.	D1.085555.	4. 4.1403.
D1.054826.	4. 9.1433.	D1.085566.	1. 3.1407.
D1.054828.	3.10.1433.	D1.092518.	22.12.1417.

4. Allgemeine Fachliteratur zur Geschichte dieser Diözese mit einigen Hinweisen auf die Jurisdiktion:

K. Juhász, *A csanádi püspökség története*, 8 Bde. (Makó 1930-47)

A. Lotz, 'A csanádi egyházmegye vázlatos története', in *Csanádi egyházmegye jubileumi évkönyve 1980* (Szeged 1980) 9-42

T. Ortvay, J. Szentkláray (ed.), *Történelmi adattár Csanád egyházmegye hajdana és jelenéhez*, 4 Bde. (Temesvár/Budapest 1871-4)

T. Ortvay, *Temes megye és Temesvár város története* 4: *Oklevelek 1183-1430* (Budapest 1896).

[17.]

1. Kalocsa, Oradea, Offizialat des Bischofs.

2. *MOL (siehe 01/2).

In diesem Archiv findet man nur einzelne Urkunden des Offizialats von Oradea. Die Liste der Urkunden wurde aufgrund des Registers "O.m., 42" (siehe: 00/1/3) zusammengestellt.

3. *1. MOL — Einzelne Urkunden*:

Alle diese Aktenstücke sind einzelne Urkunden (meistens Gerichtsurkunden), die von dem Generalvikar von Oradea ausgestellt sind.

D1.040552.	10. 6.1329.	D1.045863.	6. 2.1481.
D1.042005.	6. 5.1376.	D1.047334.	16.12.1519.
D1.043281.	10. 5.1415.	D1.047351.	11. 3.1519.

D1.047351.	20. 4.1520.	D1.086615.	22. 1.1332.
D1.050285.	29. 3.1354.	D1.086912.	24. 5.1310.
D1.050285.	25. 8.1416.	D1.086912.	11.12.1346.
D1.062305.	3.11.1451.	D1.099313.	7.11.1521.
D1.065161.	6. 6.1494.	D1.099615.	29. 3.1354.
D1.072414.	1. 3.1425.	D1.099615.	28.12.1414.
D1.074196.	10. 2.1473.	D1.099615.	9. 1.1415.
D1.074369.	20.11.1517.	D1.107383.	11. 5.1329.
D1.074442.	18.10.1369.	D1.107388.	18.10.1369.
D1.079182.	16. 1.1414.		

4. Anmerkung: Das älteste bekannte Gerichtsregister des mittelalterlichen Ungarns ist ein Protokollbuch des Kathedralkapitels von Oradea (aus den Jahren 1208-1235). Dieses "Regestrum" wurde aber längst vor der Entstehung der Offizialate zusammengestellt. Hrsg.:

J. Karácsonyi, S. Borovszky, *Regestrum Varadinense examinum ferrei candentis ordine chronologico digestum* (Budapest 1903).

Darüber siehe:

I. Zajtay, 'Le registre de Varad. Un document judiciaire du XIIIe siècle', RHD 32 (1954) 527-562

Bónis, 'Entwicklung', 193

V. Bunyitay, *A Váradi Püspökség története alapitásától a jelenkorig*, 1 (Nagyvárad 1883) 69-80.

[18.]

1. Kalocsa, Zagreb, Offizialat des Bischofs.

2. *MOL (siehe 01/2.)

In diesem Archiv findet man nur einzelne Urkunden des Offizialats von Zagreb. Die Liste der Urkunden wurde aufgrund des Registers "O.m., 42" (siehe: 00/1/3) zusammengestellt.

Für weitere Forschungen: Nadbiskupski Archiv, Zagreb und Kapitolski Archiv, Zagreb, Jugoslawien. Ein Teil des Bestandes dieser Archive ist, in Form von Mikrofilm, auch in Ungarn (MOL) zugänglich. Siehe:

I. Borsa, *Jugoszláviai levéltári anyagról készült mikrofilmek az Országos levéltár filmtárában (1963. január 1-én)* Levéltári leltárak 21 (Budapest: Levéltárak Országos Központja, 1963).

3. *1. MOL — Einzelne Urkunden*:

Alle diese Aktenstücke sind einzelne Urkunden, die von dem Generalvikar von Zagreb ausgestellt sind.

D1.066611.	29. 5.1507.	D1.101004.	28. 6.1484.
D1.082960.	s15.	D1.104282.	12. 3.1516.
D1.087913.	3. 5.1418.	D1.104413.	18. 7.1523.
D1.088361.	9. 2.1461.		

4. Zum Vikar wurde meistens, wie auch in den anderen Bischofssitzen, ein Erzdechant ernannt. Siehe:

Smičiklas, *Codex diplomaticus regni Croatiae, Dalmatiae et Slavoniae*, 17 Bde. (Zagrabiae 1904-1967) 10:278

Bónis, 'Entwicklung', 203-204 (in diesem Artikel werden auch andere Urkunden erwähnt, die nicht vom Generalvikar ausgestellt wurden, aber mit dem geistlichen Gericht von Zagreb verbunden sind).

[19.]

1. Kalocsa, Zagreb, Offizialat des Propstes von Čazma.

2. *MOL (siehe 01/2).

In diesem Archiv findet man nur einzelne Urkunden des Offizialats von Čazma. Die Liste der Urkunden wurde aufgrund des Registers "O.m., 42" (siehe: 00/1/3) zusammengestellt.

Für weitere Forschungen: Archiv Čazmanskog kaptola, Varaždin, Jugoslawien.

3. *1. MOL – Einzelne Urkunden*:

D1.045752.	23.10.1478.	D1.101230.	6. 5.1496.
D1.094840.	13. 4.1518.	D1.101255.	5. 5.1498.
D1.094843.	29. 4.1518.	D1.104007.	13. 5.1494.
D1.094853.	5. 9.1519.	D1.104196.	6. 4.1508.
D1.097695.	14. 3.1523.	D1.107118.	4. 5.1498.
D1.100913.	29. 3.1479.	D1.107608.	18. 3.1491.

4. Für die Geschichte dieses Offizialats siehe:

J. Jerney, 'A magyarországi káptalanok és konventek mint hielmes és hiteles helyek története', *Magyar Történelmi Tár* 2 (1855) 43-44

L. Balics, *A római katholikus egyház története Magyarországban*, 2.2 (Budapest 1890) 61

Ortvay, *Geographia* 2:734-737

J. B. Tkalčić, *Monumenta historica Episcopatus Zagrabiensis s. XII-XIII*, 2 Bde. (Zagrabiae 1873-1874) passim.

Anmerkung: Der Propst von Čazma residierte in Zagreb und war Mitglied des dortigen Kapitels. Der Richter des Offizialats von Čazma war der "locumtenens" des Propstes.

GIOVANNI MINNUCCI

VI. Italia

Editor's Introduction

Italy was probably the home of the first organized ecclesiastical courts in Western Europe. It is also clear that a considerable amount survives of the records of these courts. Our group was not, however, successful in obtaining many reports on the Italian archives. Dr. Minnucci promised and produced a report on the records presently contained in the state archive in Siena. For the rest, we obtained some tantalizing hints, but ultimately no reports.

For reasons discussed in the General Introduction, Italian archives are difficult. What Dr. Minnucci shows here, as Prof. Dolezalek has shown elsewhere, is that the Italian archives are rich. Clearly the history of the medieval ecclesiastical courts will not be fully known until someone can survey the holdings of the Italian archives and come to master their contents. We hope that the relative success we have had elsewhere will stimulate someone to undertake this work in Italy.

[01.]

1. Montalcino (cr. 1462), officialità del vescovo.

2. *Siena, Archivio di Stato, via Banchi di Sotto, 52, I-53100 Siena.

Alcuni documenti riguardanti la giurisdizione ecclesiastica sono conservati nel Fondo notarile ante-cosimiano. Per ogni notizia ad esso relativa e per il suo inventario v.:

G. Catoni e S. Fineschi, *Archivio notarile (1221-1862)*, Ministero dei beni culturali e ambientali, Pubblicazioni degli Archivi di Stato 87 (Roma 1975).

I numeri di riferimento che daremo qui di seguito sono tratti dall'inventario citato.

3. *762. 119 fols. 1498-1518. Atti giudiziari, inquisitorie e petizioni.

Notaio: Angelini Baldassarre di Giacomo d'Angelo da Montalcino (Siena). Fascicolo contenente 119 fogli raggruppati in vari blocchi. Numerosi i fogli sparsi e fuori posto, raramente numerati. Vi sono questioni relative a locazioni, a revoche di interdetto, a liti matrimoniali. Da notare, inoltre, una causa davanti all' "u.i.doct. d. Alexandro Petruccio" di Siena podestà e capitano della città di

Montalcino, ed una "inquisitio" per il ferimento di una persona in luogo sacro (Abbazia di S. Antimo nella diocesi di Montalcino).

*763. 197 fols. 1508-1516. Atti giudiziari, inquisitorie e petizioni.

Notaio: Angelini Baldassarre di Giacomo d'Angelo da Montalcino (Siena). Fascicolo contenente 197 fogli, alcuni dei quali raggruppati in blocchi. Fogli quasi mai numerati e moltissimi sparsi. Vi sono ad es. dispense per matrimonio, inquisizioni per percosse a religiosi. Da notare una lettera, vergata da notaio, con sigillo di "Hieronimus de Picolominibus" vescovo di Pienza e Montalcino. Uno dei blocchi, di ff. 34 (parzialmente numerato), contiene una causa nella quale è parte il cardinale Francesco Borgia in qualità di commendatario della prepositura di S. Lorenzo di Percenna della diocesi di Pienza.

[02.]

1. Siena, officialità dell'arcivescovo (vescovo fino al 1458).

2. *Siena, Archivio di Stato (vedi sopra 01/2).

3. *802. 351 fols. 1499-1508. "Cause delegate".

Notaio: Carnevali Francesco di Giacomo da Montalcino (Siena). Fascicolo contenente 351 fogli raggruppati in vari blocchi. Numerosi fogli sparsi e fuori posto, raramente numerati. Nella foderina cartacea che li raccoglie, in scrittura moderna (di mano, probabilmente, di archivista del secolo scorso che aveva tentato di riordinare il fascicolo): "Cause delegate — Rogatorie testimoniali — Inquisitorie — Processi per concessioni ecclesiastiche — Lettere compulsoriali etc." Si tratta, infatti, di richieste avanzate da ecclesiastici e da ordini religiosi all'autorità ecclesiastica per effettuare permute e vendite di terreni, contestazioni per possesso indebito, liti etc. Da notare alcune rogatorie testimoniali, relative ad una causa nella quale è parte "Hieronimus de Picolominibus Pientinensis et Ilcinensis episcopus." Solo l'ultimo blocco, costituito da 102 cc. numerate, è rilegato, anche se in maniera approssimativa, con un pezzo di pergamena sulla costola. Nel frontespizio, in alto, quasi illeggibile: "Compulsoria Constantini Petri de Sozzinis .... ‹Bindinum ?› de Thomasis."

*857. 231 fols. 1480-1515. Atti processuali del vicario generale e di commissari apostolici.

Notaio: Feliciano di ser Neri da Sarteano (Siena). Fascicolo contenente 231 fogli raggruppati in vari blocchi. Raramente i fogli sono numerati. Molti quelli sparsi. Nella foderina cartacea che li raccoglie, in scrittura moderna (v. n. 802): "Processi per concessioni ecclesiastiche — Inquisitorie — Rogatorie testimoniali — Brevi — Formule etc." All'inizio un blocco di 16 cc., rilegato in pergamena, relativo alla richiesta di una vendita di terreno fatta da un ordine religioso femminile. Troviamo, inoltre, una permuta con i monaci di Monte Oliveto Maggiore, una "inquisitio" contro un chierico per furto e sodomia, cause per debiti, una lettera con sigillo intestata: "INNOCENTIUS PAPA VIII^{s}" del 3 febbraio 1492 — anno settimo del pontificato. Vi è infine l'ultimo blocco di 70 cc. (numerate) rilegato in pergamena già scritta. Vi è annotato sulla parte anteriore, in inchiostro rosso: "Compulsorie humiliatorum."

*1027. 155 fols. 1491-1494. "Cause delegate."

Notaio: Andreucci Matteo di Gaspero da Siena. Fascicolo contenente 155 fogli raggruppati in 5 blocchi e 6 fogli sciolti. Ogni blocco è costituito da ulteriori piccoli gruppi (numerati) di fogli. Vi sono contestazioni di possesso, occupazioni indebite di proprietà ecclesiastiche. Vi è inoltre una "accusatio seu inquisitio" contro un presbitero di Rapolano reo di aggressione ai danni di un presbitero senese. Infine, lettera con sigillo del vicario generale della diocesi di Arezzo.

*1142. 56 fols. 1491-1500. Atti giudiziari di commissari apostolici.

Notaio: Selva Mattia di Cristoforo da Montefollonico. Fascicolo contenente 56 fogli, non numerati, e raccolti in 6 blocchi e 2 fogli sciolti. Vi sono richieste di essere esonerati dal pagamento di decime, di restituzione di beni indebitamente sottratti, petizioni. Interessanti 2 lettere rispettivamente del vicario generale della diocesi di Grosseto e della diocesi di Pienza. Su quest'ultima: stemma episcopale dei Piccolomini. Da notare, infine, una dichiarazione rilasciata dai Priori, Governatori e Capitano del Popolo di Siena, nella quale si afferma che il notaio "Dominicus olim Viti de Pientia" è nella matricola dei giudici e dei notai della città. In basso, a sin. della dichiarazione, grande sigillo assai sciupato.

*1333. 356 fols. 1507-1564. "Cause delegate."

Notaio: Costanti Raffaello di Cristoforo da Montalcino (Siena). Fascicolo contenente 356 fogli raggruppati in numerosi blocchi, numerati da la 68 (ne mancano però molti). Numerosi i fogli sciupati, anche con perdita di scrittura e macchie di umidità che rendono difficile la lettura. Nella foderina cartacea che li raccoglie, in scrittura moderna (v. n. 802): "Cause delegate e altri frammenti di procedimenti per vendite, permute, cambiamento di possesso di beni ecclesiastici — impedimenti matrimoniali etc. Appelli — Testimonianze." Numerose le istituzioni ecclesiastiche e gli ordini religiosi presenti come parti in causa: Monaci di Monte Oliveto, dell'Abbazia Ardenga, dell'Abbazia all'Arco (o di Santa Musticla) e "l'Operario" della chiesa cattedrale di Siena.

*1134. 466 fols. 1508-1537. "Cause delegate."

Notaio: Costanti Raffaello di Cristoforo da Montalcino (Siena). Fascicolo contenente 466 fogli raggruppati in vari blocchi. Nella foderina cartacea che li raccoglie, in scrittura moderna (v. n. 802): "Cause delegate e Atti frammentari di procedimenti per concessioni e rivendicazioni riguardanti beni ecclesiastici, annullamenti di matrimonio, censure e imputazioni d'eresia, di scandalo etc. Appelli — Rogatorie tesimoniali etc." Da notare le numerosissime lettere papali cardinalizie con le quali si rimettono le cause ai canonici senesi, o con le quali si interviene sulla causa medesima. Si segnalano una lettera di Leone X indirizzata a 2 canonici ed altre emanate sotto i pontificati di Adriano VI, Clemente VII, Paolo III. Le lettere, in pergamena, sono state quasi sempre utilizzate come rilegatura agli incartamenti nei quali si tratta delle cause a cui le lettere medesime si riferiscono.

*1335. 348 fols. 1538-1557. "Cause delegate."

Notaio: Costanti Raffaello di Cristoforo da Montalcino (Siena). Fascicolo contenente 348 fogli raggruppati in vari blocchi. Nella foderina cartacea che li raccoglie, in scrittura moderna (v. n. 802): "Cause delegate e Atti frammentari di procedimenti per concessioni e rivendicazioni riguardanti persone e beni ecclesiastici, per impedimenti matrimoniali, censure, imputazioni di eresia etc. Appelli — Protestazioni — Rogatorie testimoniali." Anche qui da notare le numerosissime lettere (valgono le considerazioni fatte per il n. precedente), fra cui una di Paolo III ed un'altra di Guido Ascanio Sforza. Vi è, infine, una causa relativa alla vendita di alcuni beni dell'Abbazia di S. Galgano.

[03.]

1. Siena (Pisa fino al 1458), Massa e Populónia, officialità del vescovo.

2. *Siena, Archivio di Stato (vedi sopra 01/2).

3. *406. 47 cc. 1434. Atti giudiziari.

Notaio: Barnaba di Giacomo da Massa (Massa Marittima in prov. di Grosseto). Il registro è di cc. 12. Vi è allegato un inserto relativo ad una contestazione di possesso della chiesa parrocchiale di S. Claudio di Mesreyo della diocesi di Sées, suffraganea della metropolitana di Rouen in Francia (1425-1440). L'inserto è composto di 35 cc. numerate da 63 a 97 (le cc. 71 e 72, bianche, sono fuori posto).

CARLA DE GLOPPER-ZUIJDERLAND

VII. The Netherlands

Editor's Preface

Until the ecclesiastical reorganization of the Low Countries in 1559, most of the modern Netherlands belonged to the diocese of Utrecht (Traiectensis in Tangl's *Provinciale* prov. Coloniensis). Since we are ignoring the post-1559 developments for purposes of these reports, gathering the surviving material for Utrecht seemed like a relatively straight-forward, if not very interesting, task. As the following report shows, it turned out to be not at all straight-forward, but of considerable interest. The reason for both the difficulty and the interest lies in the fact that considerable survivals of the records of the medieval officiality of the diocese of Utrecht have been classed with the records of its five subordinate chapters, and some of the older descriptions of these records have proved to be inaccurate. The following report, therefore, must be regarded as in the nature of work in progress. In particular, the author warns that she has not been able to go through the archives of two of the five subordinate chapters (that of the cathedral (dom) and st Marie), which may well prove to contain similar material to that discovered in the records of the chapters of Oudmunster (st Salvator), st Pieter and st Jan.

The organization of ecclesiastical jurisdiction in the diocese was somewhat unusual: It was a large diocese, divided into eleven archdeaconries. Nine of these archdeaconries were possessed corporately by collegiate churches. The canons, without participation by the bishop, elected one of their number as provost (*prepositus*), who exercised ordinary power as archdeacon. Five of these collegiate churches were in Utrecht: the cathedral, Oudmunster (st Salvator), st Pieter, st Jan, and st Marie. Four were in other cities: st Walburg in Tiel/Arnhem, st Maarten in Emmerich, st Lebuinus in Deventer, and st Plechelmus in Oldenzaal. In addition the *chorepiscopus* (a canon of the cathedral not in episcopal orders) exercised archidiaconal powers over a small group of parishes, and there was an archdeacon, called the provost of West-Friesland, who was also a canon of the cathedral. Appeal from sentences of the officials of the archdeaconries lay to the official of the bishop.

The records also mention *provisores*, who seem to have been *officiales foranei*, who were appointed by the bishop to exercise jurisdiction, in some cases *quasi-*

ordinaria, in some cases *delegata*, in certain areas. Appeal from these *provisores* also lay to the official principal in Utrecht.

[01.]

1. Köln, Utrecht, officiality of the bishop (archbishop after 1559).

In the Middle Ages most of the present-day Netherlands belonged to the diocese of Utrecht. The present Dutch secular provinces of Noord-Brabant and Limburg, however, belonged, for the most part, to the diocese of Liège, and some of the border lands of the other eastern provinces belonged to the dioceses of Osnabrück and of Münster and to that of Köln proper. In 1559, King Philip II ordered a new division of the dioceses in the Low Countries: Utrecht became a provincial see with suffragan sees in Middelburg, Deventer, Haarlem, Groningen and Leeuwarden. The present secular provinces of Noord-Brabant and Limburg became, for the most part, parts of the dioceses of Antwerpen, 's-Hertogenbosch and Roermond (province of Mechelen) and of the diocese of Liège (province of Köln).

2. *Rijksarchief in de provincie Utrecht, Alexander Numankade 201, 3572 KW Utrecht.

Most of the records of the officiality belong to the archive of the bishops of Utrecht. In medieval times the archive of the bishops was kept in different places until c1460, when the castle of Wijk bij Duurstede became the central archive depository. The archive was handed over to Charles V at the time of the coveyance of the temporalities of the see in 1528. It seems that many records were lost during the transport of the archive to Holland, while the remainder was kept in Gouda under very bad conditions. We may presume that during the Reformation people had little regard for these ecclesiastical, Catholic records, and many of them were probably simply discarded. Inventory:

S. Muller Fz., *Catalogus van het archief der Bisschoppen van Utrecht* (Utrecht 1906).

During this present research it turned out that some records of the officiality are listed among the archives of the five Utrecht chapters and that the descriptions given are sometimes erroneous. The Rijksarchief plans therefore to reconstruct, if possible, the archive of the officiality of the bishop and to compile a new inventory of the episcopal archive. Until this is done, however, all the old references remain valid.

3. *1. Case Registers:*

*Oudmunster nr. 1888. 86 fols. October 1442 - September 1445. Case register.

Register of cases of one notary, Jan Bol, in chronological order. Mostly day-by-day entries. Many pledges for payments of debts and *cautiones*, some marriage cases, some ecclesiastical cases, much procedural material. The sewing of some quires has disintegrated, and the first quire is damaged.

The second quire (Apr. - Sep. 1443) used to belong to the manuscript collection and was dated 1543, but the script and dating suggested 1443, a suspicion confirmed by the fact that one of the people mentioned was a known office-holder of the s15/m. Later on this quire turned out to be the missing part of the register of Jan Bol and was placed with it.

The other quires belong to the archive of the chapter of Oudmunster (st Salvator) and were described together as an act book of the officiality of the archdeacon of Oudmunster. But the kind of cases and the geographical data confirm that this is an act book of the officiality of the bishop, and thus it appears that this is the oldest surviving court book of the officiality.

*Oudmunster nr. 29-1. 160 fols. 1467-1469. Case register.

Register of cases by one anonymous notary. Mostly day-by-day entries. Many pledges for payments of debts, *cautiones*, some marriage cases, quarrels between clerks about vicarages and other *beneficia*.

*Bisschoppen nr. 247. Quire of 28 fols. 1468-73. Case register.

Mostly day-by-day entries by one notary, J. Vliegher. Debt transactions, marriage cases, sexual offenses. The entries are sometimes very short; they often record steps in the procedure, but do not tell what the case was about.

*Bisschoppen nr. 247-a-1. 155 fols. 1477-81. Register of cases by two notaries, Vliegher and Hoern:

fol 1-12v, Oct. 1478 - Apr. 1479: an attempt by one notary to gather together the *processus* of single cases, resulting in many blank pages.

fol 13-84v, Sep. 1477 - Jan. 1479 (the other notary, using a chronological style). Mostly civil cases: marriage, testaments, debts, property, depositions, quarrels between clerks about vicarages. The entries often record steps in the procedure, but not what the case was about.

fol 85-110, Sep. 1477 - Feb. 1479. Very short entries, mostly confessions of debt and appointments of proctors.

fol 110v-113. Blank.

fol 113v-125v, Jan. 1479 - May 1479. Like fols. 13-84v.

fol 126-128v. Blank.

fol 129-129v. *De scribis et notariis causarum*, part of the style of the court.

fol 130-134v. 1479-81. Like fols. 13-84v.

fol 135-143v. Blank.

fol 144-154v. Account of money received in various cases by notary Hoern only.

*Bisschoppen nr. 247-a-2. 31 docs. 1477-81. Docs.

With reference to cases in nr. 247-a-1, mostly concerning debts.

*Oudmunster nr. 30-1. 25 fols. 1480/ex - March 1483. Case register.

Register of cases by one notary, Maarten Kaluwe. Contents comparable to Bisschoppen nrs. 247 and 247-a-1. Contains some cases before official of archdeacon of Tiel/Arnhem.

*Oudmunster nr. 30-2. 108 fols. March 1483 - December 1485. Case register.

Register of cases, in chronological order, by one notary, Maarten Kaluwe. Contents comparable to Bisschoppen nrs. 247 and 247-a-1. Not always clear what the case was about.

*Bisschoppen nr. 249-1. 38 fols. 1496-99. Case register.

Register of cases, in chronological order, by one notary, Gerard Beyer. Contents comparable to nrs. 247 and 247-a-1. Again many debts.

fol 1-21. Jan. 1499 - May, 1499

fol 21v-24v. Blank.

fol 25-38v. 1496-99.

*Bisschoppen nr. 251-1. 117 fols. 1517. Case register.

Register of cases by one notary, Franco Beyer. Contents comparable to nrs. 247 and 247-a-1. From about fol 50 very difficult to read: damaged by water.

*Bisschoppen nr. 251-2. 15 docs. 1517. Docs.

With reference to cases in nr. 251-1.

2. *Mixed registers*:

Some notaries worked on a kind of free-lance basis for several officialities at a time and often wrote down procedural steps in different cases in one register. A list of these registers follows here:

*Oudmunster nr. 329. 283 fols (bad condition), c1350-s15/in, 1488-89. Formulary.

Formulary of notary Lambert de Weird (c1350), continued by Jacob van Scoenbreve (s14/2-s15/in). From fol. 240: letters of the chapter of Oudmunster written by notary Tielman Momfelen, 1488-89.

Mostly docs of the chapter of Oudmunster, some material of the official of the bishop and of the official of the archdeacon of Oudmunster: *citatio*, *excommunicatio*, *inhibitio*, order for *exhumatio*, *de modo appellationis super interlocutoriam*, *forme libellorum* etc.

fol 166-168v: treatise *qualiter procedatur in iudicia*. Bishop, archdeacons and deans are called *ordinarii*.

fol 169-182: examples from *processus*.

fol 221-238v: examples from officiality of archbishop of Köln.

*Oudmunster nr. 331. 210 fols. c1470-80. *Formularius novus*.

Of notary Willem Buer. Contains much judicial material from the officials of the bishop, of the archdeacon of the cathedral, of the archdeacon of Oudmunster and of the archdeacon of Deventer. *Citatio*, *inhibitio*, many *sententie*, divorce cases.

*Oudmunster nr. 32. 189 fols. 1539-60. *Minute diversorum instrumentorum constitutionum ac substitutionum*.

Of notary Jacob van Medenblick. Contains some material of the official of the bishop and of the official of the archdeacon of Oudmunster concerning vicarages: *citatio*, *inhibitio*, *sententia*.

Although the following registers date from just after our period they may contain information necessary to reconstruct the history of the medieval officialities:

*Oudmunster nr. 337-1; 337-2. 37 fols; 70 fols. March-November 1572; November 1572-March 1574. Registers of cases.

By one notary, Henric Rutghers van Ommen, in chronological order. Cases of official of the archbishop, officials of the archdeacons and of, *iudices commissarii* of different chapters. 337-1: bad condition, damaged. Not always clear for whom the notary is working and what the case was about. 337-2: much better, damaged only in the end. Gives more information about officials and cases. Marriage cases, many debts, quarrels about vicarages, cases about prebends, case about *defloratio*.

*Oudmunster nr. 34-2. 147 fols. 1574-82. Register of cases.

By one notary, Jan Mersman, in chronological order. Mostly cases of the official of the archdeacon of Oudmunster and some cases of the official of the archbishop, of the official of the archdeacon of the cathedral, of the official of the archdeacon of Arnhem and of *iudices commissarii* of different chapters. Not always clear for whom the notary is working and what the case was about. Debts, appointments of proctors, testaments, marriage cases, *cautiones*, many cases about vicarages, case about bigamy. The end of this register is damaged by water.

3. *Statutes, styles, formularies, etc.*:

*Bisschoppen nr. 248-1. 52 fols. s15/ex. *Diversorium*.

By notary Gerard ten Brink, containing:

fol 4-8. Statutes for the courts of the official of the bishop and of the official of the archdeacon of the cathedral, July 1466, with a list of costs. Ed. Joosting/Muller, *Bronnen* 6:4-18.

fol 8v-12. *Liber de processu iudicis*, style of the court. Ed. Joosting/Muller, *Bronnen* 6:219-57.

fol 37-37v. Formulae.

fol 38-40. *Fforma processus*, style of the court. Ed. Joosting/Muller, *Bronnen* 6:297-305.

fol 40-41v. Style of the court *in parvis causis*. Ed. Joosting/Muller, *Bronnen* 6:289-97.

Bisschoppen nr. 248-2. 2 docs. s15/ex. Docs.

With reference to nr. 248-1.

*Collectie handschriften nr. 300 zwart. Quire of 18 fols. Statutes.

Copy, dating from s18/e of statutes of the court by Bishop David of Burgundy, 1470. Ed. Joosting/Muller, *Bronnen* 6:20-38.

*Dom nr. 3207. 505 fols. 1525-1542. Statutes.

fol 1-21. Statutes of the court by Bishop Philip of Burgundy, c1520. Ed. Joosting/Muller, *Bronnen* 6:55-87.

fol 23v-30v. Statutes of the court by Bishop Frederick de Baden, c1506. Ed. Joosting/Muller, *Bronnen* 6:40-54.

*Bisschoppen nr. 539. Quire of 12 fols. c1540. Statutes and style of the court.

Ed. Joosting/Muller, *Bronnen* 6:87-99, 309-12.

*Bisschoppen nr. 541. Quire of 27 fols (some blank). s16/2. Style of the court, with some formulae.

*Bisschoppen nr. 250-1. 45 fols. s16/1. Formulary.

Of Gerard Beyer, notary of the court. Much procedural material: e.g., *inhibitio, citatio, littera sententie*, etc.

*Bisschoppen nr. 250-2. 210 fols. s16/1. Formulary.

Of Gerard Beyer, notary of the court. Contents comparable to nr. 250-1.

*Bisschoppen nr. 250-3. 21 docs. s16/1. Docs.

With reference to nr. 250-2.

*Bisschoppen nr. 540. Quire of 4 fols. c1560. Register.

Containing abbreviations, calendar, terms, formulae, used in the court and some notes by a notary of the court.

4. Accounts:

Bisschoppen nr. 244. 2 rolls. 1334 and 1336. Accounts of the officiality.

Both incomplete at the beginning. Ed. Muller, *Registers en rekeningen* 1:522-26.

Bisschoppen nr. 245. Quire of 10 fols with 7 docs. 1524. *Computatio jurium receptorum ratione audientiarie.*

5. Collected docs:

*Bisschoppen nr. 541a. 124 fols. 1482-1564. *Miscellanea juris canonici.*

Collection of original docs, bound together, containing: marriage cases, quarrels between clerks about vicarages, cases about acts of violence by clerks, one case about a suicide attempted by a clerk.

6. Individual docs:

*Bisschoppen nrs. 237-242. 9 docs. 1293-1451. Docs with reference to attempts to define the respective judicial powers of the bishop and of the various archdeacons.

*Dom nr. 4241. 74 fols (bound in parchment) and 20 fols. 1385, 1386. Two registers.

Containing copies of the *processus* in a case between a clerk and a layman about tithes and goods, first before the official of the bishop and then before the official of the archbishop of Köln. Full-scale *processus* with libels, etc.

Bisschoppen nr. 246. 3 docs. 1388. Confession, claim and sentence in case against a false auxiliary bishop.

Bisschoppen nr. 243b. 10 docs. c1410-1527. Letters addressed to the official of the bishop.

Dom nr. 4250. Quire of 12 fols. 1418. Depositions of witnesses about a false account.

Dom nr. 4301. Quire of 6 fols. 1495. Depositions of witnesses about a priest who wounded a woman.

*Dom nr. 4387. 28 docs. c1470-1577. Docs, mostly copies, about cases brought before the official of the bishop.

Marriage cases, debts, case between the Hospitalers and the Teutonic Order.

Bisschoppen nr. 247-a-3 to 13. 11 docs. 1472-1517. Citations.

Bisschoppen nrs. 243-243a. 62 and 26 fols. 1523-1525. Docs in jurisdictional dispute.

With reference to a disagreement about ecclesiastical jurisdiction between the bishop and the archdeacon of the cathedral, on the one hand, and the Holy Roman Emperor (Charles V), on the other.

Bisschoppen nr. 541b. 1 doc. 1531. Letter about heresy.

*Bisschoppen nr. 541c. Quire of 23 fols. 1546. Depositions of witnesses about the behaviour of someone's mistress.

Bisschoppen nr. 541d. 2 docs. 1544, 1556. Aggravations of excommunications.

The following lists individual case docs from the officiality of the bishop which are found in the archives of the Utrecht chapters of Oudmunster (st Salvator), st Pieter and st Jan. The archives of the chapters of the cathedral and st Marie have not yet been examined:

*St. Pieter nr. 384. 3 rolls (4.50, 6.15 and 28 metres long). 1344-50. Case about tithes between chapter and woman.

Almost complete *processus*; for the sentence see below nr. 385.

*St. Pieter nr. 385. 1 doc. 1350. Sentence in St. Pieter nr. 384.

*St. Pieter nr. 260. 4 docs. 1357. Tithes case between chapter and laymen.

Incomplete: *citatio, inhibitio, excommunicatio.*

*St. Pieter nr. 255. 2 docs. 1375. Sentence in tithes case between chapter and layman.

*St. Jan nr. 379. 4 docs. 1377. Case between chapter and vicar concerning land.

Taxatio expensarum, sentence.

*St. Pieter nr. 911. 1 doc. 1381. Sentence by *iudex commissarius*, appointed by official of the bishop, in case about rent between chapter and layman.

For *taxatio* see below nr. 912.

*St. Pieter nr. 912. 1 doc. 1381. *Taxatio expensarum* for St. Pieter nr. 911.

*St. Jan nr. 1244. 1 doc. 1383. *Excommunicatio* in case about land between chapter and laymen.

*Oudmunster nr. 1437. 36 fols. 1387. Case about back rent between chapter and laymen.

Copy. Complete *processus*.

*Oudmunster nr. 1436. 38 fols and 2 docs. 1387-88. Case about back rent between chapter and laymen.

Complete *processus*.

*Oudmunster nr. 907-1; nr. 907-2. 25 fols; 68 fols and 6 docs. 1394, 1396. Case about tithes in Scherpenisse between chapter and layman.

Case brought first before official of bishop and official of the archdeacon of the cathedral, then before official of archbishop of Köln (nr. 907-1), finally before papal delegate (nr. 907-2). Very complete, with some references to process before official of the bishop.

*St. Jan nr. 231. 10 docs. 1396-99. Tithes case between chapter and layman.

Only sentence of official of bishop. Other docs from the official of the archbishop of Köln.

*St. Jan nr. 504. 1 doc. 1399. Sentence in case between chapter and layman about rent.

*St. Jan nr. 1358. 2 docs. 1400. Order of official to secular judge in case between chapter and layman, that was wrongly brought before the secular judge, to give up the case.

*St. Jan nr. 137. 1 doc. 1401. Sentence in case about back rent between chapter and canon of the cathedral.

*St. Jan nr. 1416. 1 doc. 1405. *Excommunicatio* in case between chapter and laymen about seizure of land.

*St. Jan nr. 809. 5 docs. 1407-11. Case about land between chapter and woman.

Citatio, monitio, excommunicatio, settlement.

*St. Jan nr. 1242. 2 docs. 1409. *Citatio* in case about land between chapter and laymen.

*St. Jan nr. 731. 16 fols. 1412-13. Register of docs in case about land between chapter and laymen.

Complete *processus*.

*St. Pieter nr. 1072. 1 doc. 1419. Copies of docs in case about land belonging to a vicarage.

Citatio, positiones et articuli, depositions of witnesses.

*St. Pieter nr. 345. 1 doc. 1424. Sentence in tithes case between chapter and layman.

*St. Jan nr. 1254. 166 fols, bound together. 1426-66. Register.

fol 1-38. Depositions of witnesses before official of the bishop in case about payments between vicar of st Jan and laymen, with *positiones et articuli*, 1426-1432.

fol 39-60. Case of fol. 61-166 on appeal before official of archbishop of Köln, 1466.

fol 61-166. Case before official of the bishop about payments between vicar of st Jan and laymen, 1464-1466. Full scale *processus*.

*St. Pieter nr. 660. 6 quires, total 72 fols. 1434. Register.

The end is damaged. Docs in case about land between chapter and layman, first before the abbot of Oostbroek, second before the official of the bishop. Complete *processus*.

*St. Pieter nr. 331. 1 doc (damaged). 1435. Sentence in tithes case between chapter and layman.

*St. Jan nr. 733. 1 quire of 22 fols and 30 docs. 1436-64. Case about right to dig peat between chapter and local authorities of Baarn.

First before official of the bishop, later before other judges. Docs from before the official include: libels, *articuli*, depositions of witnesses, no sentence, 1436-1438.

*St. Pieter nr. 292. 10 docs. 1445-53. Tithes case between chapter and layman.

Incomplete: *sentencia, taxatio expensarum, monitio*.

*St. Pieter nr. 497. 1 doc. 1447. Sentence in case about back rent between chapter and layman.

*Oudmunster nr. 330. 47 fols. 1488-89. Inheritance case between two brothers, a clerk and a layman.

Before official of the bishop and official of the archdeacon of the cathedral, after a sentence of the *provisor* of Zuid-Beveland. Copies. Incomplete *processus*, originally there were more than 47 fols.

*St. Jan 1000-1; 1000-2; 1000-3. 140 fols; 191 fols; 84 fols, but fol 1-48 are missing. 1504-09. Case about payments between heirs of *prepositus* and local authorities of Mijdrecht.

First before official of the bishop as *iudex commissarius* of the official of the archdeacon of st Jan and then before the dean of the cathedral as *iudex commissarius* of the pope.

1000-1: official of the bishop: *libelli, positiones et articuli, taxatio expensarum*, depositions of witnesses.

1000-2: official of the bishop: replication, duplication, triplication, sentence.

1000-3: dean of the cathedral.

*St. Pieter nr. 470a. 8 quires (total: 96 fols). 1530. Depositions of witnesses in case about land between chapter and layman.

*St. Jan nr. 252. 1 doc. 1537. *Citatio* in case about church in Zoelmond.

*St. Jan nr. 253. 1 doc. 1548. *Monitio* to vicar in Zoelmond to pay debts.

*St. Pieter nr. 20. 2 quires (total: 16 fols) and 3 docs. 1569. Case about prebend between two canons.

Incomplete: judicial advice and duplication.

*Oudmunster nr. 219. 33 fols. 1573. Case about *incorporatio* of church in Vianen.

Almost complete *processus*; no sentence.

*Oudmunster nr. 338. Quire of 4 fols. 1574-75. Notes about case about prebend.

Probably extracts from a register of cases.

*Oudmunster nr. 1898. 182 fols bound together. 1574-75. Case about *ius presentationis* of church in Hagesteijn.

First before official of archdeacon of Oudmunster, then before official of the archbishop. Complete *processus*, with many depositions of witnesses.

4. There is not enough material for a full-scale history of the medieval officiality; there is hardly any material about the criminal jurisdiction, and the other material is skimpy. But with patience a researcher can draw some conclusions about the civil jurisdiction and the procedure.

Important editions are:

Joosting/Muller, *Bronnen*

Muller, *Registers en rekeningen.*

Studies of the court and the officiality:

F. Ketner, 'Het officialaat in het bisdom Utrecht', in F. Ketner, *Stichtse Studiën* (Utrecht 1974) 10-20

C.C. de Glopper-Zuijderland, 'De officiaal van Utrecht als beoorkonder van vrijwillige rechtshandelingen ten behoeve van de vijf Utrechtse kapittels in de 14[e] eeuw', *Verslagen en mededelingen van de Stichting tot uitgaaf der bronnen van het oud-vaderlandse recht* nieuwe reeks 3 (1982) 87-159.

[02.]

1. Köln, Utrecht, officiality of the archdeacon of the chapter of Oudmunster (st Salvator).

In the Middle Ages the archdeaconry of Oudmunster consisted of the region called the "Vechtstreek," a part of the present-day province of Utrecht (Wijk bij Duurstede, Werkhoven), the region around Woudrichem, the region around Driel, the region between the rivers the Hollandse Yssel and the Lek (Gouda, Lekkerkerk, Bodegraven, Linschoten, Montfoort) and the eastern half of the present-day province of Friesland, together with the islands of Ameland and Schiermonnikoog.

2. *Rijksarchief in de provincie Utrecht (see above 01/2).

Most records of the officiality belong to the archive of the chapter of Oudmunster. During this present research it turned out that records concerning the officiality are scattered all over the inventory and sometimes are mentioned in quite illogical places. Sometimes the information given in the descriptions is wrong, probably because of insufficient knowledge about the officialities.

In the archive of the chapter of Oudmunster there are some docs about cases brought before other officials. These cases are mentioned in the report concerning that specific official. Similarly, there are cases concerning the archdeacon of Oudmunster listed in the report of the bishop's officiality under "mixed registers." Inventory (available at the archive):

Jhr. dr. B.M. de Jonge van Ellemeet, *Inventaris van het archief van het kapittel van Oudmunster* (Getypt).

3. *1. Case registers*:

*Oudmunster nr. 1889-1. 262 fols. 1534-52. *Prothocollum Jacobi de Medemblick coram officiali archidiaconi Sancti Salvatoris Traiectensis.*

Register of cases in chronological order. Mostly cases about churches and vicarages and marriage cases. The entries sometimes are extensive, but sometimes they are very short, recording steps in the procedure, but not telling what the case was about.

*Oudmunster nr. 1889-2. 141 fols. 1568-73. *Prothocollum actium iudicalium mei Johannis Mersman notarii publici coram venerabili viro domino officiali Sancti Salvatoris Traiectensis habitorum et observatorum de anno domini 1568.*

Register of cases in chronological order. Contents comparable to Oudmunster 1889-1, contains also some docs of *collatio* and *presentatio*.

*Oudmunster nr. 1889-3. 6 docs. 1417; 1489/90; 1495; 1512; 1525; 1535. Fragments of older court books with some loose docs.

2. *Formularies*:

*Oudmunster nr. 1890. 42 fols. c1540-1550. Formulary.

With some procedural material: *citatio, monitio, excommunicatio*. When *officialis* is mentioned, not always clear which one.

3. *Accounts*:

*Oudmunster nr. 1740. 198 fols. 1549-82. Account book.

Of Jacob Cunretorff of his revenues and expenses both as vicar-general and official of the archdeacon of Oudmunster. Only a few notations concerning judicial cases and then mostly marriage cases.

4. *Individual docs*:

*St. Pieter nr. 249. 2 docs. 1344. Case about tithes between chapter and woman.

Libel and citation.

*Oudmunster nr. 1892. 25 docs. 1477-1563. Citations.

*Oudmunster nr. 1899. 34 docs. 1481-1583. Docs with reference to several cases brought before the official of the archdeacon.

Letters, depositions of witnesses, etc.

*Oudmunster nr. 1893. 11 docs. 1484. Case about payments between the pastor and priests of Gouda and the churchwardens.

Almost full-scale *processus*; no sentence.

*Oudmunster nr. 1894. 19 docs. 1495-98. Case about inheritance between local authorities and citizen of Gouda.

Full-scale *processus*.

*Oudmunster nr. 1895. 5 docs. 1504, 1506. Case about back rent between two laymen.

Not complete; not much judicial material.

*Oudmunster nr. 1896. 1 quire of 12 fols and 1 doc. 1508. Register, containing depositions of witnesses by the *provisor* of Rijnland, in case about vicarage in Gouda before official of archdeacon.

*Oudmunster nr. 1897. 3 docs. 1534. Docs concerning payment of costs in suit in case about misbehaviour of priest in Lexmond.

With list of all procedural steps and their costs.

*Oudmunster nr. 1878. 1 doc. 1559. Complaint of the official about violation of his jurisdiction by the procurator-general of the (secular) Court of Utrecht.

*Oudmunster nr. 1898. 182 fols bound together. 1574-75. Case about *ius presentationis* of church in Hagesteijn.

First before official of archdeacon of Oudmunster, then before official of the archbishop. Complete *processus*, with many depositions of witnesses.

4. There is not enough material for a full-scale history of this officiality, but some conclusions can be drawn. No studies.

[03.]

1. Köln, Utrecht, officiality of the archdeacon of the chapter of st Pieter.

In the Middle Ages the archdeaconry of st Pieter consisted of the present-day region of the Netherlands called the Veluwe, the region between Nijkerk, Elburg, Hattem, Zutphen, Dieren and Veenendaal.

2. *Rijksarchief in de provincie Utrecht (see above 01/2).

We know from several sources that there was an official of the archdeacon of st Pieter. There are, however, no sources of this official left in the archive of the chapter of st Pieter. But there are some docs about cases, brought before other officials. These cases are mentioned in the report concerning that specific official. Inventory:

S. Muller Fz., *Catalogus van het archief van het kapittel van St. Pieter* ('s-Gravenhage 1886).

[04.]

1. Köln, Utrecht, officiality of the archdeacon of the chapter of st Jan.

In the Middle Ages the archdeaconry of st Jan consisted of the "Proosdij van St. Jan": the region of Mijdrecht, Wilnis etc., and the western half of the present-day province of Friesland, together with the island of Terschelling.

2. *Rijksarchief in de provincie Utrecht (see above 01/2).

We know from several sources that there must have been an official of the archdeacon of st Jan. There are, however, no sources of this official left in the archive of the chapter of st Jan. But there are some docs about cases brought before other officials. These cases are mentioned in the report concerning that specific official. Inventory (available at the archive):

Jhr. dr. B.M. de Jonge van Ellemeet, *Inventaris van het archief van het kapittel van St. Jan* (Getypt 1934).

[05.]

1. Köln, Utrecht, officiality of archdeaconry of the *chorepiscopus*.

In the Middle Ages the *chorepiscopus* was one of the archdeacons in the diocese of Utrecht. His archdeaconry consisted of only eight parishes: Kockengen, Benschop, Stolwijk, Polsbroek, Kamerik, Schalkwijk, Jutfaas and Harmelen. The *chorepiscopus* was not a *prepositus* like almost all the other archdeacons; he had to be canon of the cathedral.

2. *Rijksarchief in de provincie Utrecht (see above 01/2).

There is almost no material left concerning this little officiality: only two accounts, dating from the 15th and 16th century. We know from other sources that there was already an official of the *chorepiscopus* in 1350. Inventory:

K. Heeringa, *Inventaris van het archief van het kapittel ten Dom* (Utrecht 1929)

3. *1. Accounts*:

*Dom nr. 2573-1. 12 fols. 1472-75. *De iurisdictione choriepiscopatus ecclesie Traiectensis*; account.

*Dom nr. 2573-2. 24 fols. 1504-1522. *Registrum officialitatis choriepiscopi Traiectensis*; account.

Receipts *(recepta)* from 1504-1518; expenses *(exposita)* from 1504-1522.

ISAIAS DA ROSA PEREIRA

VIII. Portugal

Editor's Note and Report

Our correspondent in Portugal was not encouraging about the survival of medieval church court records in that country. In the event, the press of other commitments made it impossible for him to undertake any visits to archives specifically for the purpose of these reports. He did, however, provide us with a brief bibliography of articles and documents that he has published and a list of documents that he currently in the process of studying. We offer them here in the form in which he sent them:

Documents et articles publiés par moi:

'Visitações de Santiago de Óbidos (1434-1481)', *Lusitania Sacra* 8 (Lisboa 1967/1969) 103-221.

'Uma visitação do archebispo de Lisboa D. João Esteves de Azambuja em 1402', *Arqueologia e História* 9ª série, 3 (Lisboa 1971) 21-30.

'Visitações de Santiago de Óbidos (1482-1500)', *Lusitania Sacra* 9 (Lisboa 1972) 79-116.

'L'Officialité diocésaine de Lisbonne au XVIe siècle', *L'Année canonique* 17 (Paris 1973) 805-815.

'Visitações das Igrejas de São Miguel de Sintra e de Santo André de Mafra (1466-1523)', *Lusitania Sacra* 10 (Lisboa 1978) 135-257.

Documents que j'étudie:

Regimento dos officiaes e pessoas que procuram no auditorio Ecclesiastico desta cidade. Ordenado pelo senhor Bispo de Coymbra: Conde Darganil (Imprimé à Coimbra, 1547).

Regimento do auditório Eclesiástico de Évora de 1535, manuscrit des Archives du chapitre d'Évora, CEC 4-VIII.

Regimento do auditório Eclesiástico de Lisboa de 1535, manuscrit des Archives du Patriarchat de Lisbonne.

Sentence du Vicaire Général de Évora, 18 février 1413, manuscrit des Archives du chapitre d'Évora, EE XII-2.

Sentence du Vicaire Général de Lisbonne, 25 mai 1414, manuscrit des Archives du chapitre d'Évora, EE XII-4.

Sentence de l'archévêque de Lisbonne, D. Jorge da Costa, 20 avril 1474, manuscrit des Archives Nationales (Arquivo Nacional da Torre do Tombo), Colegiada de S. Mateus de Santarém, caixa 2 (71-72), maço 1, nº 14.

Sentence de l'évêque de Lisbonne, D. Frei Estévão, 14 juillet 1321?), manuscrit des Archives Nationales (Arquivo Nacional da Torre do Tombo), Colegiada de S. Miguel de Torees Vedras, caixa 1 (nº 73), rollo nº 2.

Sentence du Vicaire Général de Santiago de Compostela, métropole de Lisbonne, dans une affaire entre l'évêque de Lisbonne et le Monastère d'Oya, 23 juillet 1316, manuscrit des Archives particulières de Dr. Tomaz Andrade Rocha.

Sentence du doyen et d'un chanoine de Viseu, délégués du Pape, mai 1217, manuscrit des Archives Nationales (Arquivo Nacional da Torre do Tombo), Colegiada de Santa Justa de Coimbra, caixa 32, doc. nº 3.

R.H. HELMHOLZ

IX. Spain

Editor's Preface

We were unable to obtain a correspondent in Spain. Professor Helmholz undertook two brief visits to Spain and filed the following reports. It is clear that these are only samples of what is available in the Spanish archives and that a great deal more survives in them. It also seems that progress in identifying the most fruitful areas of research will be made by those who are resident in Spain or who can spend a substantial amount of time there. Access to Spanish archives that contain this type of material is difficult for the researcher who can go to Spain only for a brief visit.

The dioceses that are covered here are listed in Tangl's *Provinciale* as follows: Burgensis (qui est domini pape) (Burgos), Barchinonensis (prov. Terrraconensis) (Barcelona), and Pampilonensis (prov. Terraconensis [vel] Caesaragustanus) (Pamplona).

[01.]

1. Burgos (exempt), officiality of the bishop.

The see was immediately subject to the papacy until 1574; thereafter it was the metropolitical see of Burgos within the province of Burgos.

2. * Archivo diocesano, Palacio Arzobispal, Burgos.

There is a good handlist available at the archive. However, almost all of the court's records are said to have perished in two fires, one in 1599, the other in 1812. The contents of the archives are therfore almost exclusively from the period after the second of these. For the pre-Tridentine period, it will not repay more than a brief visit.

3. *1. Visitation records*:

*3.2.2. 134 & 27 fols. 1492-1586. A *visita pastoral* of the cathedral.

Undertaken in 1582, the first year of the episcopate of Archbishop Christobal Vela, this visit is useful for the historian because the extent of episcopal jurisdiction, as against that of the dean and chapter, was disputed during the visitation. As a result it contains several older docs defining the jurisdictional claims of each side, and it is possible to draw some modest conclusions about ecclesiastical jurisdiction exercised within the diocese of Burgos from these docs.

2. Otros Docs (individual docs):

I was unable to consult any of the following, as the assistant archivist could not find them during my visit. They are recorded from the catalogue.

No. 68. 1434. Sentence relating to disputed *census.*

No. 54. 1459. *Processus.* Same.

No. 32. 1465. *Processus.* Same.

No. 16. 1523. Mandatum issued in a boundary dispute between parishes.

No. 59. 1527. Sentence in tithe dispute.

No. 44. 1539. Sentence issued in a dispute over *census.*

No. 60. 1561. Sentence issued in a dispute involving burial rights.

[02.]

1. Burgos, court of the cathedral chapter.

   For the history of the see, see 01/1.

2. Archivo Capitular, Catedral, Burgos.

   This archive appears to be much richer in pre-Tridentine court material than the episcopal archive. However, I was not able to see it in person, since the archivist had to leave Burgos on the day after my arrival. There is, however, a seemingly complete guide to the archive's contents:

   Demetrio Mansilla, *El archivo capitular de la catedral de Burgos* (Burgos 1956).

   I can only describe briefly what it indicates; regrettably it does not make entirely clear whether the jurisdiction of the court described was exercised over secular or spiritual pleas.

   The judicial records for the capitual court are kept in a series of *libri*, divided roughly according to subject matter. There are 77 volumes in all, about a sixth of which deal with the pre-Tridentine period. A selection of the most interesting, from the point of view of the history of the ecclesiastical courts, follows. This does *not* pretend to be a complete list, but only illustrative of the sort of material to be found in the archive. I have included the earliest dated material in each instance.

3. *1. Libros I*:

   No. 7. 889 fols. N.d. Diocesan statutes and constitutions.

   No. 12. 608 fols. N.d. Various matters concerned with ecclesiastical discipline.

No. 13. 726 fols. N.d. Docs relating to jurisdicton.

No. 19. 887 fols. N.d. Docs relating to visitations *sede vacante*.

No. 54. 1052 fols. N.d. Docs relating to episcopal jurisdiction.

No. 57. 1009 fols. N.d. Miscellaneous docs, some "sobre informaciones en derecho."

No. 62. 642 fols. N.d. Papal docs relating to justice, and local docs relating to the same.

2. Libros II:

No. 45. 533 fols. 1535-63. Visitations of benefices belonging to the chapter's jurisdiction.

No. 48. 414 fols. 1488-1558. "Diversas escrituras" dealing with capitular jurisdiction.

No. 49. 928 fols. 1516-84. Various forms (e.g. citations, inhibitions, petitions) relating to jurisdiction.

No. 50 (Part I). 554 fols. 1435-1538. "Registro de procesos criminales."

No. 50 (Part II). 1096 fols. 1435-1538. Same.

No. 51. 889 fols. 1539-46. Same.

No. 55. 665 fols. 1502-47. "Registro de procesos civiles."

No. 56. 653 fols. 1548-55. Same.

[03.]

1. Tarragona, Barcelona, officiality of the bishop.
2. *Arxiu Diocesa, Obispo Irurita 5, Barcelona, Spain.

The records of this diocese are listed in:

José Sanabre, *El Archivo diocesano de Barcelona* (Barcelona 1947).

A general, but more accessible, guide is:

Guía de los archivos y las bibliotecas de la iglesia en España (León 1972) 1:151-67.

It shows a considerable range of record material relating to diocesan administration. It also indicates the existence of material similar to that treated below in other Barcelona archives, that of the Cathedral and in some parochial archives.

The records of the bishop's courts examined consist of five classes, the class names of which seem to have been used from the time of their compilation. They are: *Registra Verbalium, Libri Testamentarum et Piarum Causarum, Registra Communium, Processus* (or *Procesos*), and *Visitas Pastorales*. All of the surviving records date from the s14/m, and continue in relatively regular but not complete sequence thereafter. The earliest *Verbalia* are less standardized in form and contain less litigation (as opposed to registration of docs) than those for the s15. There are also relatively few early s14 *procesos*, compared to the greater numbers for the end of the century and for the s15. All docs are in codex form.

What follows is a description of the docs examined. It is impossible to be sure that they are representative of the others in the same class, particularly those of later date. However, where they differ materially from others of the same class examined, this fact is specifically noted.

3. *1. Verbalia*:

*No. 1. 1344-45. Register.

Litigation and process relating to the estate of Ferrer d'Abella, former bishop of Barcelona. There are various claims against the estate, with ensuing litigation, as well as docs relating to administration of the estate.

*No. 4. 1382-88. Register of contracts, gifts, sales of goods, and miscellaneous administrative docs.

No litigation noted.

*No. 6. 1396-1401. Register.

Largely disciplinary matters involving the clergy, the entries usually consisting of a statement of the crime involved and recordation of a bond for good behavior under money penalty. Crimes noted include perjury, *fama publica* of incontinence, forgery of a seal, theft, and "excesses". Often it is said that the offender is *infra carceres episcopales*, and it seems likely that the bonds represented the conditions of release.

*No. 12. 1433-5. Register.

Instance litigation and other official court docs, such as registration of agreements or confessions of judgment. The litigation in this, and in the following registers normally took this form: complaint, answer, replication by the plaintiff (where appropriate) and court order. Virtually all the entries are quite brief, and most cases are found complete in one entry. They were not carried over from one date to another. Apparently the title *Verbalia* accurately describes the procedure used, as most answers record the formal appearance of the defendant in Latin, then move to Catalan for his actual denial or affirmative defense.

Most litigation involved at least one party in holy orders; for example, from 9 September through December 1433, only 5 of 45 cases involved laymen as both plaintiff and defendant (in 8 cases clerics were on both sides; in 8 only the defendant was a cleric; in 24 only the plaintiff was a cleric). In all, the Barcelona records show much more evidence of the exercise of jurisdiction *ratione personae* than do contemporary English records. The range of the cases found in the Register includes enforcement of parish dues, tithes, inheritance matters involving charitable bequests or debts of the testator, sworn contracts, and annual pensions.

*No. 13. 1442-5. Register.

Similar in form and contents to Reg. No. 12. Not examined in detail.

*No. 14. 1459-61. Register.

Similar in form and contents to previous two registers. There is more Catalan used than previously, often including the plaintiff's statement of claim. The *declinatio fori* was frequently used by defendants, mostly by laymen. The court sat on most days; e.g. in March 1460 there are entries for twenty days in the month, with a total of 67 matters being handled. Summary procedure was used throughout.

2. Testamenta and Causas Pias:

*No. 2. 1373-4. Register.

Docs relating to charitable bequests; also a few inter vivos transfers. Includes approval of accounts and appointment or confirmation of executors or *manuiussores* to supervise enforcement of the bequests. Charitable provisions of testaments are given verbatim.

*No. 54. 1449-54. Register.

Similar in form and contents to No. 2. Bequests of clerics and laymen included in both.

3. Communia:

*No. 56. 1453-67. Miscellaneous docs related to episcopal administration.

Appointments to office, orders to cite before the bishop, directions dealing with benefices, agreements to settle disputes or agreeing to ecclesiastical jurisdiction, questions relating to testaments. There is some doubt as to whether these registers should be included in judicial records. Although they include instances of litigation, they are not primary records in the sense that Act books are. They contain many of the same docs one would find in an English episcopal register, although without appointments to benefices or ordinations. My impression of this register does not differ noticeably from that well described and calendared in:

J.N. Hillgarth & Giulio Silano, *The Register Notule Communium 14 of the Diocese of Barcelona (1345-1348)*, Subsidia Mediaevalia 13 (Toronto 1983).

4. Procesos:

For the most part these *processus* are records of actual litigation, probably prepared for purposes of appeal. All are in codex form although occasionally stray papers from the cause are found inserted in the pages. The completeness of the records varies considerably. The fuller records contain libel, articles and positions, depositions, *acta* reciting the procedure, sentence and appeal, and even legal argument. Others contain only one of these, and it is difficult to know whether this is all that ever existed. However, since sometimes the same cause appears in several different *processus*, it seems likely that more than one volume might often be made up for a single cause. What follows is a necessarily sketchy description of the surviving s14 records. I did not have time to examine those of the s15 and s16; they are much more numerous.

*2.3.1.1/1. 1324. Rights in prebend of the cathedral.

*2.3.1.1/2. 1342. Rights in benefice in church of st Mary in Arbunto: libels and positions.

Like many of the benefice cases which follow, this one involves a dispute over the original terms of grant; the founder required that the holder of the benefice be *idoneus de cognomine suo* and the question was whether the person presented by the patron fulfilled these two qualifications. The person raising the objection claims that he has a better claim to the benefice, based on his fulfillment of the terms of the foundation charter.

*2.3.1.1/3. 1344-5. Depositions taken from apparent heresy prosecution involving Spiritual Franciscans.

Allegations recorded as having been made *coram domino inquisitore.*

*2.3.1.1/4. 1347. Long testamentary cause.

Involving dispute over whether executors had fulfilled the direction in a testament to provide a hospice for the poor.

*2.3.1.1/5. 1351-2. *Ex officio* proceeding.

Denunciation by bishop's vicar general, accusing an existing marriage of invalidity because of consanguinity. Sentence of divorce.

*2.3.1.1/6. 1358. Taxation of clerical property.

Chapter of Barcelona seeks to invoke provincial constitution agains *invasores* of ecclesiastical property to claim immunity from payment of tax on sales of meat, fish and bread in this action against the lay collectors.

*2.3.1.1/7. 1369. Rights to a benefice.

Presentation to benefice in parish church to be conferred under foundation grant upon a *presbiter ideoneus de genere vel parentela* of the founder.

*2.3.1.1/8. Other docs in same cause.

*2.3.1.1/9. 1371. Rights to benefice in parish church.

*2.3.1.1/10. 1373. Rights to benefice in parish church.

Like several others of these cases, this seems to have arisen out of competing petitions to be admitted to the benefice.

*2.3.1.1/10bis. 1376-7. Exemption to grant of tenth granted to king of Aragon by Pope Gregory XI.

Heard by papal judges delegate.

*2.3.1.1/11. 1378. Rights to two benefices in cathedral church and St Mary de Palacio.

*2.3.1.1/11bis. 1380. Clerical exemption from secular taxation of purchases of wool.

Full process is not here.

*2.3.1.1/12. 1381-3. Rights to benefice, apparently involving inheritance of the right to presentation of altar of the Holy Innocents in the cathedral.

*2.3.1.1/13. Same cause.

*2.3.1.1/14. 1382-3. *Ex officio* prosecution by denunciation against rector of parish church for neglect of clerical duties.

Citation of authorities from Roman and canon law included. Sentence in favor of the accused; guilt *non constat*.

*2.3.1.1/14bis. 1383. Spoliation of tithes.

*2.3.1.1/15. 1381. Rights to benefice.

Against executors of a testament by *procurator pauperum Christi et piarum et ultimarum voluntatum defunctorum civitatis et dyocesis Barch'.*

*2.3.1.1/15bis. 1384. Rights to benefice.

In bad condition and only briefly inspected.

*2.3.1.1/16. 1385. Disputed monastic election.

A very long *processus* not fully examined.

*2.3.1.1/17. 1385. Rights to benefice.

Only the depositions are contained in this file.

*2.3.1.1/18. 1386. Rights to benefice.

Depositions only.

*2.3.1.1/19. 1386. Sufficiency and accuracy of testamentary inventory.

Not clear whether this formed part of litigation, and if so, what part.

*2.3.1.1/20. 1391-92. Rights to benefice.

Includes mandate from the bishop to diocesan clergy to cite named persons to appear and show what right if any they had in the benefice.

*2.3.1.1/21. 1394. Rights to benefice.

Contested by claimant alleging existence of judgment in his favor at Roman court.

*2.3.1.1/22. 1395. Rights to benefice.

Mostly depositions concerned with exceptions against the persons and testimony of witnesses.

*2.3.1.1/23. 1394-95. Rights to benefice.

*2.3.1.1/24. 1395. Rights to benefice.

Appealed from the vicar general to the bishop. Mostly concerned with the legitimacy of the appeal rather than the merits of the cause.

*2.3.1.1/25. 1397. Rights to benefice in cathedral church.

*2.3.1/1/26. 1397. Rights to benefice.

Styled specifically *causa beneficialis*. Only petition for benefice and *acta* thereon included.

*2.3.1.1/27. 1397-8. Rights to benefice.

*2.3.1.1/28. Rights to benefice.

*2.3.1.1/29. 1398-1401. Rights to benefice.

*2.3.1.1/31. Depositions belonging to 1/28.

5. *Visitas Pastorales*:

*No. 9. 1388-91. Deanery of Barcelona.

Similar to No. 11; less full and more carelessly prepared.

*No. 11. 1413-15. Deanery of Barcelona.

Perhaps a fair copy. Begins with introduction and articles of inquiry to be used in visitation. Then follows the record of proceedings in each church visited. Normally the incumbent is asked about the parishioners: Are any excommunicate? Do any live in concubinage? Are there blasphemers? These produced very few positive answers, and the volume does not contain any action taken against the few presented in consequence. A far larger portion of the record is taken up by articles and depositions about the sufficiency of the parochial clergy, and large numbers of parishioners were required to respond to the articles (e.g. 29 in church of st Peter de Breha; 25 at st Stephen in Barcelona). Matters actually presented against the clergy included lack of the book of Provincial Constitutions; failure to provide church services, nonresidence, and lack of repair of parsonage. However, in some places the parishioners deposed that they were content. The entries conclude with the action taken by the visitor, usually including a fine imposed upon the incumbent and an order to amend what had been found wanting. Some of these contain references to canonical and civilian texts.

[04.]

1. Zaragoza (to 1574, Tarragona to 1318), Pamplona, officiality of the bishop.

2. * Archivo diocesano de Pamplona, Arzobispado, Plaza de Santa Maria la Real, 31001 Pamplona, Spain.

This archive contains a substantial collection of *processus*, with documentation from cases on appeal. The first date from the very end of the s15, but do not become at all numerous until the middle years of the s16. Of the 4000 or so surviving from the s16, my (rough) estimate is that about a tenth date from prior to the Council of Trent. Cases involving benefices (about *jus patronatus*, qualifications of clerics presented, or contested elections by *vecinos* who held by right of patronage) are by far the most numerous; however there are also some interesting cases involving *inter alia* marriage, burial rights, tithes, and criminal jurisdiction over the clergy.

The records at Pamplona are very well kept, and the archivist, Don José Luis Sales Tirapu, has compiled an excellent handlist of the contents of the *processus*. In my experience it was a very reliable guide, and happily there are plans afoot to have it published. There is also a brief description of the archive's contents by the same author:

'Archivo Diocesano de Pamplona', *Semana de Estudios de Historia Eclesiástica del País Vasco* (1981) 257.

The archive was open in the mornings three days a week (Monday, Tuesday and Thursday) during the spring of 1987.

Recorded below are accounts of all the docs I was able to examine personally, together with a sample of the pre-Tridentine cases in two *cajas* (Nos. 18 and 34) taken in part from the handlist. The latter is meant to give an example of the mix of materials to be found at Pamplona. However, these *cajas* contain more pre-Tridentine material than is found in most.

3. *Caja 17, No. 5. 7 fols. 1535. Dispute over rights to patronage of rectory.

*Caja 17, No. 7. 60 fols. 1541. Matrimonial; to establish validity of clandestine marriage.

*Caja 17, No. 16. 363 fols. 1548. Tithe dispute from Logroño.

Interesting legal material about the nature of tithe obligation and the force of custom allegedly contrary to the formal law of tithes.

Caja 18, No. 3. 1547. Benefice dispute.

Caja 18, No. 4. 410 fols. 1547. Benefice dispute.

Caja 18, No. 5. 1548. Dispute over parish revenues brought by absentee rector.

Caja 18, No. 6. 102 fols. 1549. Dispute over rights of precedence to seats in parish church.

Caja 18, No. 7. 95 fols. 1548. Benefice dispute.

*Caja 18, No. 8. 26 fols. 1543-9. Tithe dispute between parishioners and clergy.

The former refuse the jurisdiction of the bishop and archdeacon on grounds of the alleged interest of the latter in the outcome.

Caja 18, No. 9. 19 fols. 1549. Benefice dispute

Caja 18, No. 10. 72 fols. 1549. Benefice dispute.

*Caja 18, No. 11. 42 fols. 1548. Testamentary.

Dispute over the goods of a professed monk who had departed the monastery and died. The case passes to temporal courts.

Caja 18, No. 14. 109 fols. 1550. Benefice dispute.

Caja 18, No. 16. 23 fols. 1551. Rights of precedence to seats in parish church.

*Caja 21, No. 3. 15 fols. 1559. Matrimonial.

Process on papal dispensation permitting marriage between man and woman related by third degree of consanguinity.

Caja 34, No. 1. 46 fols. 1532. Tithes.

Rector sues parishioners for non-payment.

Caja 34, No. 2, 33 fols. 1533. Benefice dispute.

Caja 34, No. 3. 154 fols. 1533. Dispute over site of chapel to be constructed.

*Caja 34, No. 4. 30 fols. 1550. *Causa iniuriarum* between two clerics.

Caja 34, No. 5. 1551. Testamentary; related to proceeds of mass stipend.

Caja 34, No. 6. 66 fols. 1552. Disputed salary of chaplain.

*Caja 34, No. 7. 23 fols. 1552. Disputed election to rectory of Zuasti by the *vecinos*.

*Caja 34, No. 8. 4 fols. 1552. Suit by parishioners against the incumbent for neglect of his office.

Caja 34, No. 9. 66 fols. 1552. Benefice dispute.

Caja 34, No. 10. 72 fols. 1553. Benefice dispute.

*Caja 34, No. 12. 225 fols. 1553. Matrimonial; judicial separation for cruelty; division of marital property.

*Caja 34, No. 14. 78 fols. 1553. *Ex officio* proceeding against cleric for complicity in murder.

Caja 34, No. 15. 9 fols. 1553. Suit by parishioners against vicar for malfeasance in office.

*Caja 34, No. 16. 10 fols. 1553. Accounting for fruits of clerical office.

Caja 34, No. 18. 41 fols. 1556. Benefice dispute.

*Caja 75, No. 3. 7 fols. 1498–9. Disputed presentation to rectory of Guesa.

*Caja 75, No. 9. 1508. Disputed presentation to rectory of Urrizola.

*Caja 75, No. 12. 1511. Matrimonial; to enforce clandestine contract of marriage.

ANDREAS MEYER

X. Die Schweiz

Editor's Preface

This remarkable report was more thorough in its coverage both of archives and of bibliography than many of the others. Dr. Meyer has visited many of the archives in Switzerland (except those in Ticino [dioceses of Milano and Como]). He has also corresponded with and/or visited archives outside of Switzerland which he believed contained material concerning the Swiss officialities. The result is the following report, which is probably complete for the surviving records of the Swiss officialities that are contained in archives that hold all or part of what was originally in the officialities' archives. He also made one contribution to the report for Lyon (III/29), and he gives us here the only item that we have found from the archiepiscopal officiality of Besançon.

The medieval dioceses (preceded by their metropolitans) all or part of the territories of which lie in modern Switzerland follow from Tangl's *Provinciale*:

[Mainz] (Maguntina)
Konstanz (Constantiensis)
Chur (Curiensis)

[Vienne] (Viennensis)
Genève (Gebbensis)

[Tarentaise] (Tarentasiensis)
Sion (Sedunensis)

[Besançon] (Bisuntinus)
Basel (Basiliensis)
Lausanne (Lausanensis)

Einleitung

Den Archiven der geistlichen Gerichte in der Schweiz ist eines gemeinsam: sie haben in den Wirren der Reformation (Basel, Chur, Konstanz, Lausanne und Genf) oder der französischen Revolution (Basel und Konstanz) vieles eingebüßt, wobei sich die Verluste leider ebensowenig zeitlich genau datieren wie qualitativ erfassen lassen. Anders liegt der Fall beim bischöflichen Archiv von Sitten: der Brand von 1788 zerstörte den ganzen damaligen Bestand; die spärlichen Reste aus der Zeit davor, die heute in diesem Archiv liegen, sind erst später an es gefallen. Was die Reformation und die französische Revolution nicht zerstört haben, konnte wegen der Unachtsamkeit der Verantwortlichen auch im 19. Jahrhundert noch verloren gehen (Chur). Halbwegs geschlossene Bestände bestehen nur noch für die Offizialate von Basel und Konstanz im 15. und 16. Jahrhundert.

Die bisherige Forschung hat sich vor allem mit der Organisation des geistlichen Gerichts befaßt. Dabei stützte sie sich fast ausschließlich auf die urkundliche Überlieferung. Die Aktenbestände wurden bislang kaum ausgewertet, obwohl verschiedentlich auf sie hingewiesen wurde (besonders von Vasella). Zu bemerken ist, daß das bischöfliche Offizialat in den eidgenössischen Stadtorten wie Zürich und Bern nicht die bedeutende Rolle spielte, die ihm vielleicht anderswo zukam. Die Städte der Eidgenossenschaft begannen nämlich seit dem ausgehenden 13. Jahrhundert eine eigene starke Gerichtsbarkeit aufzubauen. Dabei gerieten sie mit den geistlichen Gerichten zwangsläufig in Konflikt, die weite Bereiche der weltlichen Gerichtsbarkeit (Schuldprozesse etc.) für sich in Anspruch nahmen. In dieser bis ins 15. Jahrhundert hinein dauernden Auseinandersetzung wurde die geistliche Gerichtsbarkeit im wesentlichen auf die Ehe- und Wucherprozesse beschränkt. Durch den Ausbau des städtischen Beurkundungswesens versuchte man aber auch, die freiwillige nichtstreitige Gerichtsbarkeit der Offizialate (Beurkundungswesen) auszuschalten. Eine andere Entwicklung machten in dieser Beziehung die Bischofsstädte Basel, Genf, Konstanz, Lausanne und Sitten durch. Hier behielten die bischöflichen Kurien (bzw. das Domkapitel in Sitten und die Abtei St-Maurice) durchaus ihre Bedeutung als Beurkundungsstätte.

Typisch für die schweizerischen geistlichen Gerichte scheint die enge personelle Verflechtung zwischen Offizial und Generalvikar zu sein: man findet sie in fast allen Diözesen. Dies hat zur Folge, daß sich die Aktenbestände des bischöflichen Gerichts oft nicht so leicht von jenen der bischöflichen Verwaltung trennen lassen (vgl. Konstanz und Lausanne). Obwohl schon recht früh bischöfliche Offiziale erscheinen (Sitten 1248, Genf 1250, Basel 1252, Konstanz 1256, Lausanne 1260 und Chur 1273), scheint es zu keiner klaren Ausgliederung der Kompetenzen gekommen zu sein. Ohne Parallele in der Schweiz ist die schwache Stellung des bischöflichen Offizials/Generalvikars in Sitten. Bis weit ins 15. Jahrhundert spielte er neben den beiden Dekanen des Kathedralkapitels nur eine marginale Rolle. Während der Dekan von Sitten für das Unterwallis (inkl. Sitten) zuständig war, übte der Dekan von Valeria die geistliche Gerichtsbarkeit im Oberwallis aus. Abgesehen vom Sonderfall Sitten gibt es nur ganz wenige Hinweise auf weitere geistliche Gerichte neben dem bischöflichen Offizialat in den Schweizer Diözesen. Man findet eine gewisse archidiakonale oder dekanale Gerichtsbarkeit zwar noch in den Diözesen Basel, Chur und Lausanne, es sind aber keine

Aktenbestände überliefert, so daß sich ihre ursprüngliche Rolle kaum rekonstruieren läßt. Ein Hinweis auf die in der Westschweiz reichlich vorhandenen Notarsregister, aus denen sich bestimmt weitere Erkenntnisse zur geistlichen Gerichtsbarkeit gewinnen lassen, mag genügen.

Dieser Beitrag bietet einen Überblick über die Aktenbestände der geistlichen Gerichte der Schweiz (ohne Tessin) und der nicht-schweizerischen geistlichen Gerichte, von denen sich Akten in schweizerischen Archiven befinden, unter Einbezug der Inquisitions- und Visitationsprotokolle. Das Schicksal der bischöflich-konstanzischen Akten zeigt deutlich, in welchem Maße ein ursprünglich geschlossener Bestand durch die Unbill der Zeit auseinander gerissen werden kann. Es ist also durchaus möglich (wenn auch nicht sehr wahrscheinlich), daß in hier nicht erwähnten Archiven noch weitere Quellen liegen. Die Empfängerüberlieferung (Urkunden des geistlichen Gerichts) ist hier nicht erfaßt. Es sei nur darauf verwiesen, daß sich die bibliografischen Angaben zu weiteren Urkundenbüchern am leichtesten in der *Helvetia Sacra* nachschlagen lassen. Die schweizerischen Kantonsarchive verfügen in der Regel über gute bis sehr gute Zettel- oder Buchrepertorien zu ihren Urkundenbeständen. In den von mir besuchten Archiven habe ich die urkundliche Überlieferung nur fragmentarisch (sofern keine Aktenbestände vorhanden waren) oder überhaupt nicht bearbeitet.

Allgemeine Bibliografie

Bautier/Sornay, *Sources*.

Albert Bruckner, 'Das bischöfliche Archivwesen am Oberrhein', *Archivalische Zeitschrift* 63 (1967) 46-49.

Ferdinand Elsener, 'Die Einflüsse des römischen und kanonischen Rechts in der Schweiz', *Historisches Jahrbuch der Görres-Gesellschaft* 76 (1957) 133-147.

Ferdinand Elsener, 'Der eidgenössische Pfaffenbrief von 1370: ein Beitrag zur Geschichte der geistlichen Gerichtsbarkeit', ZRG KA 75 (1958) 104-180.

Ferdinand Elsener, *Notare und Stadtschreiber: zur Geschichte des schweizerischen Notariats* (Köln/Opladen 1962).

Ferdinand Elsener, 'Die Exkommunikation als prozessuales Vollstreckungsmittel: Zur Geschichte des Kirchenbannes im Spätmittelalter', in *Festschrift für Eduard Kern* (Tübingen 1968) 69-86.

Ferdinand Elsener, *Studien zur Rezeption des gelehrten Rechts: Ausgewählte Aufsätze*, hg. von F. Ebel und D. Willoweit (Sigmaringen 1987).

F. Gabotto, 'Dissidents religieux à Genève, en Savoie et dans le Valais en 1428-1431', *Bulletin de la Société d'histoire vaudoise* 24 (1907) 3-4.

Helvetia Sacra 1/1.
Helvetia Sacra 1/3.
(Über den Stand des Projektes informiert der Jahresbericht der Redaktion der Helvetia Sacra in der SZG.)

Répertoire des statuts synodaux des diocèses de l'ancienne France du XIIIe à la fin du XVIIIe siècle éd. A. Artonne, L. Guizard, O. Pontal, 2e éd. augmentée (Paris 1969). (Enthält auch die Statuten der Diözesen Basel, Genf, Lausanne, Sion.)

Josef Schürmann, *Studien über den eidgenössischen Pfaffenbrief von 1370*, ZSKG Beiheft 6 (1948).

Sven Stelling-Michaud, *Catalogue des manuscrits juridiques (droit canon et droit romain) de la fin du XIIe au XIVe siècle conservés en Suisse* (Genève 1954).

Sven Stelling-Michaud, *L'université de Bologne et la pénétration des droits romain et canonique en Suisse aux XIIIe et XIVe siècle* (Genève 1955).

Sven et Susanne Stelling-Michaud, *Les juristes suisses à Bologne (1255-1330): Notices biographiques et regestes des actes bolognais* (Genève 1960).

Sven Stelling-Michaud, *La diffusion du droit romain en Suisse, étudiants suisses à l'étranger et leur activité professionelle ultérieure: Notariat - littérature juridique - manuscrits et bibliothèques* Ius Romanum Medii Aevi 5/12 b (Mailand 1977).

A.M. Stickler, 'Iter Helveticum', *Traditio* 14 (1958) 462-484. (Ergänzungen zu Stelling-Michaud, *Catalogue.*)

Friedrich Thudichum, *Die Diözesen Konstanz, Augsburg, Basel, Speier, Worms nach ihrer alten Einteilung in Archidiakonate, Dekanate und Pfarreien* Tübinger Studien für schwäbische und deutsche Rechtsgeschichte 1 (Tübingen 1906). (Dieses Buch bietet nur eine Übersicht über die äußeren Grenzen und die innere Einteilung der kirchlichen Organisation und keinen historischen Überblick.)

Emil Usteri, *Westschweizer Schiedsurkunden bis zum Jahre 1300* (Zürich 1955).

Oskar Vasella, *Reform und Reformation in der Schweiz: Zur Würdigung der Anfänge der Glaubenskrise* Katholisches Leben und Kämpfen im Zeitalter der Glaubensspaltung 16 (Münster 1958).

Die Visitation im Dienst der kirchlichen Reform hg. von E.W. Zeeden und H. Molitor, 2. verbesserte Auflage (Münster 1977).

[01.]

1. Besançon, Offizialat des Erzbischofs.

2. *Archives de la Ville de Lausanne, rue du Maupas 47, CH-1000 Lausanne.

Archivgeschichte:

Gilbert Coutaz, *Histoire des Archives de la Ville de Lausanne des origines à aujourd'hui, 1401-1985* (Lausanne 1986).

3. *Chavannes E 25. 146 fol. 1534. "Acta et processus causae appellationis nobilium virorum Francisci Gimelli domicelli Baillivi Lausannensis ac Johannis Costibulis eius locumtenentis appellatori contra quendam Michaelem Joutens dioc. Lausan. se pro clerico gerentem appellantem".

[02.]

1. Besançon, Basel, Offizialat des Bischofs.

2. *Staatsarchiv des Kantons Basel-Stadt, Martinsgasse 2, CH-4051 Basel [STABS].

Zur Geschichte des STABS, siehe:
Repertorium des Staatsarchivs zu Basel (Basel 1904).

*Archives de l'ancien évêché de Bâle, Hôtel de Gléresse, 10 rue des Annonciades, CH-2900 Porrentruy [AEB].

Generallandesarchiv Karlsruhe, Nördl. Hildapromenade 2, D-7500 Karlsruhe [GLAK].

Inventar des GLAK:

Manfred Krebs, *Gesamtübersicht der Bestände des Generallandesarchivs Karlsruhe* Veröffentlichungen der Staatlichen Archivverwaltung Baden-Württemberg 1-2 (Stuttgart 1954-1957).

*Aargauisches Staatsarchiv, Aargauerplatz, CH-5000 Aarau (STAAG).

3. *1. STABS*:

*Gerichtsarchiv AA 1. 1081 pp (zeitgenössischer Pergamenteinband). 1458-1470. "Sententiae coram dom. officiali in ordinariis", chronologisch geordnet, vor allem "causae matrimoniales".

*Gerichtsarchiv AA 2. 34 Hefte. 1486, 1499, 1507-1509. "Causae matrimoniales".

Protokolle der Verhandlungen *(processus)*. Pro Fall ist ein Heft angelegt.

*Gerichtsarchiv AA 3. 51 Hefte. 1510-1512. Wie AA 2.

*Gerichtsarchiv AA 4. 44 Hefte. 1513-1516. Wie AA 2.

*Gerichtsarchiv AA 5. 55 Hefte. 1517-1522. Wie AA 2.

*Gerichtsarchiv AA 6. 40 Hefte. 1523-1529. Wie AA 2.

*Gerichtsarchiv AA 7. 45 Hefte. 1508, 1530-1531. Wie AA 2.

*Gerichtsarchiv AA 8. 293 fol (zeitgenössischer Pergamenteinband). 1455-1472. "Cause delegate", chronologisch geordnet; *processus et sententiae.*

*Gerichtsarchiv AA 9. 219 fol (zeitgenössischer Pergamenteinband). 1461-1475. *Cause delegate.*

"In delegatis, diversa monitoria et inhibitiones, diverse sive in causis delegatis, diversi processus et sententie in causis appellationum coram rev. dom. nostr. Basil. et suo officiali et surrogato, item diversa alia 1461", chronologisch geordnet, wie AA 8.

*Gerichtsarchiv AA 10. 2 Hefte (89, 22 fol). 1461, 1497. Registra Processus.

"Registrum in causa appellationum coram officiali curie episcopalis Basil. iudice ordinario 1461", Zinsen. (Der Prozeß fand in erster Instanz vor dem Offizial der Kurie des Archidiakons von Basel statt.)

"(Registrum) desertionis appellationis in causa capellanie Vesselhem 1497".

*Gerichtsarchiv AA 11. 1505-1521. Prozeßschriften: *interrogatoria, appellationes, petitiones, defensiones* etc. Inhaltlich: *beneficiales, matrimoniales* etc.

*Gerichtsarchiv AA 12. 1518-1520. Inhaltlich: *beneficiales, matrimoniales, divorcii, causa appellationis ex delegatione apostolica matrimonialis, causa spolii decimarum coram iudice apostolico, testamentaria, causa hereditaria* etc., wie AA 11.

*Gerichtsarchiv AA 13. 205 fol. 1476. "Registrum in causa prophana ...;" inhaltlich: "Processus in causa censuum Ratberg".

*Gerichtsarchiv AA 14. 1464-1482. Diverse Akten, mehrere Faszikel:

fasz. 1. 75 fol. 1464-1466. "Acta cause dominarum in Klingental et Clewini Endingen": Zinsen.

fasz. 3. 1466. Beweisaufnahme über eine eheliche Geburt.

fasz. 4. 1469-70. Testamente.

fasz. 7. 1482. Darin auch Akten betreffend Andreas Zamometic.

Die meisten Akten sind nach Fällen geordnet und in Heften zusammengebunden.

*Gerichtsarchiv AA 15. 11 Hefte. 1513-1530. Diverse Akten.

Jeder Fall ist in ein Heft gebunden, inhaltlich: *beneficiales*, Zinsen.

*Gerichtsarchiv AA 16. 12 Hefte. 1485-1510. Diverse Akten; wie AA 15.

*Gerichtsarchiv AA 17. c200 fol. s/15-s/16. Diverse Akten.

Ein Konvolut von einzelnen Blättern, inhaltlich sehr heterogen, Prozeßunterlagen und ähnliches.

*Gerichtsarchiv AA 18. c800 fol (zeitgenössischer Pergamenteinband).

1471-1485. "Contractus, donationes, locationes, testamenta, precontractus, quittantie, confessata ... sub sigillo curie Basil." Chronologisch geordnet.

*Gerichtsarchiv AA 19. 4 Hefte. c300 fol. 1506-1548. Von der Hand des Kuriennotars Adalbertus Saltzman.

"Sexternus contractuum interceptus 1506: Contractuum, donacionum, locationum, testamentariorum, precontractuum, quittanciarum, confessarium 1506-1508".

"Signature coram officiali curie Basil. 1507-1515."

"Imbreviature et signature 1521-".

"Signature abbreviate 1537-1548".

*Gerichtsarchiv AA 20. 558 fol. 1470-1480, 1485-1495. "Vidimus sub titulo curie Basil."

Drei Teile: Teil 1 zeitgenössisch in Pergament gebunden.

*Gerichtsarchiv AA 22. Zeitgenössischer Pergamenteinband. 1520-1525. "Registrum thornorum pro notariis curie Basil".

Enthält: "thornus causarum matrimonialium 1521-1524, thornus causarum remissorum 1521-1525, thornus causarum arestationum 1521-1523, thornus in causis ordinariis ... 1521-1524."

2. *AEB*:

*A 85 Mappe 33. Nr. 2. 60 pp (Pergamenthandschrift). 1478-1502. "Statuta curie Basiliensis sub episcopo Casparo de Rheno".

*A 85 Mappe 35. 1482-1642 (bis 1563: pp 1-104). Verschiedene Bestallungsbriefe von Offizialen.

*A 85 Mappe 37. Diverse Faszikel:

fasz. 1. Bestallungsbrief für den Boten und Briefträger des geistlichen Gerichts 1454 (Pergament).

fasz. 3. 1492-1766 (davon neun Stücke bis 1563). Bestallungen und Reverse der Fiskalen.

fasz. 4. 1534-1774 (davon fünf Stücke vor 1563). Bestallungen und Reverse der Notare und Insiegler.

fasz. 6. 1475-1677 (Nr. 1-7 vor 1563). Bestallungen und Reverse der Prokuratoren und Advokate.

*A 85 Mappe 39. 1 Band, 13 Hefte. 1429, 1441-1500, 1521-1522. "Registra seu calculus computationum procuratoris fiscalis".

1441-1477: nur Exstanzen, danach vollständige Rechnungen. Die Rechnungen des Fiskalprokurators verzeichnen unter anderem alle Bußgeldzahlungen an die Basler Kurie, nach Jahren geordnet.

*A 85 Mappe 43. 1503/04-1516/17, 1542-1546. "Registra procuratoris fiscalis".

Vollständige Rechnungen sowie die Exstanzen 1508-1510.

*A 85 Mappe 44. 2 Hefte. 1547-1561.

"Registra omnium receptorum et expositorum per vicarium in spiritualiis et officialem ratione sigilli curie Basiliensis 1554/55-1560/61".

"Registra procuratoris fiscalis 1547-1559".

*A 85 Mappe 45. 2 Hefte. 1561-1572.

"Registrum omnium receptorum et expositorum per vicarium in spir. et officialem ratione sigille curie Basil. 1561/62-1571/72".

"Registra procuratoris fiscalis 1561/62-1569/70".

*A 85 Mappe 68. 1469-1629. "Processus de variis rebus et causis".

Darin Fragmente von Prozeßprotokollen (c150 pp) und Imbreviaturen von Sentenzen 1551-1608 (24 fol, chronologisch geordnet).

*A 85 Mappe 69, fasz 1. 8 fol. 1507. Prozeßschriften.

*A 85 Mappe 83. 1475-1563. "Acta criminalia".

fasz. 1: Prozeßschriften zu einem Sodomieprozeß von 1475, Zeugenaussagen und Sentenz, total 5 fol.

fasz. 2: Konvolut diverser Prozeßschriften 1476-1543, c30 fol.

fasc. 3: Konvolut 1544-1559, c60 fol.

fasz. 4: Konvolut 1561-1574, c10 fol bis 1563.

*A 85 Mappe 94, fasz 1. 1534-1599. "Causae matrimoniales".

Darin ein Prozeßprotokoll von 1534 (c100 fol) sowie verschiedene einzelne Akten zu anderen Fällen (bis 1563 c20 fol).

*A 104 Mappe 1. Verschiedene Stücke:

Nr. 2: "Statuta synodalia diversa" (Pergamenteinband); s13-s15, darin: pp 36-38, Sentenz des Offizials gegen die Gemeinde von Ungersheim betreffend die Ermordung des dortigen Pfarrers 1296 (gedruckt bei Trouillat, unten 02/4/5, 2:621)

Nr. 3: "Fragmenta statutorum Basil." mit Vorschriften über das Konsistorium unter den Bischöfen Friedrich zu Rhein 1437-1451 und Christoph von Uttenheim 1502-1527, 21 fol.

*A 104 Mappe 2. Pp 199-328 (Pergamenteinband). 1537. "Statuta curie episcopalis sub domino Philippo ep. Basil. composita et consistorialibus publicata".

A 142 Mappe 2. Pp 83-120. "Manuale incultum visitatorum ecclesiarum".

Siehe unten 02/4/5: Lang.

3. AEB — Nachtridentinische Bestände:

A 85 Mappen 1-32. 1570-1780. "Protocolla sententiarum de diversis causis in ep. curia, protocolla sententiarum judicalium et matrimonialium".

A 85 Mappe 36. 1575-1770. "Actes concernant la maison de l'official à Altkirch".

4. GLAK:

Gemäß brieflicher Aussage von Archivar und Amtsrat Rupp vom 2. Jan. 1987 sind in den hier aufbewahrten Beständen des Domkapitels "ganz vereinzelt Akten des bischöflichen Offizialats zu vermuten."

5. STAAG:

*6732. 1470-1471. 70 fol. "Registrum in causa beneficiali coram Friderico Frank vicario ... dni. Johannis ep. Basil. in spiritualibus generali iudice ordinario inter ... Johannem Pfeffer de Wydenberg s. Theol. professorem ordinarium eiusdem facultatis in alma universitate studii Friburgensis Constant. dioc actorem ex una et Nicolaum de Munsingen art. mag. et cler. Constant. dioc. de et super certis canonicatu et prebenda in ecclesia collegiata s. Martini Rynfeldensis Basil. dioc. reum ex alia partibus ... "

4. Bibliografie:

1. Allgemeines:

Max Burckhardt, 'Aus dem Umkreis der ersten Basler Universitätsbibliothek, mit einem Anhang: Die Bibliothek Arnolds zum Lufft', *Basler Zeitschrift für Geschichte und Altertumskunde* 58/59 (1959) 155-191 (Arnold zum Lufft war Offizial in Basel)

Jean Burcklé, *Les chapitres ruraux aux anciens évêchés de Strasbourg et de Bâle* (Colmar 1935) (besonders 311-384: Edition von Statuten aus den Jahren 1370-1777)

Anton Gössi, *Das Urkundenwesen der Bischöfe von Basel im 13. Jahrhundert (1216-1274)* Quellen und Forschungen zur Basler Geschichte 5 (Basel 1974)

Hans-Rudolf Hagemann, *Basler Rechtsleben im Mittelalter*, 2 Bde. (Basel 1981-87) (berührt das geistliche Gericht nur am Rande)

Andreas Heusler, 'Zur Geschichte des Executivprozesses in Deutschland', *Zeitschrift für Rechtsgeschichte* 6 (1867) 127-205

Katalog der datierten Handschriften in der Schweiz in lateinischer Schrift vom Anfang des Mittelalters bis 1550, Band 1, hg. von B.M. von Scarpatetti (Dietikon-Zürich 1977) (darin Nr. 181, 394, 395, 398-409, 412, 419 aus dem Besitz der Basler Offiziale Heinrich von Beinheim und Arnold zum Lufft)

Luzian Pfleger, *Die elsäßische Pfarrei, ihre Entstehung und Entwicklung. Ein Beitrag zur kirchlichen Rechts- und Kulturgeschichte* Forschungen zur Kirchengeschichte des Elsaß 3 (Straßburg 1936) (erstmals im *Archiv für Elsäßische Kirchengeschichte* 1929-1934 erschienen).

2. Archivgeschichte:

Albert Bruckner, 'Das bischöfliche Archiv von Basel', *Archivalische Zeitschrift* 63 (1967) 103-117

Marco Jorio, 'Das Schicksal des fürstbischöflich-baslerischen Archivs seit 1789, ein bewegtes Stück schweizerischer Archivgeschichte', *Basler Zeitschrift für Geschichte und Altertumskunde* 83 (1983) 85-125.

3. Zu den Offizialen:

Theodor Gottlob, 'Die Offiziale des Bistums Basel im Mittelalter', ZRG KA 69 (1952) 113-157

Wolfgang D. Wackernagel, 'Das Offizialat', *Helvetia Sacra* 1/1, 241-255 (im Anschluß daran A. Chèvre, 'Le vicariat général et l'officialité de Bâle depuis la réforme', mit summarischen Angaben zu den Archivbeständen sowie prosopographischen Bemerkungen zu den Amtsinhabern)

Wolfgang D. Wackernagel, 'Heinrich von Beinheim (1428-1435)', *Essays in legal history in honor of Felix Frankfurter* (Indianapolis 1966) 275-288.

4. Über das bischöfliche Gericht:

Karl Mommsen, 'Das Basler Kanzleiwesen des Spätmittelalters', *Basler Zeitschrift für Geschichte und Altertumskunde* 74 (1974) 159-188

Wolfgang D. Wackernagel, *Zur Geschichte der Rezeption römischen Rechts an den geistlichen Gerichten Basels: Schlußbericht an das Comité der schweizerischen Arbeitsgemeinschaft für den "Neuen Savigny"* (hektographisches Manuskript 1960).

5. Gedruckte Quellen:

Josef Hartzheim, *Concilia Germaniae*, 6 (Köln 1765) (darin, pp 2-29, Synodalstatuten von 1503)

Peter Thaddäus Lang, 'Manuale incultum visitatorum ecclesiarum: Ein bisher unbekannter Visitationstraktat aus dem späten 15. Jahrhundert', ZSKG 79 (1985) 145-162

J. Trouillat, *Monuments de l'histoire de l'ancien évêché de Bâle*, 5 vols. (Porrentruy 1852-1867)

Urkundenbuch der Landschaft Basel 708-1512, 2 Bde. (Basel 1881-1883)

Urkundenbuch der Stadt Basel 751-1797, 11 Bde. (Basel 1890-1910).

[03.]

1. Besançon, Basel, Offizialat des Archidiakons.

Die Existenz dieses Gerichtshofes läßt sich bis zur Mitte des 15. Jahrhunderts nachweisen. Ein Archiv hat aber nicht überlebt. Siehe dazu oben 02/3/1: Gerichtsarchiv AA 10.

Literatur: *Helvetia Sacra* 1/1, 301.

[04.]

1. Besançon, Lausanne, Offizialat des Bischofs.

2. *Archives de la Ville de Lausanne [AVL] (siehe 01/2).

*Archives cantonales vaudoises, rue de la Mouline 32, CH-1022 Chavannes-près-Renens [ACVD].

Archives de l'Évêche à Fribourg, rue de Lausanne 86, CH-1700 Fribourg [AEF].

*Staatsarchiv des Kantons Bern, Falkenplatz 4, CH-3012 Bern [STABE].

*Burgerbibliothek Bern, Münstergasse 63, CH-3011 Bern [BBB].

*Archives cantonales de Fribourg, Chemin des Archives 4, CH-1700 Fribourg [ACFR].

Summarisches Inventar:

Nicolas Morard und H. Foerster, *Das Staatsarchiv Freiburg, Führer durch die Bestände* (Freiburg/Ue. 1986).

*Archives de l'État de Neuchâtel, Château, CH-2001 Neuchâtel [AENE].

Archivgeschichte und summarisches Inventar:

Jean Courvoisier, *Petit guide des archives anciennes de l'état de Neuchâtel* (Neuchâtel 1981).

3. *1. AVL*:

*Chavannes E 4. c200 fol. 1398-1520. Konvolut von Einzelstücken, vor allem des Gerichts des Bailli (bischöflich-gräfliches Gericht), darin aber auch Einzelstücke der Kurie des Offizials, zB. fol 8, 74, 106 etc.

*Chavannes E 6. c80 fol (Pergamenteinband). 1450-1515. "Registre de la cour de l'official de Lausanne écrit par Jacob Richard secrétaire 1496".

Es handelt sich um ein Konvolut von Einzelstücken und Registerfragmenten des Generalvikars und des Offizials.

Der Fonds "Chavannes E 3-23" besteht fast gänzlich aus Registern des gräflichen Gerichts des Bischofs (bailli). In diesen Akten werden vereinzelt auch Urkunden des Offizials zitiert.

2. ACVD:

Ac 5. 1416-1417. Protokoll der Kirchenvisitation.

Dieses Register ist ediert worden. Siehe unten 04/4/5: *Visite*.

*Ac 29. 1 vol, 492 pp. 1438-1528. "Procédures pour sorcelleries instruites par l'inquisiteur de la foi du diocèse de Lausanne et l'official de Lausanne ainsi que devant la justice du chapitre".

c30 Prozesse, davon drei vor dem Offizial (pp 208-258).

*C IV 360. 1366. Quittung des Bischofs zugunsten seines Fiskalprokurators Olivier Joly.

*C VI b 23. Pergament. 1511. Sentenz zugunsten eines Mannes aus Paillly, den seine Frau wegen Impotenz verklagt hatte.

*C VI b 24. 1520. 23 Ladungen vor die Kurie des Offizials.

*C VI b 25. 1525. Beglaubigungsschreiben des Offizials für einen Notar.

Im weiteren befindet sich unter der Signatur Ac 6 ein Band mit dem Titel "Actes divers passés au nom de Georges de Saluces, évêque de Lausanne

(1440-1462), par R. Perrin, secrétaire de l'officialité," den Lehnherr (siehe unten 04/4/5) p 7 Anm. 1 dem Offizialat zuschreibt. Die zeitgenössische Titulatur nennt R. Perrin jedoch "secretarius officii" (so steht es auch auf dem Buchdeckel), es handelt sich vermutlich eher um einen Band aus der bischöflichen Kanzlei.

3. AEF:

Registre de l'officialité de Lausanne 1509 (ohne Signatur).

Dieses Offizialatsformularbuch ist von Yvonne Lehnherr ediert worden (siehe unten 04/4/5).

4. STABE:

*A V 1438 (= U.P. 69). 568 pp. 1508-1509. Akten des Jetzerhandels.

Hierbei handelt es sich um eine zeitgenössische Abschrift eines Inquisitionsverfahrens, das 1508 vor dem Lausanner Bischof gegen Hans Jetzer und den Berner Dominikanerkonvent (unbefleckte Empfängnis Mariens) eröffnet, seit dem 21. Mai 1508 aber vor einem Spezialgerichtshof bestehend aus den Bischöfen von Lausanne und Sitten geführt worden ist. (Die Akten sind ediert; siehe unten 04/4/5.)

5. BBB:

*Hist. Helv. III 115. 1 Band, 332 fol. 1453. Protokoll der Kirchenvisitation, die im Auftrag des Lausanner Bischofs Georges de Saluces von Franciscus de Fuste, Bischof von Granada, und Henricus de Alibertis, Abt von Filly, durchgeführt worden ist.

*Hist. Helv. I 39. 69 fol (zeitgenössischer Pergamenteinband). Constitutiones synodales (unter anderem).

fol 1-7. Constitutiones synodales des Bischofs Georges de Saluces (undatiert).

fol 42-55. 1449. Dasselbe.

6. ACFR:

*Geistliche Sachen 26. 1430. 1 Band, 85 fol, davon einige unbeschrieben, zeitgenössischer Pergamenteinband. Akten des Waldenserprozesses, durchgeführt von Ulricus de Torrente o.P. *inquisitor heretice pravitatis auct. apostolica in dioc. Lausan., Sedun. et aliis* und von Johannes de Columpnis, *lic. in decr. canonicus Lausan.* und bischöflicher Kommissar.

*Geistliche Sachen 34. 1456. Pergament. Zulassung einer Appellation an den Offizial von Besançcon.

*Geistliche Sachen 2025. 1523. 4 fol, Papier. *Constitutiones synodales* des Bischofs Sebastian von Montfaucon.

*Geistliche Sachen 2027. 1532. Pergament. Sentenz des Offizials von Lausanne in einer Benefizialsache (Schrift stark verblichen).

Ursprünglich wurde in diesem Archiv unter der Signatur Geistliche Sachen 13 (und vermutlich später unter Nr. 391) eine auf Pergament geschriebene

Prozessakte des Waldenserprozesses von 1399 aufbewahrt. Seit 1881 ist das Stück verloren, eine Abschrift findet sich im *Recueil diplomatique*, unten 04/4/5, Band 5, pp 144-178. Durchgeführt wurde der Prozeß von 1399 von Humbert Franco o.P. *inquisitor heretece pravitatis* und Vuillermus de Vuonflens o.Min., bischöfliche Kommisssare.

Zu den vielen in diesem Archiv aufbewahrten Notarsregistern seit 1356 siehe Bautier/Sornay 1353-54.

7. AENE:

* Registre du notaire Vuillème Mentha. 1395-1399. 1 vol, 75 fol.

V. Mentha war Notar des Lausanner Offizials. Sein Register beinhaltet Konzepte von Offizialatsurkunden (viele Sentenzen zu "cause matrimoniales" oder "beneficiales", auch Sentenzen des Offizials als zweite Instanz nach den Kurien der Dekane [siehe unten 06/1] und Vermerke über Appellationen an die Metropolitankurie in Besançon).

*H 7 no. 14. 1439. Pergament. Sentenz des Ulricus de Torrente "inquisitor heretice pravitatis in dioc. Lausan., Geben., et Sedun." gegen Jacquetus Doux Plain von Neuchâtel.

Gedruckt bei Matile, siehe unten 04/4/1, p 233f.

*B 23 no. 18. 1481. Papier, 6 fol. Inquisitionsprotokoll (auf französisch).

*B 23 no. 19. 1481. Papier, 6 fol. Inquisitionsprotokoll (auf französisch).

*B 23 no. 23 a-b. 1481. Papier, 8 fol. Inquisitionsprotokoll (auf französisch).

Teilweise gedruckt bei Matile, siehe unten 04/4/1, p 234-9.

*F 23 no. 23. 1481. Papier, 2 fol. Inquisitionsprotokoll (auf französisch).

4. Bibliografie:

1. Allgemeines:

Bautier/Sornay 834-852 und 1370-1372 (Notarsregister aus den Jahren 1360-1500)

Jean Pierre Graber, *Histoire du notariat dans le canton de Neuchâtel, ses origines, son évolution, son organisation* Diss. iur. Zürich 1954 (Schlieren 1957)

Auguste Matile, *Histoire des institutions judiciaires et législatives de la Principauté de Neuchâtel et Valangin* (Neuchâtel 1838)

Jean-François Poudret, 'L'heurese destinée des notaires vaudois au moyen âge', *Revue historique vaudoise* 64 (1956) 1-25

Poudret, 'Usuriers'

SMÆH 11: *Schreibschulen der Diözese Lausanne* bearb. v. A. Bruckner (Genf 1967) (besonders 110-140)

Louis Waeber, 'Les décanats de l'ancien diocèse de Lausanne et leur transformation apreès la réforme', ZSKG 35 (1941) 35-61, 98-113

Louis Waeber, 'Les décanats et paroisses de l'ancien diocèse de Lausanne', ZSGK 35 (1941) 270-308.

2. *Archivgeschichte*:

A. Millioud, 'Un ancien catalogue des archives épiscopales de Lausanne', *Revue historique vaudoise* 8 (1900) 11-16.

3. *Zu den Offizialen*:

Helvetia Sacra 1/4: *Le diocèse de Lausanne (VI*^{e} *siècle -1821), de Lausanne et Genève (1821-1924), de Lausanne, Genève et Fribourg (depuis 1924)* (Abschnitt "L'officialat (XIIIe - XVIe siècles)", im Druck)

Maxime Reymond, *Les dignitaires de l'église Notre-Dame de Lausanne jusqu'en 1536*, MDSR 2.8 (Lausanne 1912).

4. *Über das bischöfliche Gericht*:

Danielle Anex-Cabanis, 'Rapports entre l'évêque et le chapitre de Notre-Dame et Lausanne au sujet de leurs droits respectifs de juridiction', MHDB 34 (1977) 97-105

Gabriel Bise, 'Essai sur la procédure pénale en matière de sorcellerie à Fribourg du XVe aux XIXe siècles', *Annales fribourgeoises* 42 (1956) 62-73

Ferdinand Elsener, 'Die Censura ecclesiastica (Exkommunikation) in zivilrechtlichen Verträgen auf Grund eines Formularbuches des 15. Jahrhunderts aus Freiburg im Üechtland', *Festschrift Nikolaus Grass* 1 (Innsbruck-München 1974) 299-308

Gertrude Barnes Fiertz, 'An unusual trial under the inquisiton at Fribourg, Switzerland, in 1399', *Speculum* 18 (1943) 340-357

Paolo Gallone, "Les statuts de l'official de Lausanne de 1453', MHDB 34 (1977) 183-189

François Gilliard, 'Le rôle de l'officialité de Lausanne en matière d'exécution forcée', *Festschrift Karl Siegfried Bader* (Zürich 1965) 149-158

Gottlieb Friedrich Ochsenbein, *Aus dem schweizerischen Volksleben des 15. Jahrhunderts, der Inquisitionsprozeß wider die Waldenser zu Freiburg in Üechtland im Jahre 1430 nach den Akten dargestellt* (Bern 1881)

Jean-François Poudret, 'Les états de Vaud et la juridiction ecclésiastique', MHDB 34 (1977) 197-208

Peter Rück, 'Die Entstehung der nachreformatorischen dekanalen Jurisdiktion in der Diözese Lausanne', ZSKG 59 (1965) 297-327

Peter Rück, 'Die letzten Versuche Sebastians von Montfaucon (1517-1560) zur Wiederherstellung der bischöflichen Verwaltung in den katholischen Teilen der Diözese Lausanne', SZG 16 (1966) 1-19

Peter Rück, 'Die Entstehung des nachreformatorischen Generalvikariats der Diözese Lausanne aus dem Propsteigericht von Freiburg 1563-1600' ZSKG 61 (1967) 245-300

Franz Wigger, *Die Anfänge des öffentlichen Notariats in der Westschweiz* Diss. Fribourg 1951.

5. *Gedruckte Quellen*:

Die Akten des Jetzerprozesses nebst dem Defensorium hg. v. Rudolf Steck, Quellen zur Schweizer Geschichte 22 (Basel 1904)

Marius Besson, 'Les deux plus anciennes éditions imprimées des Constitutions synodales du diocèse de Lausanne', ZSKG 31 (1937) 37-44 (sie stammen aus den Jahren 1494 und 1523; der Verfasser verzeichnet auch die Aufbewahrungsorte)

Bernhard Rudolf Fetscherin, 'Visitationsbericht des Bisthums Lausanne, Bernischen Antheils, vom Jahre 1453', *Abhandlungen des Historischen Vereins des Kantons Bern* 1 (1848) 251-394

Fontes rerum Bernensium. Bern's Geschichtsquellen (bis 1390), 10 Bde. (Bern 1883-1956)

Fréd. Gingins-la-Sarra et François Forel, *Recueil de chartes et documents concernant l'ancien évêché de Lausanne* MDSR 1.7 (Lausanne 1846)

Yvonne Lehnherr, *Das Formularbuch des Lausanner Offizialats aus dem frühen 16. Jahrhundert* Diss. phil. Fribourg 1972, oder ZSKG 67 (1972) 1-159

Meinrad Meyer, 'Georges de Saluces évêque de Lausanne et ses visites pastorales ou état des églises de la campagne dans le canton de Fribourg au XVe siècle', *Archives de la Société d'histoire du Canton de Fribourg* 1 (1846-1848) 155-212, 251-327

Meinrad Meyer, 'Georges de Saluces évêque de Lausanne et ses visites pastorales ou état des églises de la campagne dans les cantons de Soleure et Neuchâtel au XVe siècle', *Archives de la Société d'histoire de Canton de Fribourg* 1 (1850) 401-426

Das Notariatsformularbuch des Ulrich Manot hg. v. Albert Bruckner, Sammlung Schweizerischer Rechtsquellen 9: Die Rechtsquellen des Kantons Freiburg 1: Stadtrechte 5 (Aarau 1958)

Othmar Perler, 'Les constitutions synodales de Sébastian de Montfaucon, évêque de Lausanne (1523)', ZSKG 37 (1943) 225-235 (Teiledition)

Recueil diplomatique du Canton de Fribourg 7 Bde. (Fribourg 1839-1683)

Les Sources du droit du Canton de Vaud, Moyen âge (X^{e} - XVIe siècle) B: *Droits seigneuriaux et franchises municipales* 1: *Lausanne et les terres épiscopales* par D. Anex-Cabanis et J.-F. Poudret, Sammlung Schweizerischer Rechtsquellen 19: Die Rechtsquellen des Kantons Waadt B.1 (Aarau 1977) vor allem 465-482

H. Türler, 'Die Lausanner Kirchenvisitation von 1416/17', *Archiv des Historischen Vereins des Kantons Bern* 16 (1900-1902) 1-41

La visite des églises du diocèse de Lausanne en 1416-1417, MDSR 2.11 (Lausanne 1921).

[05.]

1. Besançon, Lausanne, Gericht des Kapitels (Iudex spiritiualis capituli).

Von diesem Gerichtshof ist nahezu nichts überliefert. Siehe:

Peter Rück, 'Les registres de l'administration capitulaires de Lausanne (XIIIe-XVIe siècle)', *Revue historique vaudoise* 83 (1975) 135-186 (besonders 185).

Der bischöfliche Offizial war die Appellationsinstanz.

[06.]

1. Besançon, Lausanne, Gerichte der Archidiakone und Dekane.

Es sind keine geschlossene Aktenbestände überliefert; vereinzelt finden sich in den Urkundenbüchern (und vermutlich auch in den nicht gedruckten Beständen der Archive) Hinweise auf ihre Tätigkeit, zB. *Fontes rerum Bernensium* (siehe oben 04/4/5) Bd. 5 Nr. 100 und Bd. 6 Nr. 358. Im ACFR (siehe oben 04/2) sind unter der Signatur Geistliche Sachen 733 und 734 zwei Sentenzen des Dekans von Freiburg, Richter in Ehesachen, von 1557 und 1560 überliefert (beide Male Papier, 2 fol bzw. 4 fol).

[07.]

1. Mainz, Chur, Offizialat des Bischofs.

2. * Bischöfliches Archiv Chur, Hof 19, CH-7000 Chur.

Archivgeschichte:

Bruno Hübscher, 'Das Bischöfliche Archiv Chur', *Archivalia et Historica, Festschrift für Anton Largiadèr* (Zürich 1958) 33-49.

Oskar Vasella, 'Über das bischöfliche Archiv in Chur', *Archivalische Zeitschrift* 63 (1967) 58-70.

Inventar:

Im Archiv gibt es ein handschriftliches Inventar von 1888 (mit Nachträgen) für die hier aufbewahrten Urkunden. Ein Verzeichnis der bisher bekannten Offizialatsurkunden bietet Clavadetscher (1964), unten 07/4/2. Über nachtridentinische Bestände siehe: Vasella (1967), oben 07/2.

3. * Debitorium generale I. 1182 pp in 4 Teile. ca. 1504-1523. "Debitorium Generale I ad sigillum Rev. Episcopi Curiensis pro iuribus iudicii".

Nach Dekanaten und Pfarreien geordnet, verzeichnet die aufgrund eines Entscheids des bischöflichen Richters der bischöflichen Kasse geschuldeten Beträge unter Nennung der Gründe (*cause matrimoniales*, *adulteria*, Dispense etc.). In der zweiten Spalte sind die Zahlungen der Gebüßten vermerkt.

* Debitorium generale II. 460 pp. 1520-1526. "Debitorium universale seu generale II officii sigilli Rev. dom. Ep. Curiensis per eandem civitatem Curiensem atque circumcirca videlicet Rotzüns, Embs, Velsperg, Haldenstein, Thümleschg, Schambs, Rinwaldt et Maladers".

Gleich angelegt wie Debitorium I, viele leere Blätter.

* Debitorium generale III. 724 pp. 1523-1533. "Credita ad sigillum Rev. dom Episcopi Curiensis seu debita per diocesim Curiensem atque debitorium generale et prima sub parrochia s. Martini eiusdem civitatis Curiensis et extra eandem in capitulo Ruralis etc".

Gleich wie Debitorium I, viele unbeschriebene Blätter.

Debitorium II und III bilden die chronologische Fortsetzung von Debitorium I. Die drei Bände sind durch ein Ortsregister erschlossen. In diesem Register liegt ein Couvert mit 28 numerierten Privatbriefen, die sich auf Zahlungen an den bischöflichen Fiskal beziehen. Siehe: Vasella (1938), unten 07/4/2.

* Mappe 60. Mehrere Hefte vor allem aus dem weltlichen Gericht des Bischofs stammend, darunter aber:

Heft 4. 43 fol. 1472. "Acta cause hereditarie ab dem Tristenberg coram dom. Iudice curie Curien".

Heft 7. 20 fol. 1481. "Protocollum in causa Fabariensis"; beneficialis.

Heft 10. 1495. Acta et processus: Stiftung.

Heft 11. 1496. Acta et processus: Zehnt.

Heft 12. 1497. Acta et processus: Zehnt.

* Mappe 61. Mehrere Hefte vor allem aus dem weltlichen Gericht des Bischofs stammend, darunter aber:

Heft 1. 30 pp. 1505-1509. "Protocollum". Notarsregister und Formelbuch eines namentlich nicht genannten Churer Notars.

Heft 9. 11 fol. 1521. "In causa spolii inter hon. dom. Wolfgangum Rambot de Schuls agentem et Gasparem Dietegen reum"; beneficialis.

Heft 11. 38 pp. 1523-1524. Akte, Zehnt.

Heft 12. 6 fol. 1524. Akte zu einem Matrimonialprozeß, der in erster Instanz vor dem Engadiner Dekan geführt worden ist; die rechte untere Ecke fehlt.

Heft 13. 171 pp. 1524. Appellationsprozeß in Ehesachen (ab p 153 an der rechten unteren Ecke beschädigt), enthält sehr viele Zeugenaussagen.

4. Bibliografie:

1. *Allgemeines*:

SMÆH 1: *Schreibschulen der Diözese Chur* bearb. von Albert Bruckner (Genf 1935) (besonders 65).

2. *Zum bischöflichen Offizialat und den Offizialen* (judices):

Otto P. Clavadetscher, *Die geistlichen Richter des Bistums Chur: Zugleich ein Beitrag zur Geschichte des römischen Rechts im Mittelalter* Ius Romanum in Helvetia 1 (Basel 1964) (darin auf pp 121-125 ein Verzeichnis der Urkunden des geistlichen Gerichts)

Dieses Buch entfachte eine heftige Kontroverse (folgende drei Titel):

Oskar Vasella, 'Zur Geschichte des geistlichen Gerichts im Bistum Chur', ZSKG 59 (1965) 89-106

Otto P. Clavadetscher, 'Zu den geistlichen Richtern des Bistums Chur', ZSKG 60 (1966) 399-410

Oskar Vasella, 'Schlußwort über das Thema der geistlichen Richter des Bistums Chur', ZSKG 60 (1966) 411-415

Otto P. Clavadetscher und Werner Kundert, 'Das Churer Generalvikariat und Offizialat', *Helvetia Sacra* 1/1, 512-533 (inkl. nachtridentinische Zeit)

Alfons Ströbele, 'Beiträge zur Verfassungsgeschichte des Bistums Chur bis zum 15. Jahrhundert', *Jahrbuch für Schweizerische Geschichte* 30 (1905) 1-110 (besonders 94-105)

Oskar Vasella, 'Bischöfliche Kurie und Seelsorgeklerus im Bistum Chur: Nach

Briefen aus dem Beginn des 16. Jahrhunderts', ZSKG 32 (1938) 81-102 und 161-185.

3. Gedruckte Quellen:

Bündner Urkundenbuch, 3 Bde. (390-1300) (Chur 1955-1985)

Codex diplomaticus ad historiam Rhaeticam. Sammlung der Urkunden zur Geschichte Cur-Rätiens und der Republik Graubünden hg. von Th. v. Mohr und C. v. Moor, 4 Bde. (Chur 1848-1865)

J. G. Mayer, 'Synodalstatuten des Bischofs von Chur Heinrich VI. von Höwen (1491-1503)', *Anzeiger für Schweizerische Geschichte* 4 (1882-1885) 198-203

J. Muoth, 'Zwei sogenannte Ämterbücher des Bistums Chur aus dem Anfang des 15. Jahrhunderts', *Jahresbericht der Historisch-Antiquarischen Gesellschaft von Graubünden* 27 (1897), (besonders 18-25)

Rätische Urkunden aus dem Centralarchiv des fürstlichen Hauses Thurn und Taxis in Regensburg hg. v. H. Wartmann, Quellen zur Schweizer Geschichte 10 (Basel 1891)

Urkunden-Sammlungen im Staatsarchiv Graubünden 2 Teile (Chur 1975-1977)

Urkundenbuch der südlichen Teile des Kantons St. Gallen (Gaster, Sargans, Werdenberg), 2 Bde. (Rorschach 1951-1982).

[08.]

1. Mainz, Chur, Gericht des Erzpriesters im Dekanat Vintschgau.

Ein Archiv hat nicht überlebt. Der bischöfliche Offizial war zweite Instanz. Vgl. Clavadetscher (1964), oben 07/4/2, 14ff. und Helvetia Sacra 1/1, 521-525.

[09.]

1. Mainz, Chur, Gericht des Dekans im Engadin.

Ein Archiv hat nicht überlebt. Siehe oben 07/3: Mappe 61 Heft 12; Clavadetscher (1964), oben 07/4/2, 14ff. und Helvetia Sacra 1/1, 525-526.

[10.]

1. Mainz, Konstanz, Offizialat des Bischofs.

2. *Erzbischöfliches Archiv Freiburg, Herrenstraße 35, D-7800 Freiburg i. Br. [EAF].

*Zentralbibliothek Luzern, Sempacherstraße 10, CH-6003 Luzern [ZBL].

*Bischöfliches Archiv Chur [BAC] (siehe oben 07/2).

Badische Landesbibliothek, Lammstraße 16, D-7500 Karlsruhe [BLB].

Generallandesarchiv Karlsruhe [GLAK] (siehe oben 02/2).

Stiftsarchiv St. Gallen, Klosterhof 1, CH-9000 St. Gallen [SASG].

Biblioteca Apostolica Vaticana, I-00120 Città del Vaticano [BAV].

Württembergische Landesbibliothek, Konrad Adenauer-Str. 8, D-7000 Stuttgart [WLB].

3. *1. EAF*:

*Ha 125. 177 fol (ursprünglich 260). 1423-1444. Offizialatsprotokoll: 1429-1444; einzelne Stücke: 1423-1424, chronologisch geordnet.

*Ha 330 h. 348 pp. 1436-1444. *Liber sententiarum*, chronologisch geordnet.

*Ha 330 i. 1514-1517. Sentenzen, vor allem *matrimoniales*, chronologisch geordnet.

*Ha 126. 269 fol. 1518-1521. "Sententie diffinitive in cause tam matrimonialibus quam eccles. et aliis plenariis", chronologisch geordnet.

*Ha 127. 261 fol. 1522-1524/25. Wie Ha 126.

*Ha 128. 82 fol. 1551-1552. Dekrete und Sentenzen, vor allem *matrimoniales*, chronologisch geordnet.

*Ha 129. 143 fol. 1554-1555. Wie Ha 128.

*Ha 130. 133 fol. 1555-1556. Wie Ha 128.

*Ha 131. 121 fol. 1556-1557. Wie Ha 128.

*Ha 132. 102 fol. 1557-1558. Wie Ha 128.

*Ha 133. 77 fol. 1558-1559. Wie Ha 128.

*Ha 134. 118 fol. 1563-1564. Wie Ha 128.

*Ha 135-139. Bis 1574. Wie Ha 128.

Ha 342. 283 pp. 1533-1551. "Protocollum absolutionum tam presbyterorum quam laicorum, hon. viro Wolfgango notario et Johanne Alweger substituto, absolutionum de anno 1533 etc."

Ha 343. 218 fol. 1552-1562. Wie Ha 342.

Die nun folgenden "Libri conceptorum" stammen zum Teil aus der bischöflichen Kanzlei und sind daher keine eigentlichen Gerichtsakten:

*Ha 314. 146 pp. 1411, 1419-1432, 1440, 1446.

*Ha 315. 256 fol. 1441-1446.

*Ha 316. 204 fol. 1449-1460.

*Ha 317. 142 fol. 1455-1462.

*Ha 318. 168 fol. 1467-1470.

*Ha 319. 332 fol. 1481-1483. Darin fol 108 ff: "Processus contra clericos ad forum seculare in causis ecclesiasticis se trahentes" von 1482.

*Ha 320. 238 fol. 1497-1503.

*Ha 321. 517 pp. 1480-1503.

*Ha 322. 309 pp. 1516-1518. Vor allem ausgefertigte Urteile in Straffällen von Klerikern, aber auch *beneficiales*, chronologisch geordnet.

*Ha 323. 154 fol. 1518-1519. Wie Ha 322.

*Ha 324. 213 fol. 1520. Wie Ha 322.

*Ha 325. 140 pp. 1521-1523. Wie Ha 322, vor allem *beneficiales*.

*Ha 326. 71 pp. 1524-1526. Wie Ha 322.

*Ha 327. 196 pp. 1528-1530. Wie Ha 322.

*Ha 328. 236 pp. 1520-1522. Wie Ha 322.

*Ha 330 g. 327 pp. 1531.

Hinweise auf die Tätigkeit des Offizials finden sich auch in den Kopialbüchern der bischöflichen Kanzlei:

*Ha 330 a. 171 fol. 1464-1466.

*Ha 330 b. 2 Teile: 559, 273 pp. 1518-1524, 1524-1529.

*Ha 330 c. 312 pp. 1470-1481.

*Ha 330 d. 524 pp. 1496-1520.

oder in den beiden Formelbüchern und Formularsammlungen aus der bischöflichen Kanzlei:

*Ha 330 e. 418 pp. 1460-1500.

*Ha 330 f. 1450-1512.

Ha 61-78. 20 Bände. 1540-1700. Acta visitationum der Konstanzer Landkapitel (zum Teil gedruckt von Bossert, unten 10/4/5).

Kasten 98. s16-s17. Visitationsakten über Breisgauische Pfarreien, teilweise aus dem s16, vor allem aus dem s17.

2. ZBL:

*Kb Pb Msc 86 Folio. 140 fol. 1474-1480. Bischöfliches Konzeptbuch.

Aus der bischöflichen Kanzlei stammend (vgl. oben 10/3/1: Ha 330a-f).

3. BAC:

*Mappe 60 Heft 1. 224 pp. 1454-1459. Register von Johannes Hechinger, "notarius domini abbatis s. Galli necnon causarum matrimonialium ... commissarius generalis curie Constant.", chronologisch geordnet.

Das Register ist unvollständig, mindestens der Anfang fehlt. Uns interessieren hier nur die Protokolle von Zeugenaussagen (sog. "examen testium") zuhanden des Konstanzer Offizials, c50 Fälle.

4. *BLB*:

Papierhandschrift Karlsruhe 685. 333 fol. s15/ex. Enthält in alfabetischer Reihenfolge zahlreiche Formeln, notae und instrumenta. Das Formelbuch wurde von Johannes Buntz von Winterthur, Schreiber am Konstanzer Hof, verfaßt.

Nach Zapp, unten 10/4/1.

5. *GLAK*:

67/494. 193 fol. 1423-1587. Darin bis fol 132 Formularsammlung für die bischöfliche Verwaltung.

67/519. Fol 201-206. 1512/1513. Notiz über eine strittige Rechtssprechung im Thurgau vor geistlichem oder weltlichem Gericht in einem Fall von Frevel.

67/1491. 185 fol. s14-s15. Formularsammlung des Konstanzer Stadtschreibers Schulthess, darin diverse Formulare für Pfründenprozesse.

82a/B 4. Fol 105ff, 44 pp. 1550. Visitationsbericht (Breisgau und Württemberg) im Auftrag des Visitators Johannes Gumpardus vom Notar Johann Götz geschrieben.

Dieser Bericht lag bis 1932 im Staatsarchiv Zürich.

Gemäß brieflicher Aussage von Archivar und Amtsrat Rupp vom 2.1.1987 "sind in unseren Beständen Archivalien aus allen Bereichen der geistlichen und weltlichen Verwaltung des Bistums und des Domkapitels vorhanden. Allerdings sind diese Bestände nicht nach Provenienzen wie etwa "Offizialat" getrennt, sondern lediglich nach Sachrubriken untergliedert. Außerdem liegt der Schwerpunkt unserer Bestände doch im weltlichen Bereich der Verwaltung."

6. *SASG*:

Band 1011. Unpaginiert. 1503. Akten des Prozesses zwischen dem Leutpriester von St. Lorenz und dem Abt von St. Gallen über die Pfarr-Rechte der Kirche von St. Lorenz, vor den päpstlichen Delegaten Johann Hug, Propst an St. Johann in Konstanz, und Johann, Abt von Salem. (Vgl. dazu Scheiwiler, unten 11/4/1.)

7. *BAV*:

Reg. Lat. 557. Fol 39r-52r. 1500-1501. Eine Kopie der Akten des Prozesses zwischen dem bischöflichen Kommissar in Ehesachen, Petrus Numagen, und dem Zürcher Leutpriester Konrad Hofman. Letzterer hatte gepredigt, daß

Unkeuschheit bei Geistlichen nicht nur Unzucht, sondern ein Sakrileg sei. (Von Brülisauer, unten 10/4/5, pp 90-97, teilweise ediert.)

8. WLB:

HB VI 128. Fol 62-65v. 1457. Johann Zeller, Offizial: Consilium zum Streit zwischen dem Kloster Zwiefalten und König Friedrich III. um den Besitz von Kohlberg.

Id. Fol 65v-68v. c1465-1470. Jakob Grimm, Offizial: "Informaciones juris ... mag. J. G. decr. lic. in causa matrimoniali Johannis Bader alias Lantz et Eveline Vundrichin de Constant."

4. Bibliografie:

1. Allgemeines:

Johanne Autenrieth, 'Die kanonistischen Handschriften der Dombibliothek Konstanz', in *Kirchenrechtliche Texte im Bodenseegebiet. Mittelalterliche Überlieferung in Konstanz, auf der Reichenau und in St. Gallen* Vorträge und Forschungen, Sonderband 18 (Sigmaringen 1975) 5-21

Die Handschriften der ehemaligen Hofbibliothek Stuttgart 3: *Codices iuridici et politici (HB VI 1-139), Patres (HB VII 1-71)*, beschrieben von Johanne Autenrieth. Die Handschriften der Württembergischen Landesbibliothek Stuttgart 2.3 (Wiesbaden 1963) (darin Bücher aus dem Besitz der Konstanzer Offiziale Johann Guldin: HB VI 87, 93a.b, 99, HB VII 33, 67; Johann Wild: HB VI 33, 66-68; Johann Zeller: HB VI 77, 78; Leonhart Moschart: HB VI 72; Rudolf Spitzli: HB VI 69, 70, 71, 73; Andreas Wall: HB VI 69a, 125, 138; Jakob Grimm: HB VI 61, 69, 70, 71-73, 77, 78, 82-84, 86, HB VII 40)

K. Maier, 'Die Konstanzer Diözesansynoden im Mittelalter und in der Neuzeit', *Rottenburger Jahrbuch für Kirchengeschichte* 5 (1986) 53-70

Mittelalterliche Bibliothekskataloge Deutschlands und der Schweiz 1: *Die Bistümer Konstanz und Chur* bearb. von Paul Lehmann (München 1918, Nachdruck 1969) (darin pp 186-205 über die Konstanzer Dombibliothek; pp 303-387 über die Neithardsche Familie in Ulm, die in süddeutschen Bistümern viele Rechtsgelehrte gestellt hat; p 440f und p 448 über Bücher des Konstanzer Offizials Andreas Wall)

Repertorium der Kirchenvisitationsakten aus dem 16. und 17. Jahrhundert in Archiven der Bundesrepublik Deutschland 2: *Baden-Württemberg* 1 (Stuttgart 1984), (besonders 51-53)

J. Al. Scheiwiler, 'Ein st. gallischer Kirchenstreit am Vorabend der Glaubensspaltung', ZSKG 25 (1931) 81-101

Alois Schütz, 'Diplomatische Anmerkungen zu clm 21242. Ein Beitrag zur Erforschung spätmittelalterlicher Formularsammlungen', in *Grundwissenschaften und Geschichte, Festschrift für Peter Acht* (Kallmünz 1976) 189-199 (es handelt sich um einen Miszellan-Codex aus der Bibliothek der Ulmer Familie Neithard, der im frühen s14 von Heinrich von Stockach, einem Notar Heinrichs VII., und in den 40er Jahren desselben Jahrhunderts vom bishöflich-konstanzischen Notar Rudolf Lupolder zusammengesetzt worden ist)

H. Zapp, 'Bischofswahl nach einem Konstanzer Formularbuch von 1478',

Freiburger Diözesan-Archiv 100 (1980) 225-234.

2. *Archivgeschichte*:

Bernd Ottnad, 'Die Archive der Bischöfe von Konstanz', *Freiburger Diözesan-Archiv* 94 (1974) 270-516.

3. *Zu den Offizialen*:

Wolfgang Burger, 'Zeittafeln zur Geschichte der Offiziale der Bischöfe von Konstanz, von den Anfängen bis zum Jahre 1382', *Freiburger Diözesan-Archiv* 67 (1940) 346-355

Theodor Kurrus, 'Magister Johannes von Tunsel, Generalvikar und Offizial von Konstanz († 1394)', *Freiburger Diözesan-Archiv* 89 (1969) 310-356

Andreas Meyer, *Zürich und Rom: Ordentliche Kollatur und päpstliche Provisionen am Frau- und Großmünster 1316-1523*, Bibliothek des Deutschen Historischen Instituts in Rom 65 (Tübingen 1986) (enthält biografische Hinweise zu den vielen auch in Zürich bepfründeten Offizialen des s14 und s15)

4. *Über das bischöfliche Gericht*:

Arthur Bauhofer, 'Zürich und die geistliche Gerichtsbarkeit', *Zeitschrift für Schweizerische Geschichte* 16 (1936) 1-35

Eugen Baumgartner, *Geschichte und Recht des Archidiakonats der oberrheinischen Bistümer mit Einschluß von Mainz und Würzburg* Kirchenrechtliche Abhandlungen 39 (Stuttgart 1907)

Karl Brehm, 'Zur Geschichte der Konstanzer Diözesansynoden während des Mittelalters', *Diözesanarchiv von Schwaben* 22 (1904) 15-26, 44-48, 93-96, 141-144; 23 (1905) 30-32, 44-48, 60-64, 92-96, 142-144 (mit Abdruck der Synodalstatuten von c1400, 1435, 1438, 1441)

Karl Brehm, 'Nachtrag zur Geschichte der Konstanzer Synodalsynoden während des Mittelalters', *Diözesanarchiv von Schwaben* 24 (1906) 91-93

Rudolf Gmür, 'Zwei kanonische Zivilprozesse aus der Gegend des Thunersees', *Archiv des Historischen Vereins des Kantons Bern* 44 (1957-58) 289-316

Theodor Gottlob, 'Die Offiziale des Bistums Konstanz im Mittelalter', ZSKG 42 (1948) 124-144, 161-191, 257-296 (erschien auch als selbständige Schrift unter dem gleichen Titel, 1951, in Limburg an der Lahn)

Theodor Gottlob, 'Gerichts- und Kanzleiordnung des Bischofs Marquard von Konstanz aus dem Anfang des 15. Jahrhunders', ZSKG 44 (1950) 198-214

Anton Henggeler, 'Der Archidiakonat und die niedere hierarchische Ordnung in unserer Heimat, eine rechtsgeschichtliche Studie im Anschluß an eine neuere Publikation', ZSKG 1 (1907) 128-132

Eduard Otto Kehrberger, *Provinzial- und Synodalstatuten des Spätmittelalters. Eine quellenkritische Untersuchung der Mainzer Provinzialgesetzgebung des 14. und 15. Jahrhunderts, und der Synodalstatuten der Diözesen Bamberg, Eichstätt und Konstanz* Diss. phil. (Tübingen 1938)

A. Kluckhohn, 'Urkundliche Beiträge zur Geschichte der kirchlichen Zustände, insbesondere des sittlichen Lebens der katholischen Geistlichen in der Diözese Konstanz während des 16. Jahrhunderts', *Zeitschrift für Kirchengeschichte* 16 (1896) 590-626

Hans Morf, 'Obrigkeit und Kirche in Zürich bis zu Beginn der Reformation', *Zwingliana* 13 (1969-73) 164-205

Karl Otto Müller, 'Ein Landkapitel als geistliches Gericht', ZRG KA 23 (1934) 390-394 (es handelt sich dabei um einen Fall im Dekanat Hochberg am Neckar 1356 während des Bistumsstreites, als vermutlich kein Offizial amtierte)

F. Rohrer, 'Archidiaconen und Commissarien im Bisthum Constanz', *Anzeiger für Schweizerische Geschichte* 4 (1882-85) 16-19

Ernst Rüedi, 'Das geistliche Gericht zu Konstanz und seine Beziehungen zu Schaffhausen', *Schaffhauser Beiträge zur vaterländischen Geschichte* 27 (1950) 85-119.

5. *Gedruckte Quellen*:

A. J. Binterim, *Pragmatische Geschichte der deutschen National-, Provincial- und vorzüglichsten Diözesankonzilien vom 4. Jahrhundert bis zum Concil von Trient* 6 (Mainz 1845) (darin 285-294: Statuten des Bistums Konstanz von 1328)

G. Bossert, 'Die Akten der General-Kirchenvisitation der Grafschaft Hohenlohe vom Jahre 1556', *Württembergische Vierteljahreshefte für Landesgeschichte* 3 (1880) 159-170

Josef Brülisauer, *Neue Beiträge zur Biographie Conrad Hofmans (1454-1525)*, Diss. phil. Fribourg, 1970 (masch.) (darin pp 90-97 Edition der Akten des Prozesses zwischen Petrus Numagen und Konrad Hofman; siehe oben 10/3/7)

Constitutiones synodales ecclesiae Constantiensis ad laudem Dei editae anno Domini 1492 (o.O. o.J.) (Inkunabel)

Constitutiones synodales ecclesiae Constantiensis ad laudem Dei editae a. D. 1497 impressum per Erhardum Ratdolt civem Augustensem 1500

Josef Hartzheim, *Concilia Germaniae* 5 (Köln 1763) (darin pp 449-470 Synodalstatuten von 1463, pp 505-508 von 1476, pp 545-567 von 1483, pp 659-661 von 1492)

J. A. Kraus, 'Unbekannte Klerikerstatuten', *Freiburger Diözesan-Archiv* 70 (1950) 154-178 und 71 (1951) 267-282

Manfred Krebs, 'Nachlese zu den Konstanzer Bischofsregesten', *Zeitschrift für die Geschichte des Oberrheins* 98 (N.F. 59) (1950) 181-283

Die Rechtsquellen des Kantons St. Gallen 1: *Die Rechtsquellen der Abtei St. Gallen* 2.1: *Die allgemeinen Rechtsquellen der alten Landschaft* bearb. von Walter Müller, Sammlung Schweizerischer Rechtsquellen 14 (Aarau 1974), (besonders Nr. 34 pp 276 f. und Nr. 40 p 290)

O. Redlich, 'Ein oberrheinisches Formelbuch aus der Zeit der ersten Habsburger', *Zeitschrift für die Geschichte des Oberrheins* 50 (1896) 1-35, und Bemerkungen dazu von Alexander Cartellieri *ibid.* 314-317

Regesta Episcoporum Constantiensium (517-1480), 5 Bde. (Innsbruck 1895-1931)

Repertorium schweizergeschichtlicher Quellen im Generallandesarchiv Karlsruhe 1: *Konstanz-Reichenau*, 3 Bde. (Zürich 1982-84) (der vierte Band wird ein Register enthalten); 2: *Säckingen* (Zürich 1986).

[11.]

1. Tarantaise (bis 1510, danach exemt), Sion, Offizialat des Bischofs.

2. *Archives épiscopales, avenue de la Tour 12, CH-1950 Sion [AES].

Inventar und Archivgeschichte:

A. Donnet und J.-P. Hayoz, 'Catalogue des manuscrits historiques du P. Isidore Rudaz, capucin (1800-1868)', *Vallesia* 11 (1956) 155-172, besonders 163-169: 'Inventaire des archives de l'évêché de Sion'.

Peter Rück, 'Das Archiv des Domkapitels von Sitten', ZSKG 65 (1971) 114-120 (darin auch ein kurzer Abriß der Geschichte des bischöflichen Archivs).

Bernhard Truffer, 'Das Walliser Archivwesen im 16. Jahrhundert', *Vallesia* 28 (1973) 213-244, darin 229-239 ein Inventar des bischöflichen Archivs von 1428.

*Archives capitulaires, rue Mathieu Schiner 5, CH-1950 Sion (früher Archiv Valeria genannt) [ACS].

Archivgeschichte (zugleich summarisches Inventar):

Peter Rück, 'Das Archiv des Domkapitels von Sitten', ZSKG 65 (1971) 114-120.

Archives cantonales du Valais, rue des Vergers 9, CH-1950 Sion [ACVS].

Abbaye de Saint-Maurice, av. d'Agaune, CH-1890 St-Maurice [ASM].

Inventar: Bautier/Sornay 819-826.

3. *1. AES*:

*365, 01 (alte Signatur: Lade 214 Nr. 1). Pergament. 1480. Sentenz des Offizials in einem Streit zwischen zwei Junkern wegen Zinsen und Steuern.

*365, 02. Pergament. 1467. Bischof Walter bestätigt der Fransa relicta quondam Johannis Bonivini parochie de Lens, daß sie dem katholischen Glauben immer treu geblieben und daß sie keiner Ketzerei verdächtig sei.

*365, 04. 3 pp. 1554. Sentenz des Bischofs in causa matrimonialis.

*367, 09. 4 pp. 1420. Appellation des Abtes von St-Maurice an den Erzbischof von Tarantaise wegen einer Sentenz des Sittener Offizials betreffend die Kirche Bagnes.

2. ACS:

*Th 3-67. Fols 255-276. 1460. Statuta synodalia des Bischofs Walter von der Flüh.

*Th 87-22 (alte Signatur von Imesch: 8992). Pergament. 1434. Urteil des Bischofs von Sitten in einer Erbschaftssache, in der schon vor dem Gericht des Dekans von Sitten geurteilt worden war.

*Th 94-39 (Imesch 5677). 2 c15 cm breite, total c170 cm lange Papierstreifen. 1424. Vorschriften, wie eine bischöfliche Visitation vorgenommen werden sollte (in Deutsch).

Jud. Mappen 1-26. c1000 Artikel. 1340-1758. Justizsachen, zum Teil vom Offizial stammend.

Min. A 1-340 und Min. B 1-197. Vor allem s13-s16. Notarsminuten und -protokolle, Kartulare, Kanzleiregister.

Diese Geschäftsbücher (chronologische Zusammenstellung der Notarsregister bei Bautier/Sornay 1358-1368) enthalten verschiedentlich Hinweise und manchmal sogar Akten der geistlichen Gerichte der Diözese Sitten. Zwei moderne Repertorien (nach Namen und Signaturen geordnet) erleichtern die Benützung der Notariatsimbreviaturen. Es mag genügen, daß hier einige wenige Stücke aufgelistet werden:

*Min. A 10. Pp 13. 1315. Appellation an den Erzbischof von Tarantaise wegen eines Urteils des Offizials von Sitten.

*Min. A 10. Pp 103-117. "Infrascripta acta sunt coram offic. Lausan. commisario d. domini Episcopi in causa episcopali Sedun."

*Min. A 10. Pp 119-137. "Acta cause vertentis coram domino Wilhelmo de Sancto Mauritio curie s. Germani commissario in hac parte a dno. Ep. Sedun. inter dom. Rod. dictum Ubelin ex una parte et dom. Wilhelmum prepositum montis Iovis (Großer St. Bernhard) ex altera".

Commissio, memoriale, appellatio, memoriale, exceptiones, replicationes, copia insinuationis etc.

*Min. A 14. Pp 203, 187. 1513, 1514. Sprüche des Generalvikars von Sitten.

*Min. A 21bis. Pp 139-166. 1310-1347. Diverse Akten aus dem Offizialat von Sitten.

P 228: 1347, Entscheid des Offizials, einen Rentenverkauf für eine Jahrzeit betreffend.

*Min. A 92. Pp 1-158. 1451-1460. Rechnungsbuch des Johannes Jaquoti, sacerdos, über die Einnahmen aus den Siegelgebühren des Kapitels, der Dekane und des Offizials von Sitten.

*Min. 94. P 111. 1485. Zitation der Witwe des Notars Jean de Freneto im Streit gegen den Domherrn Jean Christa vor den Offizial.

3. ACVS:

Akten des bischöflichen Gerichts sind in diesem Archiv nicht vorhanden, man findet jedoch Urkunden, zB.:

AV Donum Genavense Nr. 81 und 89. Exkommunikationen.

ATL 17, Nr. 147. 1381. Quittung des Bischofs für den Sigillifer.

4. ASM:

Registres judiciaires: darin ein Register von Inquisitionsprotokollen 1453-1458.

Zur freiwilligen Gerichtsbarkeit des Abtes siehe Bautier/Sornay 1357f.

4. Bibliografie:

1. Allgemeines:

J.-B. Bertrand, 'Notes sur les procès d'hérésie et de sorcellerie en Valais', *Annales valaisannes* 3 (1920-21) 151-194

Sven Stelling-Michaud, 'Les étudiants valaisans à Bologne et la réception du droit romain au XIIIe siècle dans le diocèse de Sion', *Vallesia* 6 (1951) 59-85

Françoise Vannotti, 'Le chapitre cathédral de Sion du XIe au XIVe siècle d'après le fonds de la métralie', *Positions des thèses de l'École des chartes* (1970) 225-228

Françoise Vannotti, *Le chapitre cathédral de Sion (1043-1399). Fonds de la métralie* Thèse de l'École des chartes, 1969 (dact). (Diese Arbeit legt das Schwergewicht auf die Verwaltung und die Struktur des Grundbesitzes des Domkapitels (*métralie* kommt von *ministerialis*), sie bietet aber auch einen guten Überblick zur Geschichte und inneren Struktur des Kapitels seit dem Hochmittelalter, über die Dekane und ihre Jurisdiktion bes. pp 19-21.)

2. Zur bischöflichen Gerichtsbarkeit:

Jean Bacher, *Évolution de la législation matrimoniale dans le Valais épiscopal* Diss. iur. Fribourg (Sion 1957)

Louis Carlen, 'Das kirchliche Eherecht in der Diözese Sitten', ZSKG 49 (1955) 1-33

Louis Carlen, 'Zur geistlichen Gerichtsbarkeit in der Diözese Sitten im Mittelalter', *Blätter aus der Walliser Geschichte* 12 (1955-59) 257-290

Louis Carlen, 'Zum Offizialat von Sitten im Mittelalter', ZRG KA 77 (1960) 221-238

Louis Carlen, 'Die Generalvikare von Sitten', ZSKG 59 (1965) 1-12

Wolfgang Amadeus Liesbeskind, *Bischof Walters II. auf der Flüh Landrecht der Landschaft Wallis und Gerichtsordnung nebst einem Auszug aus seinen Synodalstatuten* (Leipzig 1930)

Poudret, 'Usuriers'

Bernhard Truffer, 'Das Wallis zur Zeit Bischof Eduards von Savoien-Achaia (1375-1386)', ZSKG 65 (1971) 1-113 und 197-301, besonders 68-77.

3. Gedruckte Quellen:

Albert Büchi, 'Ein bischöflicher Visitationsbericht vom Jahre 1509', ZSKG 7 (1913) 53-58

Albert Büchi, 'Zwei bischöfliche Visitationsberichte aus dem Anfang des XVI. Jahrhunderts', ZSKG 11 (1917) 45-54

Jean Gremaud, *Documents relatifs à l'histoire du Valais (300-1457)*, 8 Bde., MDSR 1.29-33, 37-39 (Lausanne 1875-1895) (siehe dazu auch: P.E. Martin',

Catalogue des manuscrits de la collection Gremaud conservés aux Archives d'État de Fribourg (Fribourg 1911))

Rechtsquellen des Cantons Wallis hg. von Andreas Heusler, (Basel 1890) (= Separatdruck aus der *Zeitschrift für schweizerisches Recht* N.F. 7-9).

[12.]

1. Tarantaise (bis 1510, danach exemt), Sion, Gerichte der Dekane von Sion und Valeria.

2. *Archives capitulaires de Sion (früher Archiv Valeria gennant) (siehe oben: 11/2).

3. Rechnungsbuch des Hugo, Pfarrer von Brämis. 1371-1374.

Dieses Rechnungsbuch (bei Imesch, unten 12/4/2, p 346 Anm. 1 erwähnt) war bei meinem Besuch im Archiv im Februar 1987 nicht aufzufinden.

Rechnungsbuch des Petrus Murgodi. 1386-1391.

Betrifft die Verwaltung des unteren Dekanats; siehe Imesch, unten 12/4/2, p 350 Anm. 1. Diese Rechnung war ebensowenig aufzufinden.

Imesch 6495. 1431. Zeugenverhör über die Ausübung der geistlichen Gerichtsbarkeit durch den Dekan von Valeria.

Diese Akten waren nicht aufzufinden.

*Th 40-35 (Imesch 6443). Pergament. 1357. Der Dekan von Valeria entlastet seinen Sigillifer Perrodus von Martigny.

*Th 47-17. 1 p. 1414 (bei Bautier/Sornay irrtümlich 1444). Visitation durch den Dekan von Valeria.

Zu den Beständen Min. A, Min. B und Jud. siehe oben 11/3/2.

4. Bibliografie:

1. Allgemeines:

Chantal Ammann-Doubliez, 'La chancellerie du chapitre de Sion et les débuts du notariat en Valais d'après les registres de maître Martin de Sion († 1306)', *Positions des thèses de l'école des chartes* (1986) 9-12

Bautier/Sornay 813-819 und 1357-1368 (Notarsregister aus dem 13. -16. Jh.)

SMÆH 13: *Die Schreibstätten der Diözese Sitten* bearb. von Josef Leisibach (Genf 1973), besonders 109-116: die juristische Bibliothek des Domkapitels.

2. Zur Gerichtsbarkeit der beiden Dekane:

Dionys Imesch, 'Die Würden und Würdenträger des Domkapitels von Sitten', *Blätter aus der Walliser Geschichte* 8 (1935-1938) 283-396 (besonders 340-364)

Françoise Vannotti, wie oben 11/4/1.

[13.]

1. Vienne, Genève, Offizialat des Bischofs.

2. Archives d'État de Genève, rue Hôtel-de-Ville 1, CH-1204 Genève [AEGE].

Geschichte des Archivs, zugleich auch summarisches Inventar:

Catherine Santschi, *Guide des Archives d'État de Genève* (Genève 1973).

Archives départementales de la Haute Savoie, 18 Avenue Tresume, F-74000 Annecy [ADHS].

Geschichte des Archivs, zugleich auch Inventar:

Jean Yves Mariotte et Robert Gabion, *Guide des Archives de la Haute Savoie* (Annecy 1976)

Répertoire numérique de la série G, 2 fasz. (Annecy 1926-1929).

Bibliothèque de la Société d'histoire et d'archéologie, c/o Bibliothèque publique et universitaire, 3 Place de l'Université, CH-1211 Genève [BSHG].

*Archives capitulaires de Sion [ACS] (siehe oben 11/2).

Archivio di Stato [AST], Piazza Castello, I-10100 Torino.

Siehe:

Max Bruchet, *Répertoire des sources de l'histoire de Savoie* (Paris 1935) (= Extrait de la *Revue des Bibliothèques*), besonders pp 89f., 110-116, 122; vgl. dazu Bautier/Sornay p XLIX.

3. *1. AEGE*:

Ms. hist. 47. Fol 41ff. 1435. Statuten des Bischofs François de Metz.

Ms. hist. 47. Fol 76ff. nach 1435. Statuten desselben.

Ms hist. 47. Fol 87f. 1431. Statuten desselben.

Ms. hist. 47. Fol 129-175. 1317-1470. Statuten der Genfer Bischöfe.

Ms. hist. 48. Fol 11-25. 1426-1444. Statuten des Offizialats unter Bischof François de Metz.

Ms. hist. 48. Fol 55r-126v. s15. Offizialatsformularbuch.

VIe section. Archives judiciaires: *Juridictions civiles Bm et Bn* und *Procès criminels*. Total ca. ein Dutzend Fälle. s14/ex-1536.

Siehe auch: Bautier/Sornay 1083.

X^e section. Archives notariales: Registres du notaire Jean Fusier. 5 vols. 1389-1438. Darin einige Sentenzen des Genfer Offizials zu *causae matrimoniales*, 1413.

Zu den Genfer Notariatsregistern siehe:

L. Dufour-Vernes, *Analyses des actes rédigés en latin et reçus par les notaires de Genève de 1373 à 1535*, 5 vols. et 1 vol. de table alphabétique des noms de personnes (dact).

Titres et droits, Évêché, Visites de curés et d'églises:

Nr. 1. 1411-1413, 1414. Visitationen.

Nr. 2. 1470-1471. Visitationen.

Nr. 3. 1481-1482. Visitationen.

Nr. 4. 1516-1518. Visitationen.

2. ADHS:

1 G 1. 1428-1466. Registre de minutes et d'actes de la chancellerie épiscopale.

1 G 2. 1467-1468. Registre de minutes et d'actes de la chancellerie épiscopale.

1 G 20. 1484-1487. Registre de minutes et d'actes de la chancellerie épiscopale.

Zu diesen drei Registern siehe auch Bautier/Sornay 1356.

1 G 98. 355 fol. 1443-1445. Visitationen.

2 G 1. 1450. Statuts de l'officialité de Genève: "Statuta nove reformationis curie officialatus Gebennarum".

Gedruckt in: *Les sources du droit* (unten 13/4/3).

2 G 2. 1418. Procès entre Henri de Menthon et Jean de Cluses, curé d'Olières.

2 G 3. Fragment d'une procédure entre Jean de Baresiaco, curé de Lovagny, et Pierre de Disonche.

F 195. 1526-1527. Offizialatsformularsammlung.

Dieser Kodex ist bei Lehnherr, oben 04/4/5, 6f. Anm. 2, beschrieben.

3. BSHG:

Ms. 45. 1 vol. 1430-s16. Fragments de registres des notaires épiscopaux.

4. ACS:

Tir. 3 Nr. 62. 1317-1408. Statuten der Bischöfe von Genf.

5. AST:

Genève 1 categoria, mazzo 7, no. 23. Inquisition über eine Predigt des Battista von Mantua in Genf im Jahre 1430.

Gedruckt bei Binz, siehe unten 13/4/3.

4. Bibliografie:

1. Allgemeines:

Henri Baud, *Le diocèse de Genève-Annecy* Histoire des diocèses de France 19 (Paris 1985)

Bautier/Sornay 766-772 und 1356 (Notarsregister aus den Jahren 1389-1500)

J.-P. Chapuisat, 'Pouillés des paroisses vaudoises du diocèse de Genève, XVe-XVIe siècles', ZSKG 50 (1956) 367-387

J.-P. Chapuisat, 'Visites d'églises à la Côte et au Pays de Nyon', *Revue historique vaudoise* 64 (1956) 48-64

Helvetia Sacra 1/3

Poudret, 'Usuriers'.

2. *Zum bischöflichen Gericht und den Offizialen*:

Louis Binz, *Vie religieuse et réforme ecclésiastique dans le diocèse de Genève pendant le grand schisme et la crise conciliaire 1378–1450*, 1, Mémoires et documents publiés par la Société d'histoire et d'archéologie de Genève 46 (Genève 1973), besonders 88f. und 477-488

Louis Binz, 'L'officialité du diocèse de Genève (XIIIe - XVIe siècle)', *Helvetia Sacra* 1/3, 187-216

Ferdinand Elsener, 'Justizreform in den Constitutiones et Statuta des Genfer Offizialats von 1450', ZRG KA 61 (1975) 63-83

Ferdinand Elsener, 'Die Exkommunikation als prozessuales Vollstreckungsmittel, auf Grund der Rechtsquellen von Stadt und Bistum Genf, zugleich ein Hinweis zur Frühgeschichte des summarischen Verfahrens', in *Études offertes à Jean Macqueron* (Aix-en-Provence 1970) 279-283

Gottfried Partsch, 'Un aspect général de la première apparition du droit romain en Valais et à Genève au XIIIe et au début du XIVe siècle', MHDB 19 (1957) 59-75, besonders 71-75

Jean-François Poudret, 'Un concordat entre Amadée VIII et le clergé de Savoie au sujet des compétences des cours d'église et des censures ecclésiastiques', *Mélanges offerts à Jean Dauvillier* (Toulouse 1979) 655-675

Charles-Maire Rebord, *Visites pastorales du diocèse de Genève-Annecy, 1411-1920*, 2 vols (Annecy, 1921-1922)

Catherine Santschi, 'Les officiaux du diocèse de Genève-Annecy (1545-1792, 1604-1789)', *Helvetia Sacra* 1/3, 303-322.

3. *Gedruckte Quellen*:

Louis Binz, 'Les prédications "hérétiques" de Baptiste de Mantoue à Genève, en 1430', in *Pour une histoire qualitative: Études offertes à Sven Stelling-Michaud* (Genève 1975) 15-34

Jean-Étienne Genequand, 'La visite pastorale de Saint-Gervais en 1446', *Bulletin de la Société d'histoire et d'archéologie de Genève* 14 (1968) 3-76

Édouard Mallet, *Documents inédits relatifs à l'histoire de Genève de 1312 à 1378*, Mémoires et documents publiés par la Société d'histoire et d'archéologie de Genève 18 (Genève 1872)

P. Lullin et Ch. Le Fort, *Régeste genevois ou répertoire chronologique et analytique des documents imprimés relatifs à l'histoire de la ville et du diocèse de Genève avant l'année 1312* (Genève 1866)

Les Sources du droit du Canton de Genève, 3 vols. Sammlung Schweizerischer Rechtsquellen 22: Die Rechtsquellen des Kantons Genf 1-3 (Aarau 1927-1933).

Index of Persons and Places
(Including authors of books and articles cited)

BA-Bibliographical Abbreviations; GI-General Introduction (followed by the section in which the item appears); D-Diocese List or List of Officialities, I-Introduction, P-Preface, B-Bibliography; all other references follow the system for cross-references given in the General Abbreviations. (For ease of reference, the right running heads in the text give both the report number and the section of the report treated on that page.) In subsequent references in the same string chapter and report numbers are not repeated. No indication is given if the reference appears in the numbered section more than once. References to abp, bp, dioc, prov and off are not indexed beyond the first section of a report, when the off of that abp, bp, dioc or prov is the subject of the report. Personal names of litigants mentioned in the descriptions are not indexed but officers and place-names are. All saints' names, whether personal names or place names are listed under "st", without regard to the linguistic form used in the original. In addition to the abbreviations given in the General Abbreviations, the following abbreviations are employed: abp-archbishop, adn-archdeacon, BEL-Belgium, bp-bishop, BRD-West Germany, cath-cathedral, CH-Switzerland, chap-chapter, comm-commissary, CZE-Czechoslovakia, dioc-diocese, DDR-East Germany, ESP-Spain, FRA-France, ITA-Italy, off-official or officiality, MAG-Hungary, NET-The Netherlands, ÖST-Austria, pjd-papal judge delegate, POR-Portugal, prov-province, ROM-Romania, YUG-Yugoslavia, vg-vicar general.

Aardenburg [NET], dean of, II/01/4/2, 4/5
Abella, Ferrer d', former bp of Barcelona, IX/03/3/1
Adams, N., BA, GI/01
Agram, *see* Zagreb
Agriensis, *see* Eger
Aix-en-Provence (Aquensis) [FRA], abp, dioc, prov, off of, III/00/D, 01/1, 02/1, 03/1, 04/1, 07/3/3
Alba Julia (Albensis, Karlsburg, Siebenbürgen, Transsilvaniensis, Ultrasilvanum) [ROM], bp, dioc, off of, V/00/P, D, 14/1, 15/1, 15/3/1
see also Meszes
Alexander III, pope, II/01/4/5
Alibertis, Henricus de, abbot of Filly, X/04/3/5
Allain, E., III/13/2
Altkirch [FRA], house of Basel off at, X/02/3/3
Alweger, Johannes, notary of Konstanz, X/10/3/1
Ambianensis, *see* Amiens
Ameland [NET], island, VII/02/1
Amici, Michael, seal-keeper of Brugge, II/01/3/2
Amiens (Ambianensis) [FRA], bp, dioc, off of, III/00/D, 41/1
Ammann-Doubliez, Chantal, X/12/4/1
André, Ferd[inand], III/23/2
André, Francisque, III/63/2
Anex-Cabanis, Danielle, X/04/4/4, 4/5
Anglade, A. d', III/13/2
Angoulême (Englolismensis) [FRA], bp, dioc, off of, III/00/D, 14/1
Aniciensis, *see* Le Puy
Antwerpen [BEL], dioc of, VII/01/1
adn of, II/00
Appamiarum, *see* Pamiers
Appelt, Heinrich, I/02/4
Apt (Aptensis) [FRA], bp, dioc, off of, III/00/D, 02/1
Aquensis, *see* Aix-en-Provence
Aquis, mr Raphael de, notary of Marseille, III/07/2
Aragon [ESP], king of, IX/03/3/4
Arbois de Jubainville, H. d', III/63/2
Arbunto, *see* Barcelona
Ardenga, *see* Siena, Ardenga

Arezzo [ITA], vg of dioc of, VI/02/3
Argentinensis, *see* Strasbourg
Argeş (Argensis) [ROM], off of, V/00/P, D
Arles (Arlelatensis) [FRA], abp, dioc, prov, off of, III/00/D, 05/1, 06/1, 07/1, 3/1, 08/1
Arnhem, *see* Tiel/Arnhem
Arpajon [FRA], off of bp of st Flour at, III/27/1
Artonne, A., X/00/B
Aschaffenburg [BRD], court of the adn, IV/00
Aubenas, Roger, BA, III/01/2, 3, 4, 07/2, 3/3, 4
Aufrère, Étienne, conseiller of the parlement of Toulouse, III/64/3
Augsburg (Augustensis) [BRD], bp, dioc, off of, IV/00, 01/1
Aurasicensis, *see* Orange
Aurelainensis, *see* Orléans
Austria infra Onasum, off of, *see* Passau
Autenrieth, Johanne, X/10/4/1
Autun (Eduensis) [FRA], bp, dioc, off of, III/00/D, 31/1
  chap of, III/31/3
  st Martin, abbey, III/31/3
  see also Blondel
Avignon (Avinionensis) [FRA], abp, bp, dioc, prov, off of, III/00/D, 06/1, 09/1, 10/1, 11/1, 12/1

Baarn [NET], local authorities of, VII/01/3/6
Bacher, Jean, X/11/4/2
Bács (Bachiensis) [YUG], former dioc of, V/13/4
Baden, Frederick of, bp of Utrecht, VII/01/3/3
Bagnes [CH], church of, X/11/3/1
Baiocensis, *see* Bayeux
Balics, L., V/19/4
Balázs, P., BA, V/01/2, 04/2, 08/2, 11/2
Bamberg (Bambergensis) [BRD], dioc, IV/00
Bándi, Zs., BA, V/06/2, 09/2
Barban, Guillaume, notary of Marseille off, III/07/3/1
Barcelona (Barchinonensis) [ESP], bp, dioc, off of, IX/00, 03/1
  chap of, IX/03/3/4
  deanery of, IX/03/3/5
  st Mary in Arbunto, IX/03/3/4
  st Stephen of, IX/03/3/5
  see also Abella
Baresiaco, Jean de, rector of Lovagny, X/13/3/2
Bars [CZE], county, tithes in, V/01/3/5
Basel (Basiliensis) [CH], bp, dioc, off of, III/00/D, X/00/P, I, B, 02/1
  adn, off of, X/02/3/1, 03/1
  council of, sentences of, V/01/3/5
  Phillip bp of, X/02/3/3
  see also Altkirch, Beinheim, Frank, Lufft, Rhein, Rheno, Saltzman, Uttenheim
Baud, Henri, X/13/4/1
Bauhofer, Arthur, X/10/4/4
Baumburg [BRD], adn of, I/00, 01/3/2, 07/1
Baumgartner, Eugen, X/10/4/4
Bautier, Robert-Henri, BA, GI/02, III/01/2, 02/2, 4, 03/2, 05/2, 07/3/1, 11/2, 73/2, 4, X/00/B, 04/3/6, 4/1, 11/2, 3/2, 3/4, 12/3, 4/1, 13/2, 3/1, 3/2, 4/1
Bayeux (Baiocensis) [FRA], bp, dioc, off of, III/00/D, 51/1
Beaujolais [FRA], ordonnance of the bailliage of, III/30/3/2
Beauvais (Belvacensis) [FRA], bp, dioc, off of, III/00/D, 42/1
  st Lucien, abbey, III/40/3
Becquart, Noël, III/16/2
Beinheim, Heinrich von, off of Basel, X/02/4/1
Beke, A., V/14/2
Beke, M., V/01/2
Belgradensis, *see* Beograd
Belvacensis, *see* Beauvais
Benet, A., III/31/2
Beneéthy, Matthäus, formulary of, V/01/3/3
Benschop [NET], VII/05/1
Beograd (Belgradensis) [YUG], off of, V/00/D
Berchtesgaden [BRD], provost of, I/00, 01/3/3
Bern [CH], city of, X/00/I
  Dominican convent in, X/04/3/4
Bernard, Gildas, III/63/2
Bernard, William, seal-keeper of Tournai, II/01/3/1
Bertrand, J.-B., X/11/4/1
Besançon (Bisuntinus) [FRA], abp, prov, off of, III/00/D, X/00/P, 01/1, 02/1

Besson, Marius, X/04/4/5
Beyer, Gerard, notary of Utrecht, VII/01/3/1
formulary of, VII/01/3/3
Binterim, A.J., X/10/4/5
Binz, Louis, X/13/3/5, 4/2, 4/3
Bise, Gabriel, X/04/4/4
Bisuntinus, *see* Besançon
Bituricensis *see* Bourges
Bittner, Ludwig, I/01/2
Bligny-Bondurand, E., III/39/2
Blondel, Jean, off of Autun, III/31/4
Bodegraven [NET], VII/02/1
Bogyay, T., V/13/4
Bol, Jan, notary of Utrecht, VII/01/3/1
Bónis, G., BA, V/01/2, 3/3, 4, 07/3/1, 10/3/1, 15/4, 17/4, 18/4
Bordeaux (Burdegalensis) [FRA], abp, dioc, prov, off of, III/00/D, 13/1, 14/1, 15/1, 16/1, 17/1
Borgia, cardinal Francesco, commendatario of the prepositura of st Lorenzo of Percenna (Pienza dioc), VI/01/3
Borovszky, S., V/17/3
Borsa, I., BA, V/14/2, 18/2
Borsa, Zs., V/06/2, 09/2
Bosna (Bosniensis), *see* Đakovo
Bossert, G., X/10/3/1, 4/5
Boüard, A. de, III/08/2
Bourges (Bituricensis) [FRA], abp, dioc, prov, off of, III/00/D, 18/1, 20/1, 21/1, 22/1, 23/1, 24/1, 25/1, 26/1, 27/1
st Étienne, prov chap, off of, III/19/1
Bousquet, J., III/25/2
Bouyssou, L., III/26/2
Boyé, A.J., III/13/3
Brämis, Hugo, rector of, X/12/3
Braşov (Kronstadt) [ROM], dean, off of, V/00/D, 02/1, 4
Bratislava (Posoniensis, Pressburg) [CZE], provost, off of, V/00/D, 03/1, 2, 4
Braunschweig [BRD], off of, IV/00
Breban, Jean, III/63/3
Breha [ESP], st Peter of, IX/03/3/5
Brehm, Karl, X/10/4/4
Breisgau [BRD], pastors of, X/10/3/1
Bremen (Bremensis) [BRD], dioc, IV/00
Bressanone (Brixen, Brixinensis) [ITA], bp, dioc, off of, I/00, 01/3/3, 02/1
Bretagne [FRA], offs of the bps of, III/29/3/2
Brie [FRA], off of the adn, III/58/1
Brink, Gerard ten, notary of Utrecht, VII/01/3/3
Brixen, Brixinensis, *see* Bressanone
Brouette, Émile, II/00
Brouwer, Jozef de, II/00
Bruchet, Max, X/13/2
Bruckner, Albert, X/00/B, 02/4/2, 04/4/1, 4/5, 07/4/1
Brugge [BEL], adn, city, dean, deanery, off of, II/01/3/2, 3/3, 3/4, 4/1, 4/2
hospital, Sint-Jan, II/01/4/4
see also Amici, Clapdorp
Brülisauer, Josef, X/10/3/7, 4/5
Brussel [BEL], *see* Cambrai
Brutails, J.A., III/13/2, 38/2
Bry, J., III/55/3
Büchi, Albert, X/11/4/3
Buda [MAG], council of, V/00/I
Budischin, H., IV/00
Buer, Willem, notary of Utrecht, formulary of, VII/01/3/2
Buntz, Johannes, von Winterthur, clerk of Konstanz, formulary of, X/10/3/4
Bunyitay, V., BA, V/02/3/1, 05/3/1, 17/4
Burckhardt, Max, X/02/4/1
Burcklé, Jean, X/02/4/1
Burdegalensis *see* Bordeaux
Burgensis, *see* Burgos
Burger, Wolfgang, X/10/4/3
Burgos (Burgensis) [ESP], bp, dioc, off, IX/00, 01/1
cath chap, court of, IX/02/1
see also Vela
Burgundy, David of, bp of Utrecht, VII/01/3/3
Philip of, bp of Utrecht, VII/01/3/3
see also Charles the Bold
Burias, L., III/14/2
Busquet, R., III/05/2

Cambrai (Cameracensis) [FRA], bp, dioc, off of, II/00, III/00/D, 43/1
off of at Brussel, II/00
Carnotensis, *see* Chartres
Carlen, Louis, X/11/4/2
Carpentras (Carpentoracensis) [FRA], bp, dioc, off of, III/00/D, 10/1
Cartellieri, Alexander, X/10/4/5
Cathalaunensis, *see* Châlons-sur-Marne
Catoni, G., VI/01/2
Cavaillon (Cavalicensis) [FRA], bp, dioc, off of, III/00/D, 11/1
abbey of, III/32/3

Čazma (Chasmensis) [YUG], provost, off of, V/00/D, 19/1
Cenadiensis, *see* Csanád
Cenomanensis, *see* Le Mans
Cerisy [FRA], abbey, off of, III/47/1, 49/4
Cesaragustanus, *see* Zaragoza
Chabaud, P., notary, III/11/3
Chalon-sur-Saone [FRA], bp of, III/30/3/2
Châlons-sur-Marne (Cathalaunensis) [FRA], bp, dioc, off of, GI/01, III/00/D, 44/1, 62/4
Chambéry, *see* Grenoble
Chanadiensis, *see* Csanád
Chapuisat, J.-P., X/13/4/1
Charles V, emperor, II/00, VII/01/2, 3/6
Charles VII, king of France, II/01/4/5
Charles the Bold, duke of Burgundy, II/01/4/1
Chartres (Carnotensis) [FRA], dioc of, III/00/D
 chap, off of, III/54/1
 great adn, off of, III/54/1
Cheney, C.R., GI/01
Chèvre, A., X/02/4/3
Chiemsee (Kimensis) [BRD], bp, dioc, off of, I/00, 01/3/3
 adn of, I/08/1
Chomel, V., III/73/4
Christa, Jean, canon of Sion cath, X/11/3/2
Chur (Curiensis) [CH], bp, dioc, off of, X/00/P, I, 07/1
 st Martin, church of, X/07/3
Cibiniensis, *see* Sibiu
Clapdorp, Henry, seal-keeper of Brugge, II/01/3/2
Claromontensis, *see* Clermont
Clavadetscher, Otto P., X/07/2, 4/2, 08/1, 09/1
Clermont (Claromontensis) [FRA], bp, dioc, off of, III/00/D, 20/1
 see also Rubier
Clewini Endingen, lady of, X/02/3/1
Clugny, Ferry of, bp of Tournai, II/01/4/2
Cluses, Jean de, rector of Olières, X/13/3/2
Coimbra [POR], bp, off of, VIII/00
Collier, R., III/04/2
Colocensis, *see* Kalocsa
Coloniensis, *see* Köln
Columpnis, Johannes, comm of bp of Lausanne, X/04/3/6
Como [ITA], dioc of, X/00/P
Constantiensis, *see* Konstanz
Corbie [FRA], abbey, off of, III/40/1, 47/4
 Raoul, abbot of, III/40/3
Corbigney [FRA], abbey, st Léonard, abbot of, III/31/3
Corse (Corsica) [FRA], III/00/I
Corsier, Jean, off of Toulouse, III/64/3
Courvoisier, Jean, X/04/2
Coutaz, Gilbert, X/01/2
Cristoforo da Montefollonico, Selva Mattia di, notary, VI/02/3
Csanád (Cenadiensis, Chanadiensis, Tschanad) [MAG], bp, dioc, off of, V/00/P, D, 16/1
Csontosi, J., V/10/3/1
Curiensis, *see* Chur
Cunretorff, Jacob, vg and off adn Oudmunster, account book of, VII/02/3/3

Đakovo (Bosna, Bosniensis, Diacovenis, Djakovo) [YUG], bp, dioc, off of, V/00/D
Damas [MAG], revenues from, V/01/3/5
Damme [BEL], city of, II/01/3/4
Dedek, C.L., BA
Delcambre, E., III/24/2
Delisle, Léopold, III/47/3, 70/3
Desplanque, III/38/2
Desvernay, III/30/2
Deventer [NET], dioc of, VII/01/1
 st Lebuinus, adn, chap of, VII/00, 01/3/2
Diacovenis, *see* Đakovo
Die (Diensis) [FRA], bp, dioc, off of, III/00/D, 72/1
Dieren [NET], VII/03/1
Diestelkamp, A., IV/00
Digne (Dignensis) [FRA], bp, dioc, off of, III/00/D, 28/1
Disonche, Pierre de, X/13/3/2
Djakovo, *see* Đakovo
Dolezalek, Gero, BA, GI/01, GI/02, VI/00
Dom, *see* Utrecht, cath
Domleschg (Thümleschg) [CH], valley, X/07/3
Donahue, Charles, BA, GI/01
Donnet, A., X/11/2
Doppler, Adam, I/01/3/3
Dopsch, Heinz, I/01/4
Driel [NET], VII/02/1
Ducannès-Duval, C, III/13/2
Dufour-Vernes, L., X/13/3/1

Duhamel, L., III/00/I, 02/2
Dupont, G., III/47/3
Dufresne, Jean-Luc, III/47/3
Durand, Georges, III/41/2
Durantis, William, bp of Mende, III/23/3/1, 4

Eduensis, *see* Autun
Eger (Agriensis, Erlau) [MAG], bp, dioc, off of, V/00/P, D, 07/1, 2
Eichstätt ((Eistetensis) [BRD], dioc, IV/00
Elburg [NET], VII/03/1
Elne (Elnensis) [FRA], bp, dioc, off of, at Elne and at Perpignan, III/00/D, 38/1
Elsener, Ferdinand, X/00/B, 04/4/4, 13/4/2
Ember, G., V/01/2
Embrun [FRA], prov of, III/28/1
Embs, *see* Ems
Emmerich [BRD], st Maarten, chap of, VII/00
Ems (Embs) [CH], parish, X/07/3
Endigen, Clewinus de, X/02/3/1
Engadin [CH], dean, court of, X/07/3, 09/1
Englolismensis, *see* Angoulême
Erdélyi, L., BA, V/01/3/2, 04/3/1
Érdújhelyi, M., V/13/4
Erdő, P., V/01/4
Erlau, *see* Eger
Estienne, C., III/25/2
Estienne, J., III/41/2, 42/2, 45/2
Esztergom (Gran, Strigoniensis) [MAG], abp, dioc, primate, prov, off of, GI/02, V/00/P, D, 01/1, 02/1, 4, 03/1, 04/1, 05/1, 06/1, 4, 07/1, 08/1, 09/1, 10/1, 2, 3/1, 11/1, 12/1
convent in (O.S.A.), V/01/3/5
Évora [POR], off of, VIII/00
vg of, VIII/00

Fabariensis, *see* Pfäfers
Fath, H., IV/00
Faure, C., III/29/2
Fayence [FRA], off of bp of Fréjus at, III/03/3
Fécamp [FRA], abbey, off of, III/47/4, 48/1, 49/4
Felsberg (Velsperg) [CH], parish, X/07/3
Fenzl, Annemarie, I/05/4
Fessenheim (Vesselhem) [FRA], chapel, X/02/3/1
Fetscherin, Bernhard Rudolf, X/04/4/5
Fiertz, Gertrude Barnes, X/04/4/4
Filastre, William, bp of Tournai, II/01/4/5
Filly [FRA], *see* Alibertis
Fineschi, S., VI/01/2
Fischer, Karl, I/12/4
Flanders, *see* Vlanderen
Flieder, Viktor, I/12/4
Flüh, Walter, bishop of Sion, X/11/3/1, 3/2
Foerster, H., X/04/2
Font-Réaulx, J. de, BA, III/00/I, 02/2, 09/2, 10/2, 11/2, 12/2, 72/2
Forel, François, X/04/4/5
Foroiuliensis, *see* Fréjus
Förster, H., IV/00
Fournier, Édouard, BA, III/56/3
Fournier, Paul, III/00/I
France, *see* Charles VII
Franco, Humbert, O.P., inquisitor, comm of bp of Lausanne, X/04/3/6
Frank, Fridericus, vg of Basel bp, X/02/3/5
Freiburg i. Br. [BRD], university, *see* Pfeffer
see also Fribourg
Freising (Frisingensis) (BRD), bp, dioc, off of, GI/02, I/00, 01/3/3, 03/1, IV/00
cath, provost of, *see* Hornpeck
Fréjus (Foroiuliensis) [FRA], bp, dioc, off of, III/00/D, 03/1
see also Fayence
Freneto, Jean de, notary, widow of, X/11/3/2
Frensdorff, F., IV/01/4
Fribourg (Freiburg) [CH], dean of, judge in marriage cases, X/06/1
Friedrich III, king, X/10/3/8
Friesach [ÖST], *see* Unterkärnten
Friesland [NET], secular prov of, VII/02/1, 04/1
Frisingensis, *see* Freising
Fusier, Jean, notary of Genève, X/13/3/1
Fuste, Franciscus de, bp of Granada, X/04/3/5
Fünfkirchen, *see* Pécs

Gabel, L., GI/01
Gabion, Robert, X/13/2
Gabotto, F., X/00/B
Galabert, E., III/65/2

Gallone, Paolo, X/04/4/4
Garmoisia, Jean, notary of Troyes off, III/63/3
Gars [BRD], adn of, I/09/1
Gaspero da Siena, Andreucci Matteo di, notary, VI/02/3
Gaulejac, B. de, III/25/2
Gauthier, P.F., III/29/2
Gebbensis, *see* Genève
Genequand, Jean-Étienne, X/13/4/3
Genf, *see* Genève
Gent [BEL], adn, city, dean, deanery, ?off of, II/01/4/1, 4/5
Génestal, R., GI/01
Genève (Gebbensis, Genf) [CH], bp, dioc, off of, III/00/D, X/00/P, I, B, 13/1
see also Fusier
Gescher, F., IV/00
Giacomo, Barnaba di, da Massa (Massa Marittima, prov. Grosseto), notary, VI/03/3
Giacomo da Montalcino, Carnevali Francesco di, notary of Siena, VI/02/3
Giacomo d'Angelo da Montalcino, Angelini Baldassarre di, notary of Siena, VI/01/3
Gilliard, François, X/04/4/4
Gingins-la-Sarra, Fréd., X/04/4/5
Giordanengo, Gérard, BA, III/01/2, 07/2
Giraud, P., III/05/2
Glandève [FRA], bp of, III/07/3/1
Glopper-Zuijderland, C.C. de, VII/01/4
Gmünd [ÖST], adn of, I/10/1, 11/3
Gmür, Rudolf, X/10/4/4
Godefroy, Denis, archivist (s17), II/01/2
Gombamal [*now in* Budapest, MAG], tithes, V/01/3/5
Gössi, Anton, X/02/4/1
Gottlieb, Beatrice, BA, III/44/4, 63/4
Gottlob, Theodor, X/02/4/3, 10/4/4
Götz, Johann, notary, X/10/3/5
Gouda [NET], VII/02/1
local authorities of, VII/02/3/4
rector, priests and churchwardens of, VII/02/3/4
vicarage in, VII/02/3/4
Gouget, A., III/13/2
Gouron, M., III/39/2
Graber, Jean Pierre, X/04/4/1
Gracionopolitanum, *see* Grenoble
Gran, *see* Esztergom
Grand st Bernard [CH], Wilhelm, provost of, X/11/3/2
Granada, *see* Fuste
Gravayat, P., III/19/2
Gregory XI, pope, IX/03/3/4
Gremaud, Jean, X/11/4/3
Grenoble (Gracionopolitanum) [FRA], bp, off of, at Grenoble and at Chambéry, III/73/1
Grimm, Jakob, off of Konstanz, X/10/3/8, 4/1
Groningen [NET], dioc of, VII/01/1
Grosseto [ITA], vg of dioc of, VI/02/3
Großer st Bernhard, *see* Grand st Bernard
Großwardein, *see* Oradea
Guigue, G., III/29/2
Guigue, M.C., III/29/2
Guizard, L., X/00/B
Guldin, Johann, off of Konstanz, X/10/4/1
Gumpardus, Johannes, visitor, X/10/3/5
Gurk (Gurcensis) [ÖST], bp, dioc, off of, I/00, 04/1
Gyetvai, P., BA, V/00/D, 09/4, 13/4
Győr (Jauriensis, Raab) [MAG], bp, dioc, off of, V/00/P, D, 04/3/1, 08/1

Haarlem [NET], dioc of, VII/01/1
Hagemann, Hans-Rudolf, X/02/4/1
Hageneder, Othmar, BA, GI/01, I/01/4, 05/4
Hagesteijn [NET], church in, VII/01/3/6, 02/3/4
Halberstadt (Halberstadensis) [DDR], dioc, IV/00
Haldenstein [CH], parish, X/07/3
Hamvas, J., V/13/2
Hannappel, M., IV/00
Hansen, J., IV/00
Harmelen [NET], VII/05/1
Hartzheim, Josef, X/02/4/5, 10/4/5
Hattem [NET], VII/03/1
Hayoz, J.-P., X/11/2
Hechinger, Johannes, notary of Konstanz, X/10/3/3
Heeringa, K., VII/05/2
Heinrich VII, *see* Stockach
Helmholz, R.H., GI/01
Henggeler, Anton, X/10/4/4
Herbipolensis, *see* Würzburg
Hermannstadt, *see* Sibiu
Hertogenbosch, *see* 's-Hertogenbosch
Heusler, Andreas, X/02/4/1, 11/4/3
Hildesheim (Hildeshemensis) [BRD], dioc, IV/00

Hildesheimer, Françoise, BA, III/01/2, 07/2
Hillgarth, J.N., IX/03/3/3
Hilling, N., IV/00
Hoern, notary of Utrecht, VII/01/3/1
Hofman, Konrad, lay-priest of Zürich, X/10/3/7, 4/5
Hohl, Claude, III/53/2
Hollandse Yssel [NET], river, VII/02/1
Holy See, citation to, appeal to, III/23/3/1, 32/3, V/01/3/2, 3/5, 3/6
dependence on, III/57/4
Hornpeck, Eglolf, provost of Freising cath, formulary of, I/03/4
Horváth, V., V/03/2
Hospitallers, order of, VII/01/3/6
Hours, H., III/29/2
Hübscher, Bruno, X/07/2
Huendler, Vitus, V/10/3/1
Hug, Johann, provost of st Johann in Konstanz, pjd, X/10/3/6

Imbert, L., BA, III/00/I, 02/2, 09/2, 10/2, 11/2, 12/2
Imesch, Dionys, X/12/3, 4/2
Innocent IV, pope, III/41/3
Innocent VIII, pope, VI/02/3
Ipolyi, L., V/13/4

Jacotin, A., III/24/2
Jaquoti, Johannes, accounts of, X/11/3/2
Jaroschka, dr Walter, I/00, 03/4, 05/2, 07/2
Jauriensis, *see* Győr
Jerney, J., V/19/4
Jetzer, Hans, defendant, X/04/3/4
Johanek, Ingeborg, IV/00
Joly, Olivier, fiscal proctor of bp of Lausanne, X/04/3/2
Jonge van Ellemeet, Jhr. dr B.M. de, VII/02/2, 04/2
Joosting, J.G.C., BA, VII/01/3/3, 4
Jorio, Marco, X/02/4/2
Juhász, K., V/16/4
Jutfaas, VII/05/1

Kalocsa (Colocensis) [MAG], abp, dioc, prov, off of, GI/02, V/00/P, D, 13/1, 14/1, 15/1, 16/1, 17/1, 18/1, 19/1
Kalocsa-Bács, *see* Bács, Kalocsa
Kaluwe, Maarten, notary of Utrecht, VII/01/3/1
Kamerik [NET], VII/05/1
Karácsonyi, J., V/15/4, 17/4
Karácsonyi, J., V/15/4, 17/4
Karácsonyi, R., BA
Karlsburg, *see* Alba Julia
Katona, S., V/13/4
Kehrberger, Eduard Otto, X/10/4/4
Ketner, F., VII/01/4
Keußen, H., IV/00
Kimensis, *see* Chiemsee
Klagenfurt, *see* Gurk
Klingental [CH], monastery, X/02/3/1
Kluckhohn, A., X/10/4/4
Knauz, F.(N.), BA, V/01/3/5, 03/2, 4, 3/1, 4
Knemeyer, F.-L., IV/00
Knin (Tinniniensis) [YUG], bp, dioc, off of, V/00/D
Kockengen [NET], VII/05/1
Kohlberg, possession of, X/10/3/8
Kohler, Ch., III/25/2
Koller, J., BA, V/10/3/1, 4
Köln (Coloniensis) [BRD], abp, dioc, prov, off of, II/00, IV/00, VII/01/1, 3/2, 3/6, 02/1, 03/1, 04/1, 05/1
Konstanz (Constantiensis) [BRD], bp, dioc, off of, X/00/P, I, 10/1
provincial chap, X/10/3/1
st Johann, provost of, *see* Hug
see also Alweger, Grimm, Guldin, Hechinger, Lupolder, Moschart, Munsingen, Numagen, Schulthess, Wall, Wild, Wolfgang, Zeller
Körmendy, J., V/01/2
Kortrijk [BEL], city of, II/01/4/1
Kovachich, M.G., BA, V/07/3/1
Kraus, J.A., X/10/4/5
Krebs, Manfred, X/02/2, 10/4/5
Kronstadt, *see* Braşov
Krusch, B., IV/00
Krüger, H.-J., IV/00
Kühtmann, A., IV/00
Kumorovitz, B.L., BA, V/01/2, 3/5
Kundert, Werner, X/07/4/2
Kurrus, Theodor, X/10/4/3

Lacour, R., III/29/2
Lambrecht, Daniël, II/01/3/4
Lamothe, A. de, III/39/2
Land van Waas [BEL], deanery of, II/01/4/5
Lang, Peter Thaddäus, X/02/4/5
Langres (Lingonensis) [FRA], bp, dioc, off of, III/00/D, 32/1
Latour, H., III/23/2

Laurent, Hughes, notary of Marseille, III/07/2
Lausanne (Lausanensis) [CH], bp, dioc, off of, III/00/D, X/00/P, I, B, 04/1, 11/3/2
adns and deans, courts of, X/06/1
bp, bailiff, court of, X/01/3, 04/3/1
chap, court of, X/05/1
see also Columpnis, Franco, Fribourg, Joly, Mentha, Montfaucon, Perrin, Richard, Saluces, Vuonflens
Laval, E., III/65/2
Lavant (Laventinensis) [ÖST], I/00, 01/3/3
Le Cacheux, Paul, III/47/3
Le Fort, Ch., X/13/4/3
Le Mans (Cenomanensis) [FRA], bp, dioc, off of, III/00/D, 67/1
Le Nail, J.F., III/65/2
Le Puy (Aniciensis sive Podiensis) [FRA], bp, dioc, off of, III/00/D, 24/1
Leeuwarden [NET], dioc of, VII/01/1
Lefebvre-Teillard, Anne, BA, GI/01, III/00/I, 07/4, 15/3, 19/4, 21/4, 28/4, 30/3/1, 35/1, 39/3, 40/3, 43/4, 44/4, 49/4, 58/3, 59/4, 61/4, 63/4, 68/3
Lehmann, Paul, X/10/4/1
Lehnherr, Yvonne, X/04/3/2, 3/3, 4/5, 13/3/2
Lehotská, D., V/03/2
Lejeune, Michael, II/00
Lek [NET], river, VII/02/1
Lekkerkerk [NET], VII/02/1
Lemoine, P., III/29/2
Lemovicensis, *see* Limoges
Lempereur, L., III/25/2
Lenz (Lens) [CH], parish of, X/11/3/1
Leo X, pope, VI/02/3
Leodiensis, *see* Liège
Lepage, H., III/71/2
Leuven [BEL], *see* Liège
Leux, L., III/31/2
Lexmond [NET], priest in, VII/02/3/4
Lhotsky, A., IV/00
Liège (Leodiensis) [BEL], bp, dioc, off of, GI/02, II/00, VII/01/1
off of, at Leuven, II/00
Liesbeskind, Wolfgang Amadeus, X/11/4/2
Lille [FRA], off of Tournai at, II/01/4/4
Limburg [NET], secular prov of, VII/01/1
Limoges (Lemovicensis) [FRA], bp, dioc, off of, III/00/D, 21/1
chap, off of, III/22/1
Lingonensis, *see* Langres
Linschoten [NET], VII/02/1
Lisboa [POR], abp, bp, dioc, off of, VIII/00
vg of, VIII/00
Lotz, A., V/16/4
Lovagny, *see* Baresiaco
Lufft, Arnold zum, official of Basel, X/02/4/1
Lugdunensis, *see* Lyon
Lullin, P., X/13/4/3
Lupolder, Rudolf, notary of Konstanz, formulary of, X/10/4/1
Lyon (Lugdunensis) [FRA], abp, dioc, primate, prov, off of, III/00/D, 31/1, 32/1, X/00/P
abp, conseil of, III/30/3/2
abp, off of (Cour des excès), III/34/1
abp, off of (dioc), III/33/1
abp, off of (primatial), III/29/1
abp, off of (prov), III/29/3/2
abp, off of (prov and dioc), III/30/1
abp and cath chap, off of (Cour commune), III/35/1
st Jean, chap, off of (justice du glaive spirituel), III/36/1
st Just, chap, off of, III/37/1
Lévy, J.-Ph., III/56/3
Löhr, J., IV/00

Magyi, Johannes, formulary of, V/07/3/1, 10/3/1
Maier, K., X/10/4/1
Maillezais (Malleacensis) [FRA], bp, dioc, off of, III/00/D, 15/1
Mainz (Maguntina) [BRD], abp, dioc, prov, off of, III/00/D, IV/00, 01, X/00/P, 07/1, 08/1, 09/1, 10/1
Maitre, L., III/68/2
Maladers [CH], parish, X/07/3
Malleacensis, *see* Maillezais
Mallet, Édouard, X/13/4/3
Mályusz, E., V/10/4, 11/4
Mansilla, Demetrio, IX/02/2
Mantua, Battista von, preacher, X/13/3/5
Marichal, Paul, III/56/3
Mariotte, Jean Yves, X/13/2
Marseille (Massiliensis) [FRA], bp, dioc, off of, III/00/D, 07/1
Carmelites at, III/07/3/1

chap of, III/07/3/1
hospital, st Esprit, III/07/3/3
Jews of, III/07/3/1
st Louis, convent (O.F.M), III/07/3/1
st Paule, monastery, III/07/3/3
st Victor, abbey, III/07/3/1, 3/3
cellerer of, III/07/3/3
elemosynary of, III/07/3/1
see also Acquis, Barban, Laurent, Roquevaire, Venaissini
Martigny, Perrodus von, seal-keeper of Valeria dean, X/12/3
Martin P.E., X/11/4/3
Martin, O., GI/01
Maschke, R., IV/01/4
Massa e Populónia [ITA], bp, dioc, off of, VI/03/1
Massa Marittima [ITA], *see* Giacomo
Massiliensis, *see* Marseille
Matile, Auguste, X/04/3/7, 4/1
Mauritio, *see* st Maurice
May, G., IV/00
Mayer, J.G., X/07/4/3
Mechelen [BEL], prov of, VII/01/1
Medenblick (Medemblick), Jacob van, notary of Utrecht, VII/01/3/2, 02/3/1
Melkebeek, Monique Van, *see* Vleeschouwers-Van Melkebeek
Mende (Mimatensis) [FRA], bp, dioc, off of, GI/02, III/00/D, 23/1
see also Durantis
Mentha, Vuillème, notary of Lausanne off, X/04/3/7
Menthon, Henri de, X/13/3/2
Merlet, Lucien, BA, III/54/2
Mersman, Jan, notary of Utrecht, VII/01/3/2, 02/3/1
Mesreyo (unidentified) [Sées dioc, FRA], church of st Claude, VI/03/3
Meszes [ROM], vicariat extra, off of, V/00/D, 15/1
see also Tăşnad
Metz, François de, bp of Genève, X/13/3/1
Meyer, Andreas, III/29/2, X/10/4/3
Meyer, Meinrad, X/04/4/5
Michael, dr, vicar of Pécs, formulary of, V/10/3/1
Michel, F., IV/00
Michon, L., III/31/2
Middelburg [NET], dioc of, VII/01/1
Mijdrecht [NET], region of, VII/04/1
local authorities of, VII/01/3/6
Milano [ITA], dioc of, X/00/P
Milcov (Milkoviensis) [ROM], dioc of, V/00/D
Millioud, A., X/04/4/2
Mimatensis, *see* Mende
Minden (Mindensis) [BRD], dioc, IV/00
Mohr, Th. v., X/07/4/3
Molinier, A., III/30/2
Molitor, H., X/00/B
Momfelen, Tielman, notary of Utrecht, VII/01/3/2
Mommsen, Karl, X/02/4/4
Monasteriensis, *see* Münster
Mons Pannoniae, *see* Pannonhalma
Montalcino [ITA], bp, dioc, off, VI/01/1
st Antimo, abbey, VI/01/3
see also Giacomo, Petruccio, Picolominibus
Monte Oliveto, *see* Siena, Monte Oliveto
Montefollonico, *see* Cristofero
Montfaucon, Sebastian von, bp of Lausanne, X/04/3/6
Montfoort [NET], VII/02/1
Montivilliers [FRA], abbey, off of, III/47/4, 48/4, 49/1
dean of, III/49/3
Moor, C. v., X/07/4/3
Morard, Nicolas, X/04/2
Morf, Hans, X/10/4/4
Morgand, A., III/31/2
Morinensis, *see* Thérouanne
Moschart, Leonhart, off of Konstanz, X/10/4/1
Mudrich, Andreas, I/01/4
Müller, G.E., BA, V/05/4
Müller, Karl Otto, X/10/4/4
Müller, Walter, X/10/4/5
Muller Fz., S., BA, VII/01/2, 3/4, 4, 03/2
Muller Hz., S., BA, VII/01/3/3, 4
Müller-Volbehr, J., IV/00
Munsingen, Nicolaus de, M.A., clerk of Konstanz dioc, canon of Rheinfelden, X/02/3/5
Münster (Monasteriensis) [BRD], dioc of, IV/00, VII/01/1
Muoth, J., X/07/4/3
Murgodi, Petrus, X/12/3

Nagy, G., V/10/4
Nagy, I., V/10/4, 13/4

Nagy, L., BA, V/04/2, 08/2
Nantes (Nanetensis) [FRA], bp, dioc, off of, III/00/D, 68/1
st Pierre, chap, off of, III/69/1
Narbonne (Narbonensis) [FRA], abp, prov, off of, III/38/1, 3, 39/1
Nemausensis, *see* Nîmes
Neithard, family of, in Ulm, X/10/4/1
Neri da Sarteano, Feliciano di ser, notary of Siena, VI/02/3
Neutra, *see* Nitra
Nicholas IV, pope, III/23/3/1
Nijkerk [NET], VII/03/1
Nîmes (Nemausensis) [FRA], bp, dioc, off of, III/00/D, 39/1
Nitra (Neutra, Nitriensis) [CZE], bp, dioc, off of, V/00/P, D, 09/1
Noord-Brabant [NET], secular prov of, VII/01/1
Numagen, Petrus, comm of bp of Konstanz, X/10/3/7, 4/5
Nyás, Demetrius von, formulary of, V/01/3/3

Oberwallis, *see* Sion, deans
Ochsenbein, Gottlieb Friedrich, X/04/4/4
Oldenzaal [NET], st Plechelmus, chap of, VII/00
Oláh, Nikolaus, V/06/4
Olières, *see* Cluses
Ollivant, S., BA, GI/01, GI/02
Oostbroek [NET], abbot of, VII/01/3/6
Oradea (Großwardein, W(V)aradiensis) [ROM], bp, dioc, off of, V/00/P, D, 17/1
Orange (Aurasicensis) [FRA], bp, dioc, off of, III/00/D, 08/1
Orléans (Aurelainensis) [FRA], bp, dioc, off of, III/00/D, 55/1
Ortvay, T., BA, V/03/4, 05/4, 06/4, 13/4, 16/4, 19/4
Osnabrück (Osnaburgensis) [BRD], dioc, IV/00, VII/01/1
Österreich unter der Enns, *see* Passau
Osts, Osto, promotor of off Tournai, II/01/3/4
Oswald, Josef, I/05/4
Ottenthal, Emil, I/02/4
Ottnad, Bernd, X/10/4/2
Oudenaarde [BEL], off of Tournai at, II/01/4/3
Oudenburg [BEL], deanery of, II/01/3/4, 4/2, 4/5
Oudmunster, *see* Utrecht, Oudmunster
Owen, Dorothy M., GI/01
Oya [POR], monastery of, VIII/00

Paarhammer, Hans, I/01/4
Paderborn (Padeburnensis) [BRD], dioc, IV/00
Pailhès, C., III/65/2
Paillly [CH], case from, X/04/3/2
Paix, J., III/65/2
Palacio [ESP], st Mary de, IX/03/3/4
Palustre, III/38/2
Pamiers (Appamiarum) [FRA], bp, dioc, off of, III/00/D, 65/1
Pamplona (Pampilonensis) [ESP], bp, dioc, off, IX/00, 04/1
Pannonhalma (Mons Pannoniae) [MAG], exempt abbey, off of, V/00/D, 04/1, 3/1
Paris (Parisiensis) [FRA], bp, dioc, off of, III/00/D, 29/3/2, 56/1, 60/1
adn, off of, III/59/1
cath chap, off of, III/57/1
see also Brie, st Germain
Partsch, Gottfried, X/13/4/2
Passau (Patavensis) [BRD], bp, dioc, off of, I/00, 01/3/2, 3/3, 05/1, 11/3
off for Austria below the Enns (infra Onasum, unter der Enns), I/05/1, 3/1 *(named)*
see also Rott
Paul III, pope, VI/02/3
Pavonis, John, seal-keeper of Tournai, II/01/3/1
Pécs (Fünfkirchen, Quinqueecclesiensis) [MAG], bp, dioc, off of, V/00/P, D, 10/1
see also Michael
Pelicier, P., III/44/2
Pelissier, E., III/65/2
Percenna (Siena, Pienza dioc) [ITA], prepositura of st Lorenzo, *see* Borgia
Périgeux (Petragoricensis) [FRA], bp, dioc, off of, III/00/D, 16/1
Perler, Othmar, X/04/4/5
Perpignan, *see* Elne
Perrin, R., secretary of ?bp of Lausanne, X/04/3/2
Péterffy, P.C., BA, V/00, 06/4
Peters, Henriette, I/05/4
Petit, A., III/21/2
Petit, J., off of Poitiers, III/17/3

Petit, Joseph, BA, III/00/I, 02/3, 15/3, 56/3
Petragoricensis, *see* Périgeux
Petruccio, Alexandro, u.i.doct. d., of Siena, podestà and capitano of Montalcino, VI/01/3
Petzhold, L., V/10/2
Pfäfers (Fabariensis) [CH], monastery, X/07/3
Pfeffer, Johannes, de Wydenberg, professor at university of Freiburg i. B., X/02/3/5
Pfleger, Luzian, X/02/4/1
Philip II, emperor, VII/01/1
Piccolomini, family, VI/02/3
Picolominibus, Hieronimus de, bp of Pienza and Montalcino, VI/01/3/0, 02/3
Pictaviensis, *see* Poitiers
Pientia, Dominicus olim Viti de, notary of Siena, VI/02/3
Pienza [ITA], vg of dioc of, VI/02/3
see also Borgia, Picolominibus
Piétresson de Saint-Aubin, A.-M., II/01/2
Piétresson de Saint-Aubin, Pierre, III/43/2
Pieyns-Rigo, Paulette, II/00
Pilot, J., III/73/4
Pirhala, M., V/06/4
Pisa [ITA], prov, VI/03/1
Pius II, pope, V/01/3/5
Plöchl, Willibald, I/05/4
Podiensis, *see* Le Puy
Poitiers (Pictaviensis) [FRA], bp, dioc, off of, III/00/D, 17/1
see also Petit, J.
Polsbroek [NET], VII/05/1
Pommeray, L., BA, III/59/2, 3/1, 3/3, 4
Pontal, O., X/00/B
Pontoise [FRA], off of Rouen at, III/50/1
promotor of, III/50/3
Posoniensis, *see* Bratislava
Poudret, Jean-François, X/04/4/1, 4/4, 4/5, 11/4/2, 13/4/1, 4/2
Pressburg, *see* Bratislava
Prinz, J., IV/00
Prokopp, G., V/01/2

Quantin, Michel, III/53/2
Quinqueecclesiensis, *see* Pécs

Raab, *see* Györ
Rambault, Maurice, III/01/2
Rapaics, R., BA
Rapolano [ITA], priest of, VI/02/3
Ratberg, *see* Rotberg
Ratisboniensis, *see* Regensburg
Rebord, Charles-Maire, X/13/4/2
Redet, L., III/17/2
Redlich, Oswald, I/02/4
Regensburg (Ratisboniensis) [BRD], bp, dioc, off of, I/00, 01/3/3, 06/1, IV/00
Reims (Remensis) [FRA], prov of, II/00, 01/1, III/40/1, 41/1, 42/1, 43/1, 44/1, 45/1
Rennes [FRA], delegates of abp of Tours at, III/29/3/2
Reymond, Maxime, X/04/4/3
Rhäzuns (Rotzüns) [CH], parish, X/07/3
Rhein, Friedrich zu, bp of Basel, X/02/3/3
Rheinfelden (Rynfeldensis) [CH], collegiate church of st Martin, X/02/3/5
see also Munsingen
Rheinwald (Rinwaldt) [CH], valley, X/07/3
Rheno, Caspar de, bp of Basel, X/02/3/3
Richard, Jacob, secretary of off of Lausanne, X/04/3/1
Riedner, O., IV/00
Rijnland [NET], provisor of, VII/02/3/4
Rimely, C., V/03/4
Rinwaldt, *see* Rheinwald
Robillard de Beaurepaire, C. de, III/46/2
Rodez (Ruthenensis) [FRA], bp, dioc, off of, III/00/D, 25/1
Roermond [NET], dioc of, VII/01/1
Roeselare [BEL], deanery of, II/01/4/5
Rohrer, F., X/10/4/4
Rome, *see* Holy See
Roquevaire [FRA], off of Marseille at, III/07/3/2
Rosa Pereira, Isais da, VIII/00
Rothomagensis, *see* Rouen
Rott, Mathäus, notary of Passau off, I/05/3/1
Rotzüns, *see* Rhäzuns
Rouen (Rothomagensis) [FRA], abp, dioc, prov, off of, III/00/D, 46/1, 47/1, 48/1, 49/1, 3, 50/1, 51/1, 52/1, VI/02/3
see also Pontoise
Rubier, Vincent, notary of Clermont, III/20/2
Rück, Peter, X/04/4/4, 05/1, 11/2
Rudaz, Isidore, manuscripts of, X/11/2
Rüedi, Ernst, X/10/4/4

Rupp, archivist of GLAK, X/02/3/4, 10/3/5
Rutghers van Ommen, Henric, notary of Utrecht, VII/01/3/2
Ruthenensis, *see* Rodez
Rynfeldensis, *see* Rheinfelden

's-Hertogenbosch [NET], dioc of, VII/01/1
Sagh [?Šahy, CZE], tithes of, V/01/3/5
Sagiensis, *see* Sées
Saint: for names beginning with "saint" or any variant of it, *see* st
Salem [BRD], Johann, abbot of, pjd, X/10/3/6
Sales Tirapu, José Luis, IX/04/2
Saltzman, Adalbertus, notary of Basel, X/02/3/1
Saluces, Georges de, bp of Lausanne, X/04/3/2, 3/5
Salzburg (Salzeburgensis) [ÖST], abp, dioc, prov, off of, GI/02, I/00, 01/1, 3/2, 02/1, 03/1, 04/1, 05/1, 06/1, 07/1, 08/1, 09/1, 10/1, 11/1, IV/00
suffragan bps, diocs, I/01/3/2, 3/3
Sanabre, José, IX/03/2
Santiago de Compostela [ESP], vg of, VIII/00
Santifaller, Leo, I/02/4
Santschi, Catherine, X/13/2, 4/2
Sardegna (Sardinia) [ITA], III/07/3/1
Sasad [*now in* Budapest, MAG], tithes of, V/01/3/5
Satu Mare (Szatmárnémeti) [ROM], rector of, vicar "extra Meszes", V/15/4
Sayers, Jane E., GI/01
Scarpatetti, B.M. von, X/02/4/1
Scepusiensis, *see* Spis
Schalkwijk [NET], VII/05/1
Schams (Schambs) [CH], valley, X/07/3
Scheiwiler, J. Al., X/10/4/1
Scherpenisse [NET], tithes in, VII/01/3/6
Schiermonnikoog [NET], island, VII/02/1
Schleswig (Sleswicensis) [BRD], dioc, IV/00
Schrader, G., IV/00
Schuler Libloy, F., V/05/4
Schulthess, clerk of Konstanz, formulary of, X/10/3/5
Schürmann, Josef, X/00/B
Schütz, Alois, X/10/4/1
Scoenbreve, Jacob van, notary of Utrecht, formulary of, VII/01/3/2
Seckau (Secoviensis) [ÖST], bp, dioc of, I/00, 01/3/3
Sedunensis, *see* Sion
Sées (Sagiensis) [FRA], bp, dioc, off of, III/00/D, 52/1
see also Mesreyo
Senlis (Silvanectensis) [FRA], bp, dioc, off of, III/00/D, 45/1
Sens (Senonensis) [FRA], abp, dioc, prov, off of, GI/01, III/00/D, 29/3/2, 53/1, 54/1, 55/1, 56/1, 57/1, 58/1, 59/1, 60/1, 62/1, 63/1
chap, off of, III/61/1
see also st Julien-du-Sault
Severin (Turnu Severin, Zewrinensis) [ROM], off of. V/00/D
Sforza, Guido Ascanio, VI/02/3
Sibiu (Cibiniensis, Hermannstadt) [ROM], dean, off of, V/00/D, 02/4, 05/1
Siebenbürgen, *see* Alba Julia
Siena [ITA], abp, bp, dioc, prov, off of, VI/02/1, 03/1
Arco, abbey all' (or st Musticla), VI/02/3
Ardenga, abbey of, VI/02/3
cath, operarius of, VI/02/3
Monte Oliveto Maggiore, monks of, VI/02/3
notaries of, *see* Gaspero, Giacomo d'Angelo, Giacomo da Montalcino, Neri
Priori, Governatori and Capitano del Populo, declaration by, VI/02/3
st Galgano, abbey of, VI/02/3
see also Percenna
Silano, Giulio, IX/03/3/3
Silvanectensis, *see* Senlis
Sion (Sedunensis, Sitten) [CH], bp, dioc, off of, III/00/D, X/00/P, I, B, 04/3/4, 11/1/0
deans of Sion (Unterwallis) and Valeria (Oberwallis), courts of, X/00/I, 11/3/2, 12/1
see also Martigny
see also Christa, Flüh, st Maurice
Sirimiensis, Sirmiensis, *see* Sremska Mitrovica
Sisteron (Sistericensis) [FRA], III/00/D, 04/1

Sitten, *see* Sion
Sleswicensis, *see* Schleswig
Smičiklas, T., V/18/4
Soós, I., V/07/2
Sornay, Janine, BA, GI/02, III/01/2, 02/2, 4, 03/2, 05/2, 07/3/1, 11/2, 73/2, 4, X/00/B, 04/3/6, 4/1, 11/2, 3/2, 3/4, 12/3, 4/1, 13/2, 3/1, 3/2, 4/1
Soulingeas, Y., III/24/2
Spatzenegger, dr Hans, I/00, 01/4
Speyer (Speier, Spirensis) [BRD], dioc, IV/00
Spiš [CZE], Spišská Kapitula (Scepusiensis, Zips), provost, off of, V/00/D, 06/1, 4
Sremska Mitrovica (Sirimiensis, Sirmiensis, Szerém) [YUG], bp, dioc, off of, V/00/P, D
st Bernard (Bernhard), *see* Grand st Bernard
st Blanquat, A. de, III/65/2
st Brieuc (Briocensis) [FRA], bp, dioc, off of, III/00/D, 66/1
st Elario, Nicholas, seal-keeper of Tournai, II/01/3/1
st Flour (Sancti Flori) [FRA], bp, dioc, off of, III/00/D, 26/1, 27/1
see also Arpajon
st Gallen [CH], abbot of and parish of st Lorenz in, X/10/3/6
st Germain [FRA], off of, III/60/1
st Jan, proosdij of, VII/04/1
see also Utrecht, st Jan
st Julien-du-Sault [FRA], off of, III/62/1
st Lorenz, *see* st Gallen
st Marie, *see* Utrecht, st Marie
st Maurice [CH], abbey, X/00/I
abbot of, X/11/3/1
Wilhelmus de (de sancto Mauritio), comm of bp of Sion, X/11/3/2
st Michael/Lungau [ÖST], adn of, I/11/3
st Pieter, *see* Utrecht, st Pieter
st Pölten [ÖST], dioc of, I/05/3/1
st Salvator, *see* Utrecht, Oudmunster
Steck, Rudolf, X/04/4/5
Steins, A., IV/00
Stelling-Michaud. Susanne, X/00/B
Stelling-Michaud, Sven, X/00/B, 11/4/1
Stelzer, Winfried, I/01/4
Stenzel, K., IV/00
Stickler, A.M., X/00/B
Stockach, Heinrich von, notary of Heinrich VII, formulary of, X/10/4/1
Stolwijk [NET], VII/05/1
Stransky, A., V/09/4
Strasbourg (Argentinensis) [FRA], dioc, IV/00
Straub, H., IV/00
Strigoniensis, *see* Esztergom
Ströbele, Alfons, X/07/4/2
Szabó, L.B., V/11/4
Szatmárnémeti *see* Satu Mare
Szentirmai, A., BA, V/01/4, 10/3/1, 14/4
Szentiványi, R., V/01/2
Székely, G., V/13/4
Szerém, *see* Sremska Mitrovica

Tangl, M., BA, GI/03, III/00/I, V/00/P, VII/00, X/00
Tarentaise (Tarentasiensis) [FRA], abp, prov of, X/00/P, 11/3/1, 3/2
Tarragona (Terrraconensis) [ESP], prov, IX/00, 03/1, 04/1
Tăşnad (Tasnadensis, Tasnád) [ROM], rector of, vicar "extra Meszes", V/15/3/1, 4
Terrraconensis, *see* Tarragona
Terschelling [NET], island of, VII/04/1
Tessin, *see* Ticino
Teutonic Knights, order of, VII/01/3/6
Teutsch, G.D., BA, V/02/4, 05/4
Thérouanne (Morinensis) [FRA], bp, dioc, off of, II/00
Thilliez, P., III/24/2
Tholosanus, *see* Toulouse
Thudichum, Friedrich, X/00/B
Thümleschg, *see* Domleschg
Thurgau [CH], canton, court in, X/10/3/5
Ticino (Tessin) [CH], canton of, X/00/P, I
Tiel/Arnhem [NET], st Walburg, adn, chap, off of, VII/00, 01/3/1, 3/2
Tinniniensis, *see* Knin
Tkalčič, J.B., V/19/4
Tornacensis, *see* Tournai
Torrente, Ulricus de, O.P., inquisitor, X/04/3/6, 3/7
Toul (Tullensis) [FRA], bp, dioc, off of, III/00/D, 71/1
Toulouse (Tholosanus) [FRA], abp, dioc, prov, off of, III/00/D, 64/1, 65/1
see also Aufrère, Corsier
Tournai (Tornacensis) [BEL], bp, dioc, off of, GI/02, II/00, 01/1, III/00/D

Stephen, bp of, II/01/4/1
see also Bernard, Brugge, Clugny, Filastre, Gent, Lille, Osts, Oudenaarde, Pavonis, st Elario, Vlenke
Tours [FRA], prov, off of, III/29/3/2, 66/1, 67/1, 68/1, 69/1, 70/1
see also Rennes
Traiectensis, *see* Utrecht
Trani, Geoffrey of, III/46/3/1
Trecensis, *see* Troyes
Tréguier (Trecorensis) [FRA], bp, dioc, off of, III/00/D, 70/1
Trenčín [CZE], adn of, V/01/3/2
Triesenberg (Tristenberg) [Liechtenstein], case from, X/07/3
Trier (Trevensis) [BRD], dioc, prov, III/00/D, 71/1, IV/00
Trnava [CZE], convent of (O.P.), V/01/3/2
Tropper, dr Peter, I/00, 04/2, 10/2, 10/4, 11/4
Trouillard, G., III/65/2
Trouillat, J., X/02/3/2, 4/5
Troyes (Trecensis) [FRA], bp, dioc, off of, III/00/D, 62/4, 63/1
see also Garmoisia
Truffer, Bernhard, X/11/2, 4/2
Trusen, W., IV/00
Tschanad, *see* Csanád
Tullensis, *see* Toul
Türler, H., X/04/4/5
Turnu Severin, *see* Severin

Ungersheim [CH], commune of, X/02/3/3
Unterkärnten (Friesach) [ÖST], adn of, I/11/1
Unterwallis, *see* Sion, deans
Urban V, pope, III/06/3/2
Usteri, Emil, X/00/B
Utrecht (Traiectensis) [NET], bp, dioc, off of, GI/02, VII/00, 01/1
adns, offs of, VII/01/3/2
cath (dom), adn, chap, off of, VII/00, 01/3/2
cath, dean of, pjd, VII/01/3/6
chorepiscopus, adnry, off of, VII/00, 05/1
Oudmunster (st Salvator), adn, chap, off of, VII/00, 01/3/2, 3/6, 02/1, 2
see also Cunretorff
secular court, procurator-general of, VII/02/3/4
secular prov of, VII/02/1
st Jan, adn, chap, off of, VII/00, 04/1
adn of, pjd, VII/01/3/6
st Marie, chap of, VII/00
st Pieter, off, adn, chap of, VII/00, VII/03/1
see also Baden, Beyer, Bol, Brink, Buer, Burgundy, Hoern, Kaluwe, Medenblick, Mersman, Momfelen, Rutghers van Ommen, Scoenbreve, Vliegher, Weird
Uttenheim, Christoph von, bp of Basel, X/02/3/3
Uzès [FRA], off of, III/23/3/1
Uzsai, Johannes, *ars notaria* of, V/07/3/1

Vác (W(V)aciensis, Waitzen) [MAG], bp, dioc, off of, V/00/P, D, 11/1
Vaison (Vasionensis) [FRA], bp, dioc, off of, III/00/D, 12/1
Valeria, *see* Sion, deans
Vallis [?Valsainte, FRA], Cistercians at, III/07/3/1
Vannotti, Françoise, X/11/4/1, 12/4/2
Varadiensis, *see* Oradea
Városy, J., V/13/4
Vasella, Oskar, X/00/B, 07/2, 3, 4/2
Vechtstreek [NET], region called the, VII/02/1
Veenendaal [NET], VII/03/1
Vela, Christobal, abp of Burgos, IX/01/3/1
Velsperg, *see* Felsberg
Veluwe [NET], the, region of, VII/03/1
Venaissini, Étienne, notary of Marseille off, III/07/3/1
Verden (Verdensis) [BRD], dioc, IV/00
Vesselhem, *see* Fessenheim
Veszprém (Vesprimiensis, Veszprim) [MAG], bp, dioc, off of, V/00/P, D, 12/1
Vianen [NET], church in, VII/01/3/6
Vienne (Viennensis) [FRA], prov, off of, III/30/3/2, 72/1, 73/1, X/00/P, 13/1
Vintschgau [CH], archpriest, court of, X/08/1
Viseu [POR], dean and canon of, pjd, VIII/00
Vlaanderen (Flanders) [BEL], adn of, II/01/4/4
Vleeschouwers, Cyriel, BA, GI/01, II/00
Vleeschouwers-Van Melkebeek, Monique, BA, GI/01, II/00, 01/2, 3/1, 3/3, 4/1,

4/2, 4/3, 4/4, 4/5, III/43/3, 4
Vlenke, Peter de, seal-keeper of Tournai, II/01/3/1
Vliegher, J., notary of Utrecht, VII/01/3/1
Vuonflens, Vuillermus de, O.Min., comm of bp of Lausanne, X/04/3/6
Vurum, J., V/09/4

Waciensis, *see* Vác
Wackernagel, Wolfgang D., X/02/4/4
Waeber, Louis, X/04/4/1
Wagner, C., BA, V/06/4
Waitzen, *see* Vác
Wall, Andreas, off of Konstanz, X/10/4/1
Waradiensis, *see* Oradea
Weird, Lambert de, notary of Utrecht, formulary of, VII/01/3/2
Weißensteiner, dr Johann, I/00, 05/2, 4, 12/2
Welter, L., III/20/2
Werkhoven [NET], VII/02/1
Werner, K., BA
West-Friesland [NET], adn of, VII/00
Wiedemann, Theodor, I/05/4
Wiegand, Rudolf, I/06/4
Wien [ÖST], bp, dioc, off of, seat at, I/00, 05/1, 12/1
Wieser, Franz, I/02/4
Wigger, Franz, X/04/4/4
Wijk-bij-Duurstede [NET], VII/02/1
  castle of, VII/01/2
Wijmal [now in Budapest, MAG], tithes of, V/01/3/5
Wild, Johann, off of Konstanz, X/10/4/1
Wilnis [NET], region of, VII/04/1
Winkler, P., V/13/4
Winner, Gerhard, I/05/4
Wirzeburgensis, *see* Würzburg
Wolfgang, notary of Konstanz, X/10/3/1
Worms (Wormaciensis) [BRD], dioc, IV/00
Woudrichem [NET], VII/02/1
Wunderli, Richard, GI/01
Würzburg (Herbipolensis vel Wirzeburgensis) [BRD], dioc, IV/00
Wydenberg, *see* Pfeffer

York, abp, off of, GI/01

Zagreb (Agram, Zagrabiensis) [YUG], bp, dioc, off of, V/00/P, D, 18/1
  city and chap of, 19/4
  see also Čazma
Zajtay, I., V/17/4
Zapp, H., X/10/3/4, 4/1
Zaragoza (Cesaragustanus) [ESP], prov, IX/00, 04/1
Zeeden, E.W., X/00/B
Zeller, Johann, off of Konstanz, X/10/3/8, 4/1
Zewrinensis, *see* Severin
Zimmermann, F., BA, V/02/3/1, 05/3/1, 13/4, 14/4
Zinnhobler, Rudolf, I/05/4
Zips, *see* Spiš
Zoelmond [NET], church in, VII/01/3/6
  vicar in, VII/01/3/6
Zuid Beveland [NET], provisor of, VII/01/3/6
Zürich [CH], city of, X/00/I
Zutphen [NET], VII/03/1
Zvolen [CZE], adn of, V/01/3/2
Zwiefalten [BRD], monastery, X/10/3/8

Index of Archives

Archive abbreviations are given at the beginning of each letter of the alphabet. Otherwise this index follows the principles of the Index of Persons and Places.

ABA, *see* Augsburg, Archiv des Bistums
ACFR, *see* Fribourg, Archives cantonales
ACS, *see* Sion, Archives capitulaires
ACVD, *see* Chavannes-pres-Renens, Archives cantonales vaudoises
ACVS, *see* Sion, Archives cantonales du Valais
ADA, *see* Rodez, Archives départementales de l'Aveyron
ADBR, *see* Marseille, Archives départementales des Bouches-du-Rhône
ADBRA, *see* Aix-en-Provence, Dépôt annexe des ADBR
ADG, *see* Klagenfurt, Diözesanarchiv Gurk-Klagenfurt
ADHS, *see* Annecy, Archives départementales de la Haute Savoie
ADMM, *see* Nancy, Archives départementales de la Meurthe et Moselle
ADR, *see* Lyon, Archives départementales du Rhône
ADS, *see* Amiens, Archives départementales de la Somme
ADSM, *see* Rouen, Archives départementales de la Seine Maritime
ADV, *see* Avignon, Archives départementales du Vaucluse
ADY, *see* Auxerre, Archives départementales de l'Yonne
AEB, *see* Porrentruy, Archives de l'ancien évêché de Bâle
AEF, *see* Fribourg, Archives de l'Évêché
AEGE, *see* Genève, Archives d'État
AEMF, *see* München, Archiv des Erzbistums
AENE, *see* Neuchâtel, Archives de l'État
AES, *see* Sion, Archives épiscopales
AN, *see* Paris, Archives Nationales
ASM, *see* st Maurice, Abbaye de
AST, *see* Torino, Archivio di Stato
ASV, *see* Città del Vaticano, Archivio Segreto Vaticano
AVL, *see* Lausanne, Archives de la Ville
Aarau [CH], Aargauisches Staatsarchiv (STAAG), X/02/2, 3/5
Aix-en-Provence [FRA], Dépôt annexe des ADBR (ADBRA), III/01/2, 3
Alba Julia [ROM], Bibliotheca Batthyanyana (BBAJ), V/01/2, 3/3
Capitul rom. cat., V/14/2
Alençon [FRA], Archives départementales de l'Orne, III/52/2
Amiens [FRA], Archives départementales de la Somme (ADS), III/41/2, 4
Angoulême [FRA], Archives départementales de la Charente, III/14/2
Annecy [FRA], Archives départementales de la Haute Savoie (ADHS), X/13/2, 3/2
Aschaffenburg [BRD], Stiftarchiv, IV/00
Augsburg, Archiv des Bistums (ABA), IV/01/2, IV/01/3/1
Aurillac [FRA], Archives départementales du Cantal, III/26/2, 27/2
Auxerre [FRA], Archives departementales de l'Yonne (ADY), III/53/2, 3/2, 61/2, 62/2
Avignon [FRA], Archives départementales du Vaucluse (ADV), III/00/I, 02/2, 3/1, 06/2, 3/2, 08/2, 3/2, 09/2, 10/2, 4, 11/2, 12/2

BAC, *see* Chur, Bischöfliches Archiv
BAV, *see* Città del Vaticano, Biblioteca Apostolica Vaticana
BBAJ, *see* Alba Julia, Bibliotheca Batthyanyana
BBB, *see* Bern, Burgerbibliothek
BFL, *see* Pannonhalma, Bencés Föapátsági Levéltár
BHA, *see* München, Bayerisches Hauptstaatsarchiv
BLB, *see* Karlsruhe, Badische Landesbibliothek
BMC, *see* Carpentras, Bibliothèque municipale
BML, *see* Lyon, Bibliothèque municipale
BMT, *see* Toulouse, Bibliothèque municipale
BN, *see* Paris, Bibliothèque Nationale
BSG, *see* Paris, Bibliothèque st Geneviève
BSHG, *see* Genève, Bibliothèque de la Société d'histoire et d'archéologie
Barcelona [ESP], Arxiu diocesa, IX/03/2
Basel [CH], Staatsarchiv des Kantons Basel-Stadt (STABS), X/02/2, 3/1
Bayerisches Hauptstaatsarchiv, *see* München, Bayerisches Hauptstaatsarchiv
Beauvais [FRA], Archives départementales de l'Oise, III/42/2, 45/2
Bern [CH], Burgerbibliothek (BBB), X/04/2, 3/5
Staatsarchiv des Kantons (STAGE), III/29/2, 3/3, X/04/2, 3/4
Bolzano (Bozen), ITA, Staatsarchiv, I/02/2
Bordeaux [FRA], Archives départementales de la Gironde, III/13/2
Bourges [FRA], Archives départementales du Cher, III/19/2
Bozen, *see* Bolzano
Bregenz [ÖST], Vorarlberger Landesarchiv, I/00
Bressanone (Brixen) [ITA], Diözesanarchiv, I/00, 02/2
Brugge [BEL], Rijksarchief, II/01/4/4
Stadsarchief, II/01/2, 3/4
Brussel [BEL], Algemeen Rijksarchief, II/00
Budapest [MAG], Magyar Országos Levéltár (MOL), V/01/2, 3/4, 03/2, 3/1, 06/2, 3/1, 07/2, 3/1, 08/2, 3/1, 09/2, 3/1, 10/2, 3/1, 11/2, 3/1, 12/2, 3/1, 13/2, 3/1, 14/2, 3/1, 15/2, 3/1, 16/2, 3/1, 17/2, 3/1, 18/2, 3/1, 19/2, 3/1
Burgos [ESP], Archivo capitular, IX/02/2
Archivo diocesano, IX/01/2

Carpentras [FRA], Bibliothèque municipale (BMC), III/02/2, 3
Châlons-sur-Marne [FRA], Archives departementales de la Marne, III/44/2
Chartres [FRA], Archives départementales d'Eure et Loire, III/54/2
Chavannes-pres-Renens [CH], Archives cantonales vaudoises (ACVD), X/04/2, 3/2
Chur [CH], Bischöfliches Archiv (BAC), X/07/2, 10/2, 3/3
Città del Vaticano, Archivio Segreto Vaticano (ASV), III/03/2, 06/2, 3/1
Biblioteca Apostolica Vaticana (BAV), III/08/2, 3/1, X/10/2, 3/7
Clermont-Ferrand [FRA], Archives départementales du Puy-de-Dôme, III/20/2
Cluj-Mănăştur (Kolozsmonostor) [ROM], Konventarchiv, V/14/2

DAW, *see* Wien, Diözesanarchiv
Digne [FRA], Archives départementales des Alpes de Haute Provence, III/04/2, 28/2

EAF, *see* Freiburg, Erzbischöfliches Archiv
EPL, *see* Esztergom, Esztergomi Prímási Levéltár
Eger [MAG], Egri Érseki Levéltár, V/07/2
Eisenstadt [ÖST], Diözesanarchiv, I/00
Erfurt [DDR], archiv, IV/00

Esztergom [MAG], Esztergomi Prímási Levéltár (EPL), V/01/2, 3/1, 3/2
Főkáptalani Levéltár (FKL), V/01/2, 3/5, 10/2, 3/1
Főszékesegyházi Könyvtár (FKE), V/01/2, 3/3
Évora [POR], Archives du chapitre, VIII/00

FKE, *see* Esztergom, Főszékesegyházi Könyvtár
FKL, *see* Esztergom, Főkáptalani Levéltár
Foix [FRA], Archives départementales de l'Ariège, III/65/2
Freiburg im Breisgau [BRD], Erzbischöfliches Archiv (EAF), X/10/2, 3/1
Fribourg [CH], Archives cantonales de (ACFR), X/04/2, 3/6, 06/1
Archives de l'Évêche (AEF), X/04/2, 3/3

GKL, *see* Győr, Győri Káptalani Levéltár
GLAK, *see* Karlsruhe, Generallandesarchiv
Gent [BEL], Rijksarchief, II/01/2, 3/4
Genève [CH], Archives d'État de Genève (AEGE), X/13/2, 3/1
Bibliothèque de la Société d'histoire et d'archéologie (BSHG), X/13/2, 3/3
Gouda [NET], archive at, VII/01/2
Graz [ÖST], Steiermärkisches Landesarchiv, I/00
Grenoble [FRA], Archives départementales de l'Isère, III/73/2
Gurk, *see* Klagenfurt
Győr [MAG], Győri Káptalani Levéltár (GKL), V/08/2, 3/2

Hannover [BRD], IV/00
Hildesheim [BRD], IV/00

Innsbruck [ÖST], Tiroler Landesarchiv, I/00, 02/2

KAS, *see* Salzburg, E.B. Konsistorial Archiv
KKP, *see* Pécs, Klimó Könyvtár
KLA, *see* Klagenfurt, Kärntner Landesarchiv
Karlsruhe [BRD], archives at, IV/00
Badische Landesbibliothek (BLB), X/10/2, 3/4
Generallandesarchiv (GLAK), X/02/2, 3/4, 10/2, 3/5
Klagenfurt [ÖST], Kärntner Landesarchiv (KLA), I/00, 04/2, 11/2, 11/3/1
Diözesanarchiv Gurk-Klagenfurt (ADG), I/00, 10/2, 11/2
Klosterneuburg [ÖST], Stiftsbibliothek (SKÖ) V/10/2, 3/1
Kolozsmonostor, *see* Cluj-Mănăştur
Köln [BRD], Stadtarchiv, IV/00

La Rochelle [FRA], Bibliothèque municipale, III/15/2
Laibach, *see* Ljubljana
Lausanne [CH], Archives de la Ville (AVL), X/01/2, 04/2, 3/1
Le Puy [FRA], Archives départementales de la Haute-Loire, III/24/2
Levoča [CZE], Štátny Oblastný Archív, V/06/2
Lille [FRA], Archives départementales du Nord, II/01/2, III/43/2
Limoges [FRA], Archives départementales de la Haute-Vienne, III/21/2, 22/2
Linz [ÖST], Oberösterreichisches Landesarchiv, I/00
Lisboa [POR], Archives du patriarchat, VIII/00
Archives particulières de Dr. Tomaz Andrade Rocha, VIII/00
Arquivo Nacional da Torre do Tombo, VIII/00
Liège [BEL], Archives de l'État
Ljubljana (Laibach) [YUG], Landesarchiv, I/02/2
Luzern [CH], Zentralbibliothek (ZBL), X/10/2, 3/2

Lyon [FRA], Archives départementales du Rhône (ADR), III/29/2, 3/2, 30/2, 3/2, 33/2, 34/2, 35/2, 36/2, 37/2
Bibliothèque municipale (BML), III/29/4, 30/2, 3/1, 33/4

MOL, *see* Budapest
Marseille [FRA], Archives départementales des Bouches-du-Rhône (ADBR), III/01/2, 05/2, 07/2
see also Aix-en Provence, Dépôt annexe des ADBR
Mechelen [BEL], Aartsbisschoppelijk Archief, II/00
Mende [FRA], Archives départementales de la Lozère, III/23/2
Mons [BEL], Archives de l'État, II/01/2, 3/4
München [BRD], Archiv des Erzbistums München und Freising (AEMF), GI/02, I/00, 01/2, 3/4, 03/2, 3/1, 08/2, 09/2
Bayerische Staatsbibliothek, I/03/4
Bayerisches Hauptstaatsarchiv (BHA), GI/02, I/00, /02/2, 03/2, 3/2, 4, 05/2, 3/2, 07/2, 3/1, IV/00, 01/2, 3/2
Mâcon [FRA], Archives départementales de Saône-et-Loire, III/31/2

NBÖ, *see* Wien
Nancy [FRA], Archives départementales de la Meurthe et Moselle (ADMM), III/71/2, 3/2
Nantes [FRA], Archives départementales de la Loire Atlantique, III/68/2, 69/2
Neuchâtel [CH], Archives de l'État de Neuchâtel (AENE), X/04/2, 3/7
Nîmes [FRA], Archives départementales du Gard, III/39/2

Oudmunster (st Salvator), *see* Utrecht, Oudmunster

Pamplona [ESP], Archivo diocesano, IX/04/2
Pannonhalma [MAG], Bencés Főapátsági Levéltár (BFL), V/04/2, 3/1
Paris [FRA], Archives Nationales (AN), III/56/2, 57/2, 58/2, 59/2, 60/2
Bibliothèque Nationale (BN), III/18/2, 29/3/1, 32/2, 40/2, 46/2, 3/1, 51/2, 53/2, 3/1, 64/2, 3, 66/2, 67/2, 70/2, 71/2, 3/1
Bibliothèque st Geneviève (BSG), III/25/2, 3/1, 64/2, 3
Pécs [MAG], Klimó Könyvtár (KKP), V/07/2, 3/1
Périgueux [FRA], Archives départementales de la Dordogne, III/16/2
Perpignan [FRA], Archives départementales des Pyrénées-Orientales, III/38/2
Poiters [FRA], Archives départementales de la Vienne, III/17/2
Porrentruy [CH], Archives de l'ancien évêché de Bâle (AEB), X/02/2, 3/2, 3/3

Regensburg [BRD], Bischöfliches Zentralarchiv, I/06/2
Rodez [FRA], Archives départementales de l'Aveyron (ADA), III/25/2, 3/2, 4
Rouen [FRA], Archives départementales de la Seine Maritime (ADSM), III/46/2, 3/2, 4, 48/2, 49/2, 50/2

SASG, *see* st Gallen, Stiftsarchiv
SKÖ, *see* Klosterneuburg
STABE, *see* Bern, Staatsarchiv des Kantons
STABS, *see* Basel, Staatsarchiv des Kantons
STAAG, *see* Aarau, Aargauisches Staatsarchiv
Salzburg [ÖST], E.B. Konsistorialarchiv (KAS), I/00, 01/2, 3/1, 3/2, 3/3, 02/2, 07/2
Siena [ITA], Archivio di Stato, VI/00, 01/2, 02/2, 03/2
Sion [CH], Archives cantonales du Valais (ACVS), X/11/2, 3/3
Archives capitulaires (ACS), X/11/2, 3/2, 12/2, 13/2, 3/4
Archives épiscopales (AES), X/11/2, 3/1

Speyer [BRD], archives at, IV/00
st Gallen [CH], Stiftsarchiv (SASG), X/10/2, 3/6
st Lô [FRA], Archives départementales de la Manche, III/47/2
st Maurice [CH], Abbaye de (ASM), X/11/2, 3/4
Strasbourg [FRA], *former* Bezirksarchiv, IV/00
Stuttgart [BRD], Württembergische Landesbibliothek (WLB), X/10/2, 3/8, 4/1

Torino [ITA], Archivio di Stato (AST), X/13/2, 3/5
Tours [FRA], Bibliothèque municipale. III/55/2
Toulouse [FRA], Bibliothèque municipale (BMT), III/64/2, 3
Troyes [FRA], Archives départementales de l'Aube, III/63/2

Utrecht [NET], Rijksarchief in de provincie Utrecht, VII/01/2, 02/2, 03/2, 04/2, 05/2
  archive of bps of, VII/01/2
  cath (dom), archive of, VII/01/3/6
  Oudmunster (st Salvator), archive of chap of, VII/01/3/1, 3/6, 02/2
  st Jan, archive of chap of, VII/01/3/6, 04/2
  st Marie, archive of chap of, VII/01/3/6
  st Pieter, archive of chap of, VII/01/3/6

VKL, *see* Veszprém, Veszprémi Káptalani Levéltár
VPL, *see* Veszprém, Veszprémi Püspöki Levéltár
Valence [FRA], Archives départementales de la Drôme, III/72/2
Varaždin [YUG], Archiv Čazmanskog kaptola, V/19/2
Veszprém [MAG], Veszprémi Püspöki Levéltár, V/01/2, 3/5
  Veszprémi Káptalani Levéltár (VKL), V/01/2, 3/5

WLB, *see* Stuttgart, Württembergische Landesbibliothek
Wien [ÖST], Diözesanarchiv (DAW), I/00, 05/2, 3/1, 12/2
  Haus-, Hof- und Staatsarchiv, I/02/2
  Nationalbibliothek (NBÖ) V/07/2, 3/1
  Niederösterreichisches Landesarchiv, I/00
Würzburg [BRD], Kreisarchiv, IV/00
  Staatsarchiv, IV/00
  Stadtarchiv, IV/00

Xanten [BRD], Domarchiv, IV/00

ZBL, *see* Luzern, Zentralbibliothek
Zagreb [YUG], Kapitolski Archiv, V/18/2
  Nadbiskupski Archiv, V/18/2

MIX
Papier aus verantwortungsvollen Quellen
Paper from responsible sources
FSC® C105338

Printed by Libri Plureos GmbH
in Hamburg, Germany